370.18
Oe8r   73164

DATE DUE		
Mar 9 '72	Apr 12 '76	
Mar 24 '72	Apr 18 77	
Apr 10 '72	Apr 3 78	
Apr 24 '72	Apr 21 81	
Apr 24 '74		
Mar 19 '74		
Apr 7 '75		
Jan 26 '76		
Feb 9 '76		
Mar 22 '76		
Apr 5 '76		

GAYLORD M-2   PRINTED IN U.S.A.

Harvard Studies in Technology and Society

The volumes in this series present the results of
studies conducted at the Harvard University Program
on Technology and Society. The Program was established
in 1964 by a grant from the International Business
Machines Corporation to undertake an inquiry in depth
into the effects of technological change on the economy,
on public policies, and on the character of the society,
as well as into the reciprocal effects of social progress on
the nature, dimensions, and directions of scientific and
technological developments.

Run, Computer, Run

The Mythology of Educational Innovation

An Essay by Anthony G. Oettinger

with the collaboration of Sema Marks

Harvard University Press
Cambridge, Massachusetts

370.18
Oebn
73164
Jan., 1971

To Doug and Margie,
whom the fuss is all about

Foreword

A number of facile, one-dimensional views about the relationship between technology and society confront the scholar who seeks to do systematic research in this area. In one such view, technology is an unalloyed blessing that promises an end to human drudgery and a solution to our social problems. Another view is that technology is an autonomous force that is destroying human values. In a third view, technology is undeserving of special attention, since it has been with us at least as long as the Industrial Revolution. Not surprisingly, these same views are reflected in much of what is currently being said about educational technology: that computers and systems analysis will be the salvation of education, or that they will displace teachers and turn children into robots, or that nothing can ever replace the book as the dominant tool of education.

Run, Computer, Run cuts across such oversimple views. Anthony G. Oettinger argues that contemporary instructional technology can lead to genuine improvements in education, provided it is not force-fed, oversold, and prematurely applied. He also finds that it is being force-fed, oversold, and prematurely applied at the present time, most notably by some branches of the U.S. Office of Education, by the new breed of learning corporations, and by many of the technical leaders in the field.

The author denies neither the inherent excitement nor the long-term promise of experiments with the use of computers, assorted teaching machines, and systems analysis in secondary education. When he turns from experimental possibility to large-scale practical application, however, he concludes that while education is badly in need of salvation the probability is slight that its ills will soon yield to the kind of quick technological fix advocated by the most enthusiastic proponents of educational innovation.

Unlike many books about education, *Run, Computer, Run* is not about a few avant-garde experimental schools where new technology can be nurtured as in a hothouse. Nor is it about those hopeless schools where the problem is less to save education than to save the children. The book deals with the vast ground between these extremes, that is, with the schools that the vast majority of American children go to.

This average American school inspires neither passionate praise nor passionate denunciation, mainly because it is so familiar. It is disquietingly like the schools we went to thirty years ago. Peace, quiet, and order are prominent among its objectives. The librarian is happiest when all the books are in their proper places on the shelves. The science teacher keeps to the lesson plan no matter what the children may be interested in. The new textbooks are six weeks overdue and both the record player and projector are broken.

Will computer terminals in every classroom change all this? The advocates say yes, with conviction. This book says no, pugnaciously. It does so by puncturing some of the myths that have grown up around education and educational technology and by casting doubt on some too-facile notions about how technology can serve social purposes.

For example, cannot systems analysis contribute at least as much to educational policy as it has to our national security policy? Perhaps, but consider the staggeringly greater complexity of the educational "system." It comprehends the pupils, the teacher, the principal, the parents, the school board, city hall, the taxpayer, the foundations, and the federal government, all of whom have different ideas about the proper ends of education. This is not to mention the neighborhood bookie, television, comic books, the local drug trafficker, Selective Service, the professions and disciplines, the hit parade, the nation's foreign policy, the Urban League, and the John Birch Society, which must also be taken into account at some point. It is an extraordinarily complex system, and the techniques have yet to be developed that can subject it to a genuinely exhaustive systems analysis.

At the Harvard Program on Technology and Society, where the research for this book was conducted, we construe technology as more than hardware alone. We understand it as tools in a general sense, including machines, but also including intellectual and linguistic tools and the latest analytic and mathematical techniques. In short, we define technology as the organization of knowledge for practical purposes.

Sharing this approach, Professor Oettinger examines not only the new educational hardware but also the institutional setting into which it is being introduced. Just as the school's movie projector represents an organization of our knowledge of physics, chemistry, optics, and perception for the practical purpose of presenting a moving image, so can the school and the American educational system as a whole be seen as organizations of our knowledge of learning, teaching, and administration for the purpose of transmitting to the young the accumulated knowledge and values of society.

Both are found wanting. The hardware itself is as yet much more primitive than is generally appreciated, so that fragile, unreliable, and expensive devices often gather dust in a classroom corner once the enthusiasm that greeted their arrival has subsided. Knowledge about how to apply the technology is even more primitive; teaching methods and curriculum contents remain virtually unmodified by the availability of new devices. The biggest obstacle to the rapid and effective introduction of technology into the schools, however, is the structure of the American school system itself, which, in Oettinger's words, "seems ideally designed to resist change."

It succeeds in combining the rigidity of a military service and the fragmentation of small business, without either the centralized authority that can make the military move or the initiative and flexibility of response of the innovative entrepreneur.

The author concludes that neither educational technology nor the school establishment is ready to consummate the revolution in learning that will bring individualized instruction to every child, systematic planning and uniform standards to 25,000 separate school districts, an answer to bad teachers and unmovable bureaucracies, and implementation of a national policy to educate every American to his full potential for a useful and satisfying life. Major institutional change that can encourage experimentation, flexibility, variety, and competition seems called for before the new technology can contribute significantly to education. The book ends with some suggestions about the form that such institutional changes might take.

This will no doubt be a controversial book and those who disagree with its conclusions may find the author's tone immoderate. Yet the credentials of both book and author are beyond question. *Run, Computer, Run* was not conceived and was never thought of as a report of exhaustive empirical research into every educational experiment with modern instructional technology. As noted in the author's preface, however, the manuscript emerged improved but unscathed in its essentials from a searching examination by twenty of the most respected and exacting experts in education and educational technology in the country. That said, the book remains an essay, in the best sense of that half-forgotten term: it is a careful personal statement by a thoughtful and knowledgeable man about some of the contemporary uses and misuses of technology in education. The tone is also personal, as is appropriate to the genre, and has the further virtues of adding literary quality to the book and, it may be hoped, carrying-power to its message.

The objectives of the Harvard University Program on Technology and Society are to discern the implications of technological change on a number of society's processes and institutions and to lend clear voice to significant conclusions revealed by the details of its research. In both these respects, *Run, Computer, Run* is a fitting start to this new series of Harvard Studies in Technology and Society.

Emmanuel G. Mesthene, Director
Harvard University Program on
Technology and Society

Preface

Two prologues, both previously published papers of mine, are presented to establish a common perspective with the reader. Two appendices, both accounts of first-hand experiences, are presented to set a common background. Prologue I, "A Vision of Technology and Education," describes my initial approach to the subject of this essay, which might therefore have been titled "The Vision Revisited." Prologue II, "The Uses of Computers in Science," was written to explain to readers of the *Scientific American* how computers, properly used, might alter the course of science by stretching human reason and intuition and thereby creating effects as far-reaching as those of the invention of writing. Appendix A is a report of first-hand impressions of two inner-city schools, while Appendix B is an account of a personal battle with one elementary form of educational technology. The experiences reflected in the prologues and appendices roughly define the viewpoint from which I wrote this essay.

I wrote "A Vision of Technology and Education" late in 1965. Earlier that year, Emmanuel G. Mesthene, Director of the Harvard University Program on Technology and Society, had invited me to join with Charles T. W. Curle, David Landes, Seymour Martin Lipset, John R. Meyer, and Richard S. Rosenbloom in weekly discussions of the relations between technology and society. These discussions, with my experiences as a user of the experimental Multiple-Access Computing system of Project MAC at M.I.T., and my own research efforts in Project TACT (Technological Aids to Creative

Thought) under a contract between Harvard University and the Advanced Research Projects Agency of the Department of Defense, stimulated the "Vision."

I wrote it to "present a vision of technological possibility deliberately unclouded by economic or temporal realism." I explored "both some effects this vision, if realized, might have on the fabric of society and some of the factors likely to inhibit its realization." While I did recognize that there might be some problems in making the vision come true, I tended to focus on rather grand questions. I said, for example, that "a system based on remote information storage might make control over subject matter far easier than it is in our present society. One need only picture the use a Hitler or a Stalin could have made of a national educational information pool to understand the seriousness of this problem." It now seems to me after more than two years of study more sensible to assume that neither Hitler nor Stalin could have found the right button to push, at least in the short run.

This present essay will show that some of the difficulties in realizing the vision are also grand and that, furthermore, the accumulation of a myriad of frustrations and inadequacies, however minor in isolation, creates a problem the complexity of which goes far beyond that of any system-design problem with which we have successfully grappled to date.

I admitted that the questions raised in the "Vision" were at best first-order questions or, as I wrote, "superficial questions whose interactions with one another are ignored." *Run, Computer, Run* reports on the fruits of my effort to analyze these interactions in greater depth.

This effort began in 1966-67 with a year of research and weekly discussions by a group created under the Program on Technology and Society. My principal partners in this group were Howard Gruber, now Professor of Psychology at the Institute for Cognitive Studies at Rutgers University; Donald Meals, now on the staff of Arthur D. Little, Inc., Cambridge, Massachusetts; and Samuel Nash, now Director of Program

Planning for the New Haven Public Schools. Jan ter Weele, now Assistant Superintendent of Schools in Hanover, New Hampshire, and Irene Taviss, Head of the Program's Information Center, contributed actively, as did Sema Marks, a doctoral candidate at the Harvard Graduate School of Education, whose collaboration in the writing of this essay began at that time. Juergen Schmandt, Associate Director of the Program, and Arthur Trottenberg, now Vice President for Administration at the Ford Foundation, participated on several occasions.

A first draft of the manuscript was completed in January 1968. That draft was circulated for critical review to a wider audience at a two-day conference in Cambridge, Massachusetts, on May 1 and 2, 1968. I am much indebted to the following participants in that conference both for their criticisms of the draft and for the deeper insights the wide-ranging conference discussions afforded me: James Becker, Research for Better Schools; Louis Bright, U.S. Office of Education; Harvey Brooks, Harvard University; Charles Brown, Newton, Massachusetts, School System; Ned Bryan, U.S. Office of Education; John B. Carroll, Educational Testing Service; George D'Ombrain, McGill University; Robert Dreeben, Harvard University; David Engler, McGraw-Hill Book Company; Robert Glaser, University of Pittsburgh; Harold Gores, Ford Foundation; Howard Gruber; Gerald Holton, Harvard University; J. C. R. Licklider, Massachusetts Institute of Technology; Robert Locke, McGraw-Hill Book Company; Sema Marks; John Mays, Office of Science and Technology, Executive Office of the President; Donald Meals; Emmanuel G. Mesthene; George Papadopoulos, Organisation for Economic Cooperation and Development; Juergen Schmandt; Charles Silberman, *Fortune* magazine; Theodore Sizer, Harvard University; B. F. Skinner, Harvard University; Lyle Spencer, Science Research Associates; Lawrence Stolurow, Harvard University; Patrick Suppes, Stanford University; Irene Taviss; and Jan ter Weele.

Emmanuel Mesthene also invited James Becker, Robert Locke, David Engler, Patrick Suppes, and Robert Schaefer and Francis Ianni of Columbia University to prepare written critiques of the manuscript. These critiques served as points of departure for the May conference. In addition, they not only sharpened my own thinking but, in several welcome instances, rescued me from error. I am most grateful to their authors.

The January 1968 draft was the basis for an article, "The Myths of Educational Technology," which appeared in the *Saturday Review* of May 18, 1968. I am indebted to Peter Schrag, then the magazine's Editor for Education, for his valuable substantive and editorial comments.

Excerpts from the same draft were used as bait for a discussion in the pages of the Fall 1968 issue of the *Harvard Educational Review*. Participants in this debate included James Becker and Patrick Suppes, who contributed the critiques they had prepared for the May 1968 conference; and Warren Bennis, State University of New York at Buffalo, Allan Ellis, Harvard University and New England Education Data Systems, and Robert Glaser, who were invited by the editors of the *Review* to fire additional shots. Sema Marks and I wrote a rebuttal.

This set of conferences and debates revealed agreement with many of the observations made in *Run, Computer, Run* but also many varied points of sharp disagreement. Except for correcting some clear-cut errors, I did not, however, feel compelled to alter my point of view or my conclusions to any significant extent. I do hope that the style and the clarity of this book now come closer to meeting the exacting standards of many of the critics who bravely ran the obstacle course I set for them in the first draft.

I am grateful to J. C. R. Licklider, Edwin Taylor, and Jerrold Zacharias for the opportunity to test my ideas in the spring of 1968 as the first speaker in the colloquium series, "Education and Computers," which they organized at M.I.T. More people than I can list by name helped me by arranging site visits, through conversations, critical readings of various drafts, editorial comments, and similar services of great value. I take this opportunity to thank them all.

Jane Draper made all the excellent arrangements for the May conference and, with Mitzi Gerrish, capably marshaled all the secretarial assistance and other amenities that smoothed the course of this work, while Joyce Sulahian unfailingly kept my other affairs in order. Tom Parmenter, Associate for Publications at the Program on Technology and Society, gave me much valuable editorial advice, applying to many an awkward passage the touch of his felicitous style. I am grateful to Nancy Clemente, of the Harvard University Press, for speeding the manuscript through the Press. The Xerox copier, Scotch tape, Avery self-adhesive correction tape, Swingline stapler, and Wiss scissors gave invaluable technological support to the preparation of the manuscript.

I owe a special debt to Irene Taviss, not only for gathering and interpreting the material used in Section 1.3, but also for encouraging me in dark moments and for her penetrating criticism of every part of every draft. This essay could not have been written without the creative contributions which my collaborator, Sema Marks, made to every stage of research and of writing. As a trained mathematician, a sometime high school teacher, an expert computer programmer and now a doctoral candidate in the Harvard Graduate School of Education, she combines those high qualities of intellect, of education, and of action which the new breed of school people must have if technology and the schools are to get along with one another productively.

To my wife, Marilyn, my love and my thanks for bearing with me once again through a period of deep absorption in my work.

Anthony G. Oettinger

Cambridge, Massachusetts
January 6, 1969

Contents

Contents

Prologues

Prologue I

A Vision of Technology and Education

INTRODUCTION

Without an understanding of the dynamics of interactions between technological and social change, views concerning these interactions tend to be polarized and naive. To those "outside," major technological programs such as the Lunar Landing Program appear to be the product of lobbying by powerful special interest groups, advocating big spending by the government and social change at any cost, without seriously considering the consequences of such spending or change, and thereby imposing on the market rather than catering to it. Viewed from the "inside," social reaction to potential technological change may seem short-sighted if not downright Luddite. For example, the reaction to potential large-scale introduction of atomic power led to efficiency increases and cost reductions by the conventional power

The preparation of this paper was supported in part by the Advanced Research Projects Agency under Contract SD-265 with Harvard University. Reprinted by permission of the Association for Computing Machinery, New York, New York, from *Communications of the ACM,* July 1966, pp. 487-490; copyright © 1966 by the Association for Computing Machinery, Inc.

industry which have effectively delayed the introduction of nuclear power into the mainstream of peacetime affairs.

In approaching the problem of the interaction of educational technology with society, I shall first present a vision of technological possibility deliberately unclouded by economic or temporal realism. I shall then explore both some effects this vision, if realized, might have on the fabric of society and some of the factors likely to inhibit its realization. The questions raised will be at best first-order questions, that is, superficial questions whose interactions with one another are ignored. It is very unlikely that so simple-minded a view gets close to reality, but no more seems possible at this time.

THE VISION

In the first tableau of our vision, we see that it is technically possible for sound, pictures, and even objects stored at appropriate centers to be available with the greatest of ease and negligible cost at innumerable local points of access, first perhaps in schools, libraries, or factories and only a little later, as seen from our visionary perspective, in every home. The cost of getting there is one of the things that should give us pause, but potential means, safely short of involving extrasensory perception, are now at our command. Once this much is granted, an entirely new look at the means for education is possible.

Note that it does not matter for our purpose whether or not we assume that computer technology will replace libraries as we now know them. Reasons of cost and reliability might lead us to prefer storing information on microscopic film or in solid-state devices and transmitting it by electronic means rather than propelling conventional books hither and yon through a national network of huge pneumatic tubes, but this choice need not concern us here. Careful design might well require that certain frequently used materials be available in local depositories, but the basic assumption we need to go on is simply that anything available in any library can be made available to anyone anywhere within what he thinks is a reasonable time.

In the next tableau we see individual consoles linked to the common information pool serving as the basic tool for virtually all formal education. The key idea is that by pushing buttons or otherwise signalling from a suitable terminal a student has access to:

1. The catalogs of great libraries, hence access to their collections.

2. The catalogs of new video tape or film libraries, hence access to the collections which include recorded lessons on specialized topics (possibly in the manner of an illustrated encyclopedia) and also source materials such as records of significant contemporary events, of outstanding dramatic productions, of clinical recordings (perhaps of a difficult operation particularly well performed in a leading hospital), and so on.

3. Teaching programs of the kind already in widespread experimental use.

4. Tools to aid symbol manipulation and concept formation such as numerical and algebraic manipulators, dictionaries, thesauri, editing programs, and so forth.

The teaching programs give routine directions through the maze of materials. However, many of the documents in the consulting collections may, in themselves, contain references to other entries. The library system is thus visualized as a kind of gargantuan version of Vannevar Bush's Memex.

The local teacher gives guidance, perhaps after having mastered the materials himself as part of a machine-aided program of continuing education. Indeed, guidance is all important since the individual has greater responsibility for his own education than he has had in the past; the teacher's role thus becomes far more humanistic and far less mechanical than it is now.

The manipulative tools are very important both for education and for research. At present, visual display systems are useful in helping men understand the results of experiments or calculations; they may be used by students of introductory differential equations to generate direction fields and thus to gain immediate insight into the global character of the solutions to these equations; they may be used by research scientists, perhaps to make visible various proposed structures for complex organic molecules and to view these from arbitrary orientations and across arbitrary sections. Such tools enable the easy confrontation of model and reality, as in the visual superposition of calculated streamlines on those in a real fluid flowing around a real obstacle in a real tank. To those who have observed them, such confrontations have dramatic immediacy and perspicuity. There is here a means for expanding man's consciousness and giving him a new way of grasping ideas that is especially valuable where scientists must use intuition and complex calculations to study phenomena increasingly remote from what is immediately evident to the unaided senses.

The system we see also provides expert help for both ends of the ability scale. Special materials are available for the very advanced or the particularly slow. Outstanding people or trained remedial specialists are provided for consultation via a directory of consultants incorporated in the system.

Students who are now at the low end of the scale but who do have intellectual potential could be reached by the new techniques. Such students have been shown to respond well to individualization of education, especially when personal contact with a teacher keeps learning from being a fearful experience. The teacher, released from routine chores for guidance activities, can provide much more individual attention than now.

For some, although obviously not for all, the unassisted machine carries the impersonality of the confessional or the couch to its logical and beneficial extreme. Finally, the use of reinforcements designed to appeal to the culturally deprived might also reach students in this category.

In certain areas, notably in mathematics and in the fields of application of mathematics, the student may use computers associated with this system not only as tools for tackling and solving more exciting and deeper problems than can now be handled, but also as a means for remembering techniques which he has developed. The computer puts these techniques at the student's fingertips throughout his school career and beyond, on the assumption that the system remains available to him wherever he goes. This availability obviously requires a national or worldwide system of standardized consoles and the cheap communication channels we have already postulated.

Such an approach fundamentally changes the entire teaching process. To the extent that teaching by rote is necessary, it can be handled by the programmed teaching devices incorporated in the system. But far beyond this, people can learn to use library resources of all types and can master the manipulative tools put at their disposal. The system helps them remember both the tracks they and others pursued while browsing and the problem-solving techniques they developed for their own individual purposes.

The system could thus be regarded as the crude beginnings of a cultural or social memory, comparable in complexity and accessibility to that of the individual human being. Such a collective mind already exists in a sense in libraries and in the complex organism we call scientific literature, but with much more limited powers of recall and of articulation than are envisioned here.

One immediate interesting consequence of these visions is that they leave no obvious intellectual need for the separation of children in grades or for other forms of lockstep. The child can progress through the system as rapidly as he is able or wishes to.

Another interesting feature of the system is that it relieves the school of what is the bulk of its concern today, namely the abstract and the verbal. The school may concentrate instead on the concrete, the social, and the human. In principle, everything that has been described heretofore could be done as well in the home as in the school. Such learning would be an individual activity; the long use in Europe of individual tutoring as the primary means of education shows that group activity is not always necessary for learning. The school would, however, continue to provide for what Buckminster Fuller has called the baby-sitting function; this, and also for the meeting, the rubbing, and the blending of individuals who must later take places as partners in society.

The school thus becomes more of a model of society. The transition from school to job would be far less traumatic; the continuum of learning would be more obvious and the tools and techniques of learning and of access to knowledge would carry over to higher education or to professional activities without severe discontinuities. The materials used may change but the methods need not. In a job interview, the student might describe the materials he has mastered and, perhaps, demonstrate directly that he can use the techniques on problems relevant to the job.

Some might insist on grading in the form of a profile of the levels of achievement or of familiarity in various directions available in the system. Such a profile need not pretend to quantify proficiency but, by pointing to those areas in the common information pool which a student has reached, simply make plain where his strengths and weaknesses lie. Although the greater snob value attached to certain profiles might affect a student's choice of subject, the system nevertheless allows a greater scope for individual freedom and greater opportunity for the student to match himself to the outer world rather than to the mores of a school than is possible today. This flexibility can be a relief since, for many people today, things are never again quite so grim as in school.

The school, free to concentrate on guidance and counseling, may also emphasize such concrete matters as laboratory exercises in the sciences or student productions of plays, poetry readings, and discussions of books in the humanities. Picture the student who has seen video lectures on certain physical principles presenting himself to the laboratory instructor and claiming that he is ready to perform a certain experiment. This is one of the points at which the teacher can check the student's progress since, if the student fumbles miserably in the laboratory, he can be sent back for further study at the machine. Furthermore, the student's progress and the outcome of his experiment might well determine the path of his future inquiries into the machine pool of knowledge.

The emphasis on the concrete within the school has two desirable social effects. First, it tends to reduce the upper-class aversion to science and technology that makes these children shy away from these subjects. Second, the undesirable barrier between the academic school and the vocational school can disappear. While the better-off students would be faced with the concrete in the laboratory, those hitherto relegated to vocational schools might, through initial exposure to concrete mechanisms, devices, demonstrations, and so on, then be stimulated to a deeper abstract understanding of such phenomena by exposure to appropriately leveled sources in the machine bank of information.

A student who has used a wrench to loosen a rusty bolt or to tighten one would, either on his own or with the guidance of his sympathetic teacher, quickly notice that the longer the handle on the wrench the easier it is to turn the bolt. The step from this experience to motivation for looking at a video tape of an elementary lecture on simple machines is a small one, but rarely taken in the present-day vocational school where the teacher, although sympathetic, is usually unable to supply the lecture himself. The student so stimulated might then, if he has the innate intellectual equipment, be able to catch up to others on his own time and in privacy.

The difference between being in and out of school is reduced since industrial plants have access to the same information and education system. Hence, where a man has achieved his level profile becomes less relevant than what the level is. An easy flow back and forth between school and work is conceivable for people of all ages.

THE COLD WATER

Little need be said of feasibility and economics. Though everything described in the preceding section can be done in principle, doing it is a matter of enormous funds and effort. If the vision is to come true at all, most likely it will come about through an evolutionary process and, in the course of evolution, deviate radically from its present innocent state. Many specific criticisms can obviously be leveled at the vision. The following is merely a sample.

What, for example, guarantees that such a system could work in practice as well as in principle? The information available at the terminals will be prepared by people, and it is questionable whether the available people will have enough ideas and enough command of the technology to do a job good enough to interest the students.

Where, indeed, do the teachers come from? What degree of contact can remain between really good, sensitive teachers and the students when the machines frequently know more than the teacher? How can student-teacher contact be encouraged? How, in the long run, can teacher training be pointed toward guidance in the creative arts and laboratory work? And what about the transitional problem of re-educating teachers of the old school?

The teacher in the wrench example of the preceding section would have to be able to move freely between the abstract and the concrete, a knack which all too few possess. Hence, in spite of the high degree of automation of the visionary system, there might not be enough talent to start it. The vision implicitly assumes that teachers will be able to guide students from all walks of life and levels of competence. If this ideal is unattainable, it would quickly seem more efficient to group students by ability for clustering around an appropriate advisor. Thus, grading and lockstep would be reinvented.

The new system might overcome the current great importance of factors of birth in determining which students receive higher education but it might also leave far behind the student without intellectual potential. The natural elitism of the educated might therefore be sharpened. In the light of present parent agitation against grouping by ability, the very possibility of implementing an ability-oriented system within the American social structure must be seriously questioned. Elected school boards are not likely to take kindly to some of the implications of the vision, and its implementation might require either a tremendous education of the public or an authoritarian educational system. The problems of fluoridating water would pale in this context.

It is conceivable that terminals in the home would lead to serious problems of addiction and of competition. With home and school indistinguishable, the tendency to stay glued to the console might be irresistible for those with a competitive bent and hence would have a marked effect on the quality of life.

A system based on remote information storage might make control over subject matter far easier than it is in our present society. One need only picture the use a Hitler or a Stalin could have made of a national educational information pool to understand the seriousness of this problem. Using regional rather than national information centers, or foreign as well as domestic sources, might reduce this uniformity. Indeed, some of the homogeneity now evident in the lower schools might be alleviated by a system which can give access to a much wider range of literature than a bigoted local school board would allow today.

Nevertheless, new technology tends to produce greater interdependence and uniformity. Teaching all children the same history might be all too easy and gaining control of the mind of a nation all too possible unless this question is most carefully studied and intellectual freedom most jealously guarded. The vision includes discussion and questioning in the school and diversity in the system, but the impersonal use of canned materials on a large scale might produce in students the illusion of infallibility, since the printed, recorded, or filmed word or action often seems to wield greater authority than does the fumbling middle-aged type at the blackboard or in the kitchen.

Finally, to hint for once at a second-order effect, it seems likely that any partial step toward the vision would be based on an evaluation of the educational system and of the economics of computers, communications, and so on, as they are now. It should be clear that the prospect of a system which might radically alter patterns of book distribution and hence the stability of the book trade would lead to a reaction that might alter the assumption on which original plans are based so significantly as to preclude their rational implementation.

Unfortunately, little is now available to help answer these questions.

Prologue II

The Uses of Computers in Science

In its scientific applications the computer has been cast in two quite distinct but complementary roles: as an instrument and as an actor. Part of the success of the computer in both roles can be ascribed to purely economic factors. By lowering the effective cost of calculating compared with experimenting the computer has induced a shift toward calculation in many fields where once only experimentation and comparatively direct measurement were practical.

The computer's role as an instrument is by far the more clear-cut and firmly established of the two. It is in its other role, however, as an active participant in the development of scientific theories, that the computer promises to have its most profound impact on science. A physical theory expressed in the language of mathematics often becomes dynamic when it is rewritten as a computer program; one can explore its inner structure, confront it with experimental data, and interpret its implications much more easily than when it is in static form. In disciplines where mathematics is not the prevailing mode of expression the language of computer programs serves increasingly as the language of science. I shall return to the subject of the dynamic expression of theory after considering the more familiar role of the computer as an instrument in experimental investigations.

The advance of science has been marked by a progressive and rapidly accelerating separation of observable phenomena from both common sensory experience and theoretically supported intuition. Anyone can make at least a qualitative comparison of the forces required to break a matchstick and a steel bar. Comparing the force needed to ionize a hydrogen atom with the force that binds the hydrogen nucleus together is much more indirect, because the chain from phenomenon to observation to interpretation is much longer. It is by restoring the immediacy of sensory experience and by sharpening intuition that the computer is reshaping experimental analysis.

The role of the computer as a research instrument can be readily understood by considering the chain from raw observations to intuitively intelligible representations in the field of X-ray crystallography. The determination of the structure of the huge molecules of proteins is one of the most remarkable achievements of contemporary science. The highlights of this work have been reported in a number of articles in *Scientific American,* notably "The Three-dimensional Structure of a Protein Molecule," by John C. Kendrew (December 1961), and "The Hemoglobin Molecule," by M. F. Perutz (November 1964). The labor, care, and expense lavished on the preparation of visual models of protein molecules testify to a strong need for intuitive aids in this field. The computational power required to analyze crystallographic data is so immense that the need for high-speed computers is beyond doubt.

The scope and boldness of recent experiments in X-ray crystallography have increased in direct proportion to increases in computer power. Although computers seem to be necessary for progress in this area, however, they are by no means sufficient. The success stories in the determination of protein structures have involved an interplay of theoretical insight, experimental technique, and computational power.

In work of this kind a rotating protein crystal is bombarded by a beam of X rays; the rays diffracted by the crystal are recorded on a photographic plate, where they produce characteristic patterns of bright spots on the dark background. Measurements of the relative positions and intensities of the spots in the diffraction pattern are the raw material for calculations that have as their result a table of coordinates of the three-dimensional distribution of electrons in the molecule. The electron-density data are then used to draw density-contour maps, which are interpreted as a three-dimensional model of the particular protein molecule under study.

Many of the links in this chain are now automated. The laborious manual measurement of photographs, for example, is no longer necessary. In the laboratory of William N. Lipscomb, Jr., at Harvard University, a mounted crystal is rotated automatically through the required sequence of orientations while a photomultiplier tube measures the intensity of the diffracted X rays. Machines convert information about position and intensity into digital form and record it on punched cards for input to a computer.

At the other end of the chain Cyrus Levinthal of the Massachusetts Institute of Technology and Robert Langridge of Harvard have used the time-shared computer and display facilities of M.I.T.'s Project MAC to develop a remarkable set of programs that accept electron densities calculated for a three-dimensional region and turn these into an image of molecular structure on an oscilloscope. Gone is the time-consuming task of drawing and building the electron-density map. Once the picture of a molecule has been calculated for a standard orientation the orientation can be changed at will by simple controls that actuate special circuits for transforming the coordinates of the picture before displaying it. Slight motions provide excellent depth perception without the expense of stereoscopic image pairs. The molecule can be turned in order to view it from any angle, or it can be sliced by a plane in order to see it in cross section.

Joining these two links is the next step. A new coaxial-cable network will soon carry Lipscomb's raw data directly to a computer at the Harvard Computing Center. No technical obstacle bars the further transmission of calculated electron densities to the system at M.I.T., where the molecular display could be prepared and then sent back for direct viewing on a screen at the experimental site. Once the time-shared computer utility emerges from its present experimental stage to spread throughout institutions and regions, such doings will very likely be commonplace. It is only tame speculation to visualize a graduate student "looking through" a computer at a protein molecule as directly as he now looks at a cell through a microscope.

The metaphor of the transparent computer describes one of the principal aims of contemporary "software" engineering, the branch of information engineering concerned with developing the complex programs (software) required to turn an inert mound of apparatus (hardware) into a powerful instrument as easy to use as pen and paper. As anyone can testify who has waited a day or more for a conventional computing service to return his work only to find that a misplaced comma had kept the work from being done at all, instant transparency for all is not yet here. Nevertheless, the advances now being made toward making computer languages congenial and expressive, toward making it easy to communicate with the machine, and toward putting the machine at one's fingertips attest to the vigor of the pursuit of the transparent computer.

A few critics object to the principle of transparency because they fear that the primary consequence will be atrophy of the intellect. It is more likely that once interest in the *process* of determining molecular structure becomes subordinate to interest in the molecule itself, the instrument will simply be accepted and intellectual challenge sought elsewhere. It is no more debasing, unromantic, or unscientific in the 1960's to view a protein crystal through the display screen of a computer than it is to watch a paramecium through the eyepiece of a microscope. Few would wish to repeat the work of Christian Huygens each time they need to look at a microscope slide. In any case, computers are basically so flexible that nothing but opaque design or poor engineering can prevent a person from breaking into the chain at any point, whenever he thinks human intuition and judgment should guide brute calculation.

It is essential, of course, for anyone to understand his instrument well enough to use it properly, but the computer is just like other commonplace instruments in this regard. Like any good tool, it should be used with respect. Applying "data reduction" techniques to voluminous data collected without adequate experimental design is a folly of the master not to be blamed on the servant. Computer folk have an acronym for it: GIGO, for "garbage in, garbage out."

X-ray crystallography is the most advanced of many instances in which similar instrumentation is being developed. Four experimental stations at the Cambridge Electron Accelerator, operated jointly by Harvard and M.I.T., are currently being connected to a time-shared computer at the Harvard Computing Center to provide a first link. A small computer at each experimental station converts instrument readings from analogue to digital form, arranges them in a suitable format and transmits them to the remote computer. There most data are stored for later detailed calculation; a few are examined to instruct each of the small local machines to display information telling the experimenter whether or not his experiment is going well. Heretofore delays in conventional batch-processing procedures occasionally led to scrapping a long experiment that became worthless because poor adjustments could not be detected until all calculations were completed and returned.

This type of experiment is described as an "open loop" experiment, since the computer does not directly affect the setting of experimental controls. Closed-loop systems, where the experiment is directly controlled by computer, are currently being developed. Their prototypes can be seen in industrial control systems, where more routine, better understood devices, ranging from elevators to oil refineries, are controlled automatically.

The problem of "reading" particle-track photographs efficiently has been a persistent concern of high-energy physicists. Here the raw data are not nearly as neat as they are in X-ray diffraction patterns, nor can photography as readily be bypassed. Automating the process of following tracks in bubble-chamber photographs to detect significant events presents very difficult and as yet unsolved problems of pattern recognition, but computers are now used at least to reduce some of the tedium of scanning the photographs. Similar forms of man-machine interaction occur also in the study of brain tumors by radioactive-isotope techniques. Where the problem of pattern recognition is simpler, as it is in certain types of chromosome analysis, there is already a greater degree of automation.

Let us now turn from the computer as instrument to the computer as actor, and to the subject of dynamic expression of theory. To understand clearly words such as "model," "simulation," and others that recur in this context, a digression is essential to distinguish the functional from the structural aspects of a model or a theory.

A robot is a functional model of man. It walks, it talks, but no one should be fooled into thinking that it is a man or that it explains man merely because it acts like him. The statements that "the brain is like a computer" or that "a network of nerve cells is like a network of computer gates, each either on or off," crudely express once popular structural theories, obviously at different levels. Both are now discredited, the first because no one has found structures in the brain that look anything like parts of any man-made computer or even function like them, the second because nerve-cell networks were found to be a good deal more complicated than computer networks.

A functional model is like the electrical engineer's proverbial "black box," where something goes in and something comes out, and what is inside is unknown or relevant only to the extent of somehow relating outputs to inputs. A structural model emphasizes the contents of the box. A curve describing the current passing through a semiconductor diode as a function of the voltage applied across its terminals is a functional model of this device that is exceedingly useful to electronic-circuit designers. Most often such curves are obtained by fitting a smooth line to actual currents and voltages measured for a number of devices. A corresponding structural model would account for the characteristic shape of the curve in terms that describe the transport of charge-carriers through semiconductors, the geometry of the contacts, and so forth. A good structural model typically has greater predictive power than a functional one. In this case it would predict changes in the voltage-current characteristic when the geometry of the interfaces or the impurities in the semiconductors are varied.

If the black box is opened, inspiration, luck, and empirical verification can turn a functional model into a structural one. Physics abounds with instances of this feat. The atom of Lucretius or John Dalton was purely functional. Modern atomic theory is structural, and the atom with its components is observable. The phlogiston theory, although functional enough up to a point, evaporated through lack of correspondence between its components and reality. Although the description of the behavior of matter by thermodynamics is primarily functional and its description by statistical mechanics is primarily structural, the consistency of these two approaches reinforces both.

The modern computer is a very versatile and convenient black box, ready to act out an enormous variety of functional or structural roles. In the physical sciences, where the script usually has been written in mathematics beforehand, the computer merely brings to life, through its program, a role implied by the mathematics. Isaac Newton sketched the script for celestial mechanics in the compact shorthand of differential equations. Urbain Leverrier and John Couch Adams laboriously fleshed out their parts in the script with lengthy and detailed calculations based on a wealth of astronomical observations. Johann Galle and James Challis pointed their telescopes where the calculations said they should and the planet Neptune was discovered. In modern jargon, Leverrier and Adams each ran Neptune simulations based on Newton's model, and belief in the model was strengthened by comparing simulation output with experiment. Computers now routinely play satellite and orbit at Houston, Huntsville, and Cape Kennedy. Nevertheless, there is little danger of confusing Leverrier, Adams, or a computer with any celestial object or its orbit. As we shall see, such confusion is more common with linguistic and psychological models.

The determination of protein structures provides an excellent example of how computers act out the implications of a theory. Finding a possible structure for a protein molecule covers only part of the road toward understanding. For example, the question arises of why a protein molecule, which is basically just a string of amino acid units, should fold into the tangled three-dimensional pattern observed by Kendrew. The basic physical hypothesis invoked for explanation is that the molecular string will, like water running downhill, fold to reach a lowest energy level. To act out the implications of this hypothesis, given an initial spatial configuration of a protein chain, one might think of calculating the interactions of all pairs of active structures in the chain, minimizing the energy corresponding to these interactions over all possible configurations, and then displaying the resultant molecular picture. Unfortunately this cannot be done so easily, since no simple formula describing such interactions is available and, with present techniques, none could be written down and manipulated with any reasonable amount of labor. Sampling more or less cleverly the energies of a finite but very large number of configurations is the only possibility. An unsupervised computer searching through a set of samples for a minimum would, more likely than not, soon find itself blocked at some local minimum — unable, like a man in a hollow at the top of a mountain, to see deeper valleys beyond the ridges that surround him.

The close interaction of man and machine made possible by new "on-line" time-sharing systems, graphical display techniques, and more convenient programming languages enables Levinthal and his collaborators to use their intuition and theoretical insight to postulate promising trial configurations. It is then easy for the computer to complete the detail work of calculating energy levels for the trial configuration and seeking a minimum in its neighborhood. The human operator, from his intuitive vantage point, thus guides the machine over the hills and into the valley, each partner doing what he is best fitted for.

Even more exciting, once the details of the interactions are known theoretically, the X-ray diffraction pattern of the molecule can be calculated and compared with the original observations to remove whatever doubts about the structure are left by ambiguities encountered when going in the other direction. This closing of the circle verifies not only the calculation of molecular structure but also the theoretical edifice that provided the details of molecular interactions.

In this example the computer clearly mimics the molecule according to a script supplied by underlying physical and chemical theory. The computer represents the molecule with a sufficient degree of structural detail to make plausible a metaphorical identification of the computer with the molecule. The metaphor loses its force as we approach details of atomic structure, and the submodels that account for atomic behavior are in this case merely functional.

The remarkable immediacy and clarity of the confrontation of acted-out theory and experiment shown in the preceding example are by no means isolated phenomena. Similar techniques are emerging in chemistry (see "Computer Experiments in Chemistry," by Don L. Bunker, *Scientific American*, July 1964), in hydrodynamics (see "Computer Experiments in Fluid Dynamics," by Francis H. Harlow and Jacob E. Fromm, *Scientific American*, March 1965), and in other branches of science. It is noteworthy, as Don L. Bunker has pointed out, that computers used in this way, far from reducing the scientist to a passive bystander, reinforce the need for the creative human element in experimental science, if only because witless calculation is likely to be so voluminous as to be beyond the power of even the fastest computer. Human judgment and intuition must be injected at every stage to guide the computer in its search for a solution. Painstaking routine work will be less and less useful for making a scientific reputation, because such "horse work" can be reduced to a computer program. All that is left for the scientist to contribute is a creative imagination. In this sense scientists are subject to technological unemployment, just like anyone else.

In the "softer" emerging sciences such as psychology and linguistics the excitement and speculation about the future promise of the computer both as instrument and as actor tend to be even stronger than in the physical sciences, although solid accomplishments still are far fewer.

From the time modern computers were born, the myth of

the "giant brain" was fed by the obvious fact that they could calculate and also by active speculation about their ability to translate from one language into another, play chess, compose music, prove theorems, and so on. That such activities were hitherto seen as peculiar to man and to no other species and certainly to no machine lent particular force to the myth. This myth (as expressed, for example, in *New Yorker* cartoons) is now deeply rooted as the popular image of the computer.

The myth rests in part on gross misinterpretation of the nature of a functional model. In the early 1950's, when speculation about whether or not computers can think was at the height of fashion, the British mathematician A. M. Turing proposed the following experiment as a test. Imagine an experimenter communicating by teletype with each of two rooms (or black boxes), one containing a man, the other a computer. If after exchanging an appropriate series of messages with each room the experimenter is unable to tell which holds the man and which the computer, the computer might be said to be thinking. Since the situation is symmetrical, one could equally well conclude that the man is computing. Whatever the decision, such an experiment demonstrates at most a more or less limited functional similarity between the two black boxes, because it is hardly designed to reveal structural details. With the realization that the analogy is only functional, this approach to the computer as a model, or emulator, of man loses both mystery and appeal; in its most naive form it is pursued today only by a dwindling lunatic fringe, although it remains in the consciousness of the public.

In a more sophisticated vein attempts continue toward devising computer systems less dependent on detailed prior instructions and better able to approach problem-solving with something akin to human independence and intelligence. Whether or not such systems, if they are achieved, should have anything like the structure of a human brain is as relevant a question as whether or not flying machines should flap their wings like birds. This problem of artificial intelligence is the subject of speculative research that has been described by Marvin L. Minsky (see "Artificial Intelligence," *Scientific American*, September 1966). Once the cloud of misapplied functional analogy is dispelled, the real promise of using the computer as an animated structural model remains.

Mathematics has so far made relatively few inroads in either linguistics or psychology, although there are now some rather beautiful mathematical theories of language. The scope of these theories is generally limited to syntax (the description of the order and formal relations among words in a sentence). Based as they are on logic and algebra, rather than on the now more familiar calculus, these theories do not lend themselves readily to symbolic calculation of the form to which mathematicians and natural scientists have become accustomed. "Calculations" based on such theories must generally be done by computer. Indeed, in their early form some of these theories were expressed only as computer programs; others still are and may remain so. In such cases the language of programs is the language of science; the program is the original and only script, not just a translation from mathematics.

Early claims that computers could translate languages were vastly exaggerated; even today no finished translation can be produced by machine without human intervention, although machine-aided translation is technically possible. Considerable progress has been made, however, in using computers to manipulate languages, both vernaculars and programming languages. Grammars called phrase-structure grammars and transformational grammars supply the theoretical backdrop for this activity. These grammars describe sentences as they are generated from an initial symbol (say *S* for sentence) by applying rewrite rules followed (if the grammar is transformational) by applying transformation rules. For example, the rewrite rule *S → SuPr*, where *Su* can be thought of as standing for subject and *Pr* as standing for predicate, yields the string *SuPr* when it is applied to the initial symbol *S*. By adding the rules *Su → John* and *Pr → sleeps* one can turn this string into the sentence "John sleeps." Transformations can then be applied in order to turn, for example, the active sentence "John followed the girl" into the passive one "The girl was followed by John."

Under the direction of Susumu Kuno and myself a research group at Harvard has developed, over the past few years, techniques for inverting this generation process in order to go from a sentence as it occurs in a text to a description of its structure or, equivalently, to a description of how it might have been generated by the rules of the grammar. Consider the simple sentence "Time flies like an arrow." To find out which part of this sentence is the subject, which part the predicate and so on, a typical program first looks up each word in a dictionary. The entry for "flies" would show that this word might serve either as a plural noun denoting an annoying domestic insect or as a verb denoting locomotion through the air by an agent represented by a subject in the third person singular.

The specific function of a word in a particular context can be found only by checking how the word relates to other words in the sentence, hence the serious problem of determining which of the many combinations of possible functions do in fact fit together as a legitimate sentence structure. This problem has been solved essentially by trying all possibilities and rejecting those that do not fit, although powerful tests suggested by theory and intuition can be applied to eliminate entire classes of possibilities at one fell swoop, thereby bringing the process within the realm of practicality.

A grammar that pretends to describe English at all accurately must yield a structure for "Time flies like an arrow" in which "time" is the subject of the verb "flies" and "like an arrow" is an adverbial phrase modifying the verb. "Time" can also serve attributively, however, as in "time bomb," and "flies" of course can serve as a noun. Together with "like" interpreted as a verb, these yield a structure that becomes obvious only if one thinks of a kind of flies called "time flies," which happen to like an arrow, perhaps as a meal. Moreover, "time" as an imperative verb with "flies" as a noun also yields a structure that makes sense as an order to someone to take out his stopwatch and time flies with great dispatch, or like an arrow.

A little thought suggests many minor modifications of the grammar sufficient to rule out such fantasies. Unfortunately too much is then lost. A point can be made that the structures are legitimate even if the sentences are meaningless. It is, after all, only an accident of nature, or for that matter merely of nomenclature, that there is no species of flies called "time flies." Worse yet, anything ruling out the nonexisting species of time flies will also rule out the identical but legitimate structure of "Fruit flies like a banana."

Still more confusing, the latter sentence itself is given an anomalous structure, namely that which is quite sensible for "Time flies . . ." but which is nonsensical here since we know quite well that fruit in general does not fly and that when it does, it flies like maple seeds, not like bananas.

A theory of syntax alone can help no further. Semantics, the all too nebulous notion of what a sentence means, must be invoked to choose among the three structures syntax accepts for "Time flies like an arrow." No techniques now known can deal effectively with semantic problems of this kind. Research in the field is continuing in the hope that some form of man-machine interaction can yield both practical results and further insight into the deepening mystery of natural language. We do not yet know how people understand language, and our machine procedures barely do child's work in an extraordinarily cumbersome way.

The outlook is brighter for man-made programming languages. Since these can be defined almost at will, it is generally possible to reduce ambiguity and to systematize semantics well enough for practical purposes, although numerous challenging theoretical problems remain. The computer is also growing in power as an instrument of routine language data processing. Concordances, now easily made by machine, supply scholars in the humanities and social sciences with tabular displays of the location and context of key words in both sacred and profane texts.

Psychologists have used programming languages to write scripts for a variety of structural models of human behavior. These are no more mysterious than scripts for the orbit of Neptune or the structure of hemoglobin. The psychological models differ from the physical ones only in their subject and their original language. Convincing empirical corroboration of the validity of these models is still lacking, and the field has suffered from exaggerated early claims and recurrent confusion of the functional with the structural aspects of theory. Psychology and the study of artificial intelligence are both concerned with intelligent behavior, but otherwise they are not necessarily related except to the extent that metaphors borrowed from one discipline may be stimulating to the other.

In actuality it is the languages, not the scripts, that are today the really valuable products of the attempts at computer modeling of human behavior. Several languages, notably John McCarthy's LISP, have proved invaluable as tools for general research on symbol manipulation. Research on natural-language data processing, theorem-proving, algebraic manipulation, and graphical display draws heavily on such languages. Nevertheless, the computer as instrument is rapidly making a useful place for itself in the psychology laboratory. Bread-and-butter applications include the administration, monitoring, and evaluation of tests of human or animal subjects in studies of perception and learning.

The business of science, both in principle and in practice, is inextricably involved in the business of education, particularly on the university level. The paradigm of the computer as instrument and as actor, although described in terms of research, seems to apply to instruction as well. Because on-line, time-shared systems are still experimental and expensive, especially with graphical display facilities, their use for instruction lags somewhat behind their use for research.

Hopes for computers in education at the elementary or secondary level have been described by Patrick Suppes (see "The Uses of Computers in Education," *Scientific American,* September 1966). My own current exploration of the potential value of technological aids to creative thought focuses on the undergraduate or graduate student and on the transition from learning in the classroom to learning when practicing a profession.

The desire to keep labor within reasonable bounds generally leads to oversimplified and superficial experiments in student laboratories. Where the observation and intelligent interpretation of a variety of significant phenomena are the primary objectives of a laboratory exercise, using a transparent computer should reduce unnecessary drudgery to the point where judgment and interpretation, even of realistic experiments, can prevail.

The transparent computer also promises to be effective as a kind of animated blackboard. This hardly implies the disappearance of chalk, films, or books. The computer merely adds another powerful and versatile tool to the teacher's kit. In fact, where repetition or polish is necessary, the computer itself can serve to make films or equivalent visual recordings. Whereas films cannot be interrupted or altered, a recorded computer sequence can easily be stopped in response to a student's question; the lecturer can then explore alternatives by returning either to the informal direct use of the computer or to the conventional blackboard. The prerecorded sequence can then be resumed.

Best of all, there need be no distinction between the classroom tool and that available to students for homework assignments, laboratory calculations, or individual research projects. The transition from classroom to life therefore promises to be made smoother. Since computers are not yet either as transparent or as cheap as one might wish, many problems of technique and finance remain to be faced. In any case, no panacea has been found for education's ills, only a richer range of choices to be made.

An example based on my experimental use in Harvard classrooms of a keyboard-and-display system developed by Glen Culler at the University of California at Santa Barbara will illustrate both the promise and the problems. Because the static printed page cannot adequately portray the effect of dynamic display, the problems may be more evident than the promise. The topic chosen is mathematical in nature, since such problems are best suited for the equipment currently available. The objective is to develop a natural and perspicuous presentation of topics traditionally reserved for more advanced treatment, to develop others in greater depth than conventional methods allow, and to stimulate the student's intuition and his resourcefulness in solving problems. The objective is not to eliminate theory and rigor in favor of witless calculation, but rather to restore the close link between theory and calculation that characterized mathematics before the advent of rigor late in the nineteenth century led to the aberrant but currently fashionable split between pure and applied mathematics.

It is well known that any periodic function can be approximated by the sum of a series of terms that oscillate harmonically, converging on the curve of the function. Culler's apparatus makes possible quick intuitive exploration of the nature of this approximation. Consider, for example, the square wave shown in Figure 1. The accompanying computer-generated curves show the effect of increasing the number of terms in the partial sum of the series. The spikes near the corners of the square wave are caused by nonuniform convergence near a discontinuity. For the pure mathematician this

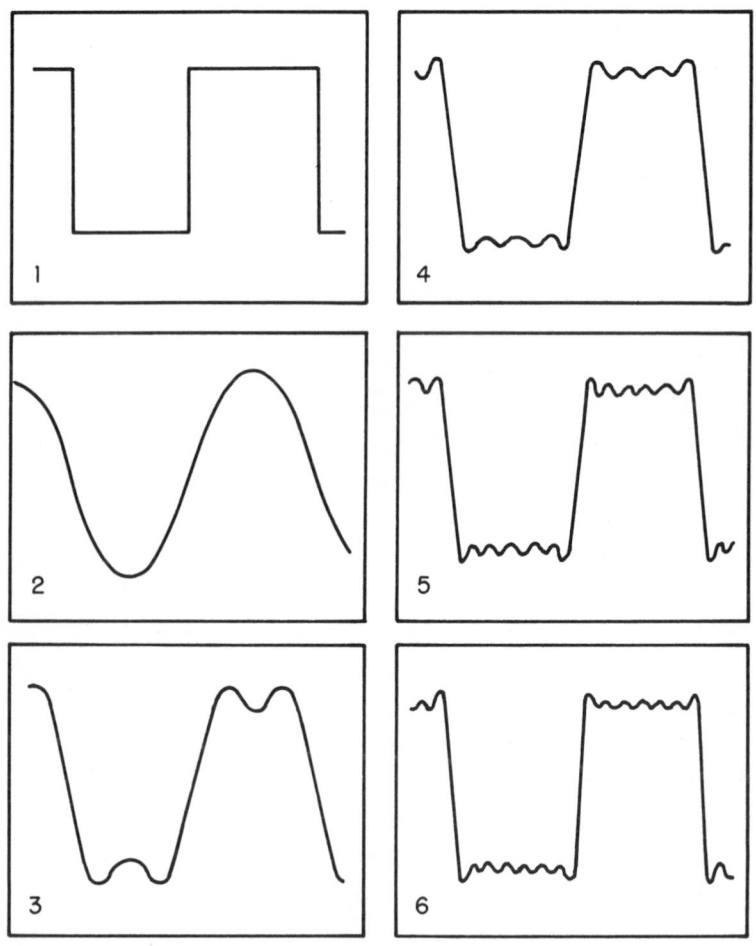

FIGURE 1. Successive Fourier Approximations to a Square Wave

demonstration can motivate a more formal treatment of non-uniform convergence. For the engineer the phenomenon can be clarified by displaying the components of the approximation in such a way as to make it obvious intuitively why the spikes occur. In principle the instructor, or an interested student on his own, could follow up such a demonstration by modeling the effect of a linear circuit element, say a resistor or a simple amplifier, on a square wave, on its individual components and on their sum.

At present any concurrent formal algebraic manipulations require pencil or chalk. Current progress toward machine-aided algebraic manipulation raises the exciting possibility that machines will eventually help with both symbolic and numerical manipulation and with easy transitions between these two modes of expression. Working in both modes simultaneously or in whatever combination rigor and intuition demand would profoundly affect the thought of pure and applied mathematicians alike.

Other types of teaching experiment can be conducted by building an appropriate structural model into the computer. One might assume the structure and examine its behavior, as is frequently done in management games, or one might treat only the behavior as observable, leaving the model to be determined as an exercise in theory-building. As paradigms are developed by research in some area, these paradigms could then be applied as well to teaching in that area. It will be interesting, for example, to experiment with the teaching of a foreign language for which a transformational grammar of the type I described earlier has been implemented on a computer.

It is also interesting to speculate on the use of on-line computers as tools for the investigation of the psychology of learning and problem-solving. Experiments in this area have been difficult, contrived, and unrealistic. When the interactive computer serves as a problem-solving tool, it is also easily adapted to record information about problem-solving behavior. Here again the problem will not be the collection of data but rather devising appropriate experimental designs, since an hour's problem-solving session at a computer console can accumulate an enormous amount of data.

In short, computers are capable of profoundly affecting science by stretching human reason and intuition, much as telescopes or microscopes extend human vision. I suspect that the ultimate effects of this stretching will be as far-reaching as the effects of the invention of writing. Whether the product is truth or nonsense, however, will depend more on the user than on the tool.

Run, Computer, Run

Come, Dick. Come, Jane.
See Spot run.
Run, Spot, run!

Introduction

To pick up almost any current magazine or to listen to eminent researchers and educational spokesmen is to be persuaded that, thanks to the wonders of modern technology, the necessary educational revolution is just around the corner. But is it? The introduction of technology into education is an age-old process alternately exhilarating and depressing. The vastness of prevailing ignorance about both education and technology is matched only by the acrimony of debate about the value of educational technology, a debate blighted by a persistent confusion of ultimate promise with immediate possibility. Scientists or engineers who believe that quick but expensive technological remedies are all that's needed to cure education confront businessmen and school board members at ease with the status quo and anxious only to keep both the budget and the kids in line. Teachers are helpless in the middle.

We cannot ignore the fact that technology *does* offer us hitherto undreamt of possibilities. At the same time, there is merit in the common-sense conclusion that buying some gadget or following some fad *today* might only waste money.

That is one reason why it is vital to distinguish carefully between the long-range promise of educational technology and the technology that is ready for immediate delivery. One purpose of this essay is to sharpen this distinction and to examine the causes of prevalent confusion. Toward this end, it has been necessary to explain some technology to educators, some education to technologists, and to inform both about their master, the polity that educational devices and processes are to serve. With this varied audience in mind, I do not regret seeming naive when I explain to one party some details of what may be all too obvious to another. Educators need not be told what a mess the schools are in. Many of them have said so, loud and often. Scientists need to hear little about the limits of their knowledge. They know better than anyone else how close at hand these lie. Lay decision-makers are no longer surprised by the limitations of experts. They muddle through making the best choices they can, as always.

The need to convince laymen, particularly the lay President and lay Congress and the lay members of the country's 25,000-plus school boards, of the value of basic research often leads scientists and educators into exaggerations that may begin as well-intentioned rhetorical devices but often end in self-delusion. Expediency likewise leads politicians into waving the scientific or technological flag in order to help pass a bill, win an election, or soften the impact of social reform. The rhetoric of educational technology becomes more intelligible once we understand that much of it is fund oriented, social-policy oriented, politically oriented, and not truth oriented. Its context is the opposing rhetorics of needs versus resources, of immediate versus long-term gains.

When a President and Congress set great store in education as a weapon of social reform, agencies like the U.S. Office of Education or the National Science Foundation are put under great pressure to produce immediate results. But when a program must be successful by definition, the need for a good show often overwhelms scientific objectivity; after the curtain falls, little remains either of practical value or of added insight. It may be politically expedient, when poverty is In, to seek support of educational technology on the ground that it will solve the problems of our inner cities and then to use it as a Trojan horse for wheeling in needed reforms. If this leads to demands for an immediate return on investment, however, and if failure to produce this return is both probable and verifiable, then the expedient is really not good strategy. Ideas that are promising as objects of research and honest experiment tend to give birth, through artificial dissemination, to broods of depressing fads. There is then the danger that an angry reaction will kill the promise along with the fads.

Here is an example. In March 1968, the U.S. Office of Education sponsored a conference titled "An Educational System for the Seventies" (fashionably shortened to "ES '70"). The tenor of the conference was typical of the state of thinking in much of the education establishment. I do not want to make too much of this happening — in fact, my point is that not much *can* be made of it — but it will serve the purposes of my argument better than any straw man imagination could conjure up.

Note, for instance, the implicit suggestion in a *pre-conference* announcement that ES '70 already had a concrete existence: "It is hoped that the conference will serve these objectives: 1) to get consultative thinking from various groups about priority goals and outcomes for *ES '70* [emphasis added] in their subject matter area; 2) to provide practice in articulating desired student outcomes in terms of behaviors, values, attitudes, transfer to life situations, citizen role;

3) to provide cross-group communication and efforts at integrative thinking in exploring the realities of *the organic curriculum* [emphasis added]; 4) to provide a limited yet critical exposure of the organic curriculum to secondary school leadership, teachers, and policymaking citizen groups."[1]

A basis for belief in the concrete existence of ES '70 and of *the* organic curriculum was supplied in a document accompanying the statement of conference objectives and claiming that "various elements of the educational process, such as team teaching, programmed instruction, flexible scheduling, computer-assisted teaching, and individualized curricula have recently been examined by researchers *and judged to be important additions to current practice* [emphasis added]."[2]

This belief was further supported, with an air of authority and finality, by the statement that an "overall plan, the first phase of which is almost completed, will identify all of the activities that must be completed before the total new curriculum can become operational." The very next sentence, however, said that "these activities can roughly be classified as research, development, or demonstration," meaning that no one really knew what to do next.

This uncomfortable inconsistency was clarified by the following much more illuminating words from a pre-conference report on secondary education in the United States:

> Educational researchers have made significant findings about the learning process, curriculum innovation, and educational technology. Yet, it is distressing when one considers the tremendous time lag between initial research findings and the implementation of these findings. Even with a rapid escalation of federal research funds for education, the return on this investment has been inconsequential. In short, it seems that a massive and radical redesign of

the secondary education program is imperative. To bring this about, a coordinated planning and development effort, involving a variety of social institutions, is necessary.[3]

This paragraph raises very interesting questions: *Have* researchers indeed "made significant findings about the learning process . . . and educational technology?" *Why* is there a "time lag" between initial research findings and their implementation? *Has* the return on investment of federal research funds for education been "inconsequential," and if so, *why*? Are "significant findings" at hand to justify a "massive and radical redesign" of education programs?

These questions – the reworded *assumptions* of ES '70 – are so important, in fact, that the future of education, and therefore of education research, rests on their answers. And, education itself is of such a magnitude that even minor changes, if extended throughout the system, entail a commitment of major economic and social resources and affect all of society. *Changing education policy is comparable in impact to changing national defense policy.*

Many have therefore thought it appropriate to apply to education an intellectual tool strongly identified with defense policy, namely systems analysis. Scientific methods, in recent years rechristened as systems analysis, can indeed help us understand something of the complexity of American education on the national scale. In the simplest language, the systems analyst says: "It is better to see the whole problem than just a part of the problem." In education, we must recognize that the proper sphere of explicit quantitative analysis is still severely limited. Beyond that sphere, as within it, a scientific viewpoint is merely an aid to clear thinking. It does reveal quickly that technology alone cannot fix education because it makes us see clearly that the schools and the polity are so tightly intertwined as to preclude any change that is resisted by any one of the multitude of participants in the educational enterprise. Where every partner has veto power, none alone can proceed toward change. The prevalent notion that the possession of technological devices is sufficient impetus to change is thus revealed as an illusion.

The prospects for change are also depressing when one looks at schools district by district and sees a tangle of authorities who feel mostly threatened, conservative, and broke. School administrators and teachers are fearful, filled with legitimate concerns for the safety of their jobs and of their persons. Professional accomplishment is neither stimulated nor rewarded. These key people are ill-disposed, by both background and training, to innovation, with or without the devices of new technology. Their opportunities for continuing their own education are most meager.

Local rhetoric about educational goals and possible new technologies is sharply at variance with the reality of schools. Before we allow ourselves to be dazzled by new technology, let us note that the single most common technological tool of education, the book, which is also the most ancient, has been and still is being misused. Libraries are impregnable citadels; use by students is constrained because it might wear out the books, get them out of proper shelf position, or lead the students away from the lesson plan. Why should we expect more from more "exciting" technological innovations? Much-advertised new curricula, such as the Physical Science Study Committee (PSSC) physics, have been adopted in name only. Lip service paid to the individual and to individualization of instruction masks business as usual: regimentation and the primacy of discipline over intellect or action still prevail.

It is for this reason that all the current talk and writing about individualization is so hard to follow. But some sense appears when we distinguish between universal and particular goals of education, between mass production and tailoring in the processes of education, and between group and lone learning. Making these distinctions, and defining complementary technical factors, *begins* the necessary task of producing effective means for matching educational goals with the people, the processes, and the devices of educational technology that we have to work with.

The plight of the schools then becomes evident as one sees that they are being asked to do custom tailoring economically in diversified groups while aiming at both universal and particular goals. Technology seems exciting because it appears to resolve the conflicts and to let us do just that. The nature of the gap between appearance and real possibility must be understood if real progress is to be made toward satisfying society's urgent desire. Otherwise, my conclusion that educational technology can *now* be little more than a placebo for an ailing system will be interpreted as a denial of its potential value, and will be construed, wrongly, as a reinforcement of the conservative argument against further investment for "inconsequential" returns.

Some analysis of ongoing experiments quickly outlines this gap. It is clear that the problems of logistics and the costs of individualization in every form conspire toward relapse into lockstep. Many educators see individualization in terms of independence and creativity as vital to our society. How to achieve independence or creativity through formal schooling is not understood and measuring either is still impossible. Many experiments in this realm are thought to be promising. They tend, however, to become mired in their own platitudes under the gun of those who will believe nothing that cannot be operationally defined, quantified, and measured. It is difficult to see among these promising experiments any important additions to *general* practice. Their effective implementation depends on the energies of a charismatic individual or on a specially receptive atmosphere and they tell us nothing of how to go from prototype to full production.

Other educators prefer rote, in practice if not in theory. Creativity and rote are the extremes of a structure whose shape is scarcely discernible, but whose elements supply the stuff of education. The extreme advocates of creativity have a hard lot. Measurable results come easier with rote. It's easy to say, "The Pilgrims landed at Plymouth Rock in 1620"; and when the job's done there's something almost tangible and to a degree useful to show off. But if one says to students, "From a contemporary point of view, just what is interesting and important about the Pilgrims?" one is in for a siege of creativity that is all too likely to have little to do with either learning or with the Pilgrims. Many experiments have staked out territory between these extremes. The description of some experiments in individualized mass production and in tailoring conveys the flavor of these efforts.

Take, for instance, an experiment conducted in elementary schools. Widely described as promising, it has addressed itself to reaching measurable universal goals through processes created by mass production and applied by mass production at custom-tailored rates to pupils grouped by the level of their attained "behavioral objectives" rather than by their chronological ages. The teachers in this experiment behave like machines. Though they are successful in some respects, their work is washed out by the leveling influence of the unexperimental high school. This experiment again does not represent an important addition to current *general* practice. Nonetheless, the pressure for quick returns on investment has increased the number of participating schools from 23 to 88, with 1,000 more innovation-drunk schools clamoring to take part. By diverting resources into premature dissemination, these pressures for quickie cure-alls threaten to stop further progress with this promising form of mass production while imposing on pupils and taxpayers yet another change in form without change in substance.

A look at another experiment done in a collegiate setting shows what an important difference it makes to have human and material resources of high quality on hand and to be free from disciplinary and scheduling constraints. In this experiment, the process is created by custom tailoring and applied through an ingenious combination of rate tailoring and mass production. The goals are prescribed but, since they apply to a group self-selected for homogeneity, the distinction between the universal and the particular is not important. Learning takes place through a combination of lone and group activities. From the point of view of public elementary and secondary schools, the minimal requirements for even attempting emulation of this experiment are a description of Utopia. But they are not sufficient. The successful export of such an experiment to the schools as they are is therefore most unlikely.

There is a tendency nowadays to equate educational technology with inert *devices*. Devices are important, but worthless without people and processes. It should go without saying that a system intended for human use should be adapted to humans and not vice versa. Beyond that rather obvious but often ignored point, the system should be *transparent* in the sense that the system should not obscure the student's view of the subject. Few of the multitude of systems based on devices from chalk to television are now transparent enough for service in the schools.

To help in understanding educational devices and in telling how effectively they can be matched with the goals, the people, and the processes of education, I shall present a profile of their significant technical characteristics. At present, novelty and glamor are the best known properties of these devices. Cost and value are of obvious importance, but an adequate profile requires rating more technical factors as well. The factors to be considered are flexibility, generality, scheduling, parallelism, amount, physical accessibility, reliability, maintenance, complexity, comfort, standardization, integration, and content.

These factors interact with one another and with chosen goals, processes, and groupings in complex and ill-understood ways. One thing is clear: Maximizing some of these factors will interfere with freedom of choice and with maximizing other factors. The need to reconcile conflicting demands leads to what in the jargon of systems analysis is called "tradeoff studies." Said plainly, this means that when you can't have everything, you must find out how to make the most of what you've got.

A detailed case study of language laboratory devices specifically illustrates some significant general tradeoffs. In particular, it confirms what is already evident from the analysis of various processes, namely that greater individualization and greater cost necessarily go hand in hand. Reliability is a sine qua non. It is rarely found in practice, although it is among the key factors distinguishing a laboratory prototype carefully kept alive by attentive parents, relatives, and friends from a production model ready to face all comers however careless or ill-willed. Even if genuine researchers have judged a prototype to be an important addition to current practice, much time and effort remains ahead before the fledgling can leave the nest without dropping into the mouth of the nearest cat. Prototypes with merit need a long period of tender and expensive care. However distressing the tremendous time lag between initial research findings and their implementation may be, the engineering lead time between prototype and production model is a fact of life. With devices, as with people and processes, lead time is necessary to turn ultimate promise into immediate possibility.

Enter the computer. The promise seems immense, hence the excitement is great. Like books or tutors, computers can serve any goals. They are indifferent to how the processes they apply are created. The man-made programs that control computers can embody universal or particular goals; they can either be mass produced or hand-tailored on the spot. Like a book, a computer can perform for either a group or a lone individual.

Stored-program technology endows any one computer with great flexibility; it is at least as general as a blackboard. Multiple access and communications techniques promise parallelism, that is, simultaneous availability to many students, and also easy physical accessibility. A computer itself is potentially an excellent tool for scheduling anything, including itself. Like good tutors, who can marshal resources beyond their own, computers can marshal most other educational devices and make them perform at their command. Computers have given other devices—slide projectors and tape recorders, even blackboards — renewed dignity as part of the world of technological innovation.

More subtle qualities make computers capable of profoundly affecting education by stretching human reason and intuition. A wide latitude of processes permits balancing costs and needs as appropriate in various circumstances. A computer *need not* play favorites with educational goals or processes. Specific examples of learning situations, based on observing various mathematical phenomena through a computer, suggest that the computer's ultimate effects will be as far-reaching as those of the invention of writing.

The prospects are exciting indeed. But, although computers may revolutionize possibilities, they alter the facts of life not at all. When we go to schools where computers are actually in use, we find them serving as expensive page turners, mimicking programmed instruction texts. Yes, computers have practically infinite branching capabilities, but this matters little when we are unable to foresee more than a very few of the most common possible learner responses. Restricted to narrow ranges of preordained alternatives, the learner is constrained to answer in the program's terms. Computers are being used simply to churn out masses of data of doubtful value. Moreover, even with computers, the facts of life reassert themselves in the shape of cost, amount, reliability, maintenance, complexity, comfort, standardization, integration, and content. In short, much lead time is still between us and the reduction of experiments to practice. We shall see that time and again in the brief history of computing, glowing experimental results have lost their meaning in the translation from pilot study to useful operating size. Much of what computer-aided instruction and learning needs is still in the laboratory. Costs are high though decreasing, and hopes for personnel savings are largely illusions. Even computers are subject to all the usual social problems.

If we want real technological change – not just the appearance of it – we must, as in all enterprises, invest money in better ideas and better people. The scale of investment is bound to be large. With 46.5 million pupils expected in public elementary and secondary schools by 1975, each additional dollar to be spent on one child translates into $46.5 million on a national scale. Given this massive multiplier and the knowledge that ideas, people, and money have little effect if used inefficiently, it is clear that when and how resources flow is decisive for economically efficient progress.

Some policies are therefore suggested as more conducive to efficient progress than current ones. We must support promising ideas longer than either private or government programs now permit. We must support risk-taking and cushion failure. All partners in the educational enterprise must share the dangers, the costs, and the credit or blame attendant on changing technology. Though we may want *technological* change, we must, nonetheless, chart our course by *human* judgment. We must follow through in depth with a small number of distinct alternatives.

In our still profound ignorance, who can prescribe the right path to take? The best intentioned orthodoxy is bound to fail. Both nature and the ideology of free enterprise suggest turning to competition. An argument for competition in education cannot be based solely on faith in the market mechanism, which has declined in areas where a need for more deliberate government intervention and control has been felt. It depends also on the belief that a system whose basic existence is assured no matter how badly or how unresponsively it performs can benefit from some elements of market competition, with careful checks and controls built in.

We must encourage as much diversity as possible – as many paths, as many different outlooks, as many different experiments, as many different initiatives as we can afford once the demands of education have been balanced against those of other needs of our society. How we might get there from here is examined in the last chapter.

1 The School Setting

1.1 SYSTEMS ANALYSIS

That is common knowledge, so common in fact, that it may not even be true. — *Donald Barthelme,* Snow White*

There is today a widely held point of view from which most anything, and education in particular, can be described as a collection or system of interdependent parts belonging to a hierarchy in which a system may have subsystems of its own while acting as a mere part of a suprasystem. The process of analyzing or synthesizing such systems, called "systems analysis" for short, is touted as one of the shiniest of new technologies.

To some extent, speaking of systems is little more than appealing to a fashionable metaphor for the sake of snowing someone. Even then, this fad is not without merit as an antidote to that other pseudo-scientific fad, the precise and exhaustive analysis of an insignificant isolated effect under artificial conditions. Thinking "systems" at least reminds one that everything is related to everything else. Although always necessary in practice, ignoring any of these relations can be perilous; thinking "systems" alerts us to this peril.

*New York: Atheneum, 1967, p. 44.

Systems analysis cannot be dismissed as modern gadgetry. Its best formulations are indistinguishable from descriptions of the scientific method and thus have roots reaching back through Roger Bacon to Aristotle and not, as some believe, just to the RAND Corporation. At its best, the systems approach, applying well-developed, proved research and design tools to problems, solves them far more satisfactorily than naked intuition.

The mathematical methods of control-systems theory, for example, are very effective in designing speed controls for engines, or process controls for certain chemical plants, or in plotting optimal trajectories for missiles. Whether the spectacular failures of electrical-power distribution systems in the late sixties were due to failures of the methods or to failures in their application is still hotly disputed. Other quantitative techniques, linear programming, for instance, have had some successful applications to decision-making, although the range of reality which they can depict faithfully is limited. Computer-aided games and simulation are other recent additions to the tool kit of the hopeful systems student.

All these techniques have serious limitations. The widespread belief that there exists a general body of well-defined and effective systems theory that may be applied by powerful computers to the analysis or synthesis of any system whatsoever is a myth. This belief is really valid for only a relatively small class of very simple systems like those mentioned in the preceding paragraph. There is more wishful thinking than validity in claims for the success of the systems approach in the design, management, and control of entire space and military systems, in spite of the repeated citation of these enterprises as paradigms for educational and other social systems.

At least three conditions must be satisfied for the systems approach to be more than an apt metaphor:

1. The system being studied must be independent enough of the systems which combine with it to form a suprasystem for interactions among these systems to be either satisfactorily accounted for or else ignored without dire consequences.

2. The system being studied must be one for which well-developed and proved research and design tools exist.

3. When designing a system, we must know explicitly what it is for.

The first two conditions may conflict: Such tools as we have work best on simple systems, but dissecting a simple system out of its complex natural environment is an operation which the patient may not survive. The third condition is perhaps the most stringent. We must know what a system is for, and know it far more explicitly than when navigating by intuition. When we ask what it means to know objectives explicitly, we shall see that such knowledge is hard to come by in the educational sphere.

Education is not unique in this respect. Describing the Planning-Programming-Budgeting System (PPBS) he developed for former Secretary of Defense Robert S. McNamara, Charles Hitch introduces it as "a combination of two management techniques which are related and mutually supporting, but distinct; in fact, they are so distinct that it is possible to use either without the other." The first of these techniques, program budgeting, need not concern us here. Hitch tells us that the second "is called systems analysis, cost-effectiveness analysis, or cost-benefit analysis, as well as various other names, including operations or operational research. The whole system seems to be singularly plagued by terminological confusion. I hope," he goes on, "that, as someone said of the music of Wagner, it is better than it sounds."

The systems analyst's job, as the Pentagon is reputed to put it, is simply to meet goals with a maximum ratio of effectiveness to cost. Fortunately for this nation, the Defense Department's application of PPBS is not quite so simple-minded, or at least was not at its inception. To the extent that PPBS is used in the Defense Department as an analytic technique rather than as an administrative club, its value depends on the possibility of doing what Hitch defines as "explicit, quantitative analysis, which is designed to maximize or at least increase the value of the objectives achieved by an organization, minus the values of the resources it uses."

To this definition of systems analysis Hitch himself has added caveats that many witless disciples have apparently forgotten and which therefore bear repeating:

> However, there are risks and dangers as well as opportunities in the application of new management techniques — including the risk of discrediting the techniques, if one tries to move too far too fast. Although it did not appear easy at the time, there is no doubt in my mind that the Department of Defense, or much of it, is easier to program and to analyze quantitatively than many areas of civilian government. For example, it is certainly easier than the foreign affairs area. Quite apart from these difficulties, the substantive problems in other areas are different and new. In Defense, we had several hundred analysts at the RAND Corporation and elsewhere developing programs and systems analysis techniques for a decade before the department attempted any large-scale general application.

Although the U.S. Office of Education, the Bureau of the Budget, and others nowadays set great store on systems analysis, PPBS, cost-effectiveness, or the same thing by some other name, the evidence suggests that the continuation of Hitch's comment is valid for education: "No remotely similar preparatory effort has gone into any other governmental area and the number of trained and skilled people is so limited that they are inevitably spread far thinner in other departments of government than they were and are in Defense."[1]

The "systems" label should therefore not be given too much significance: it can produce no miracles; you can't just "feed it to the computer." But neither should "systems" be ignored. Despite obvious limitations, taking some of the systems viewpoint—as by agreeing in principle that it is better to think about a problem in its whole context than not—is the best available attitude toward any subject whose literature is characterized by the idée fixe (individualized instruction), the panacea (applying computers to education can bring a powerful new force to bear on the central-city problem), and the empty label (organic curriculum). Thoughtful and thorough engineering is always good practice.

In summary, dealing with the mythology of systems analysis requires making a distinction as delicate as that between ultimate promise and immediate possiblity. The myth surrounding systems analysis holds that educational salvation lies in applying to education the planning and control techniques commonly believed to have been successful in the defense and aerospace industries. Advocating Systems Analysis (capital "S," capital "A") as a panacea is very much like Making the World Safe for Democracy, Unconditional Surrender, and Massive Retaliation; all are experiments in delusion for political ends. Yet, not to believe in the usefulness of systems analysis (lower-case "s," lower-case "a") is to deny the value of reason, common sense, and indeed, of the scientific method.

1.2 SCHOOLS AS SYSTEMS IN A CHANGING WORLD

It may never have crossed your mind to think that other universes of discourse distinct from your own existed, with people in them, discoursing—Donald Barthelme, Snow White*

Once agreed that it is better to think about a problem in its full context than not, one must ask what is the context of schools and of what are schools the context? My primary interest in this essay is in the schools as a context for technological innovation. In his essay "Social Problems and National Socio-Technical Institutes," Alvin Weinberg, Director of the Oak Ridge National Laboratory, suggests that "many problems that are traditionally viewed as being primarily social possess stronger technological components than one at first suspects." He goes on to say that "they therefore may admit to techno-logical palliatives, or even 'fixes,' which hopefully can buy the time necessary to get at the cause of the social problem."

The thrust of Weinberg's optimistic argument for "techno-logical fixes" is that *if* a technological solution to an apparently social problem can be found, *then* there are many reasons why "in general, a technological invention is easier to make and put into use than is a social invention." The examples he cites are revealing: "Many fewer people were involved in our decision to go ahead with the Manhattan Project than were

*New York: Atheneum, 1967, p. 44.

involved in our decision to adopt the pay-as-you-go income tax. In consequence, it was easier to start on the atomic bomb than to modify the income tax laws."[2] The observation that decisions were made by relatively few people is true of most of the major military-industrial developments of recent decades, including not only the Manhattan Project, but the development of the national air-defense system — with its subsystems of ballistic missiles and command-and-control — the design of the Polaris submarine, and the race for the moon.

Few major projects, however, can achieve the magnificent isolation of the Manhattan Project, an isolation secured only with considerable difficulty, even under wartime conditions favorable to secrecy. The space effort, although run far more openly, nevertheless involves matters sufficiently arcane to be beyond the comprehension or the immediate experience of most taxpayers. Consequently, with strong Presidential support, the space program was launched after persuading only a relatively small number of scientists, engineers, administrators, and Congressmen. The novelty of the effort initially removed it from the restraints of tradition. Only fairly recently has the very success of the space program and its obvious and geographically widespead economic benefits put it in the pork barrel with all the post offices, federal office buildings, rivers, and harbors.

The setting of education differs radically. A study by the staff of the Denver Research Institute has pinpointed some of the shortcomings of defense management techniques in the civilian sphere. The study, *Defense Systems Resources in the Civil Sector: An Evolving Approach, An Uncertain Market,* emphasizes the difficulties which multiple jurisdiction, decentralization, and localism in decision-making create in the civilian sector: "The hierarchical and authoritarian structure, as well as the often classified nature of military systems contracts, precludes much public debate and minimizes the number and variety of audiences for the report. Yet, almost all civil systems work must be responsive to many sets of requirements and many audiences — a problem which constitutes much of the so-called communications gap between defense systems people and civil servants."[3]

Within the educational system, it is difficult to find an appropriate audience and, still more difficult, a boss to satisfy. Schools belong to everyone's experience. Consequently, everyone is aware of them and has an opinion about them. The very crude schema of the school system and the community presented in Figure 2 suggests the complexity inherent in the strong linkages and mutual interactions among the various elements. Technological change in education is therefore very closely coupled to the polity within which educational policies and procedures are developed.

The strength and multiplicity of these linkages enforces stability. Changing school hours affects not only pupils and school personnel but every mother as well. Introducing the "new math" shakes up every parent in town. Attempting administrative decentralization stirs storms of union protests. Ability grouping invites federal court decisions prohibiting it. If part of the high school burns down, it is cheaper for taxpayers in some localities to build a new one because the state contributes to new construction but not to renovation. An experiment with a new high school curriculum raises the specter of low performance on College Boards. And, most obvious, the people who make up every other institution, from the family to the Presidency, are products of the schools.

Granted the complexity of the system it becomes obvious that any change in either school or society which alters, or even threatens to alter, established linkages between them will meet at best with the delays inherent in explaining any change to those affected and at worst with fierce resistance. Whenever some external sector of society or the schools themselves press for change in the schools, then the schools must in turn make their peace with all other linked sectors of society. Without external pressures or alliances the schools themselves rarely initiate change. If the change seems undesirable to the schools but the external pressures are strong, the schools, like any institution, tend to adopt evasive tactics which take the form of change without commitment to its substance.

There is a great deal of critical opinion to the effect that this indeed is what happens. We read, for instance, that:

> Boston—and other cities—like to talk innovation. Innovation has become fashionable and profitable. The federal government will pay for almost anything billed as new or experimental. In the past two years more than two billion dollars have gone to programs associated with education for "disadvantaged youth." Around the urban school systems are magnificent necklaces of special programs, head starts, pilot schools, enrichment classes; but the body of education and the results produced remain almost unchanged. In Boston, which has enough trial programs and experiments to fill a book, the life of the average child in the average classroom is virtually unaffected. The teachers, the curriculum, the school committee are the same. The books are the same. The attitudes are the same.[4]

Implicit in such commentaries is the notion that the educational establishment itself is the sole obstacle to wanted

FIGURE 2. The Public School and Its Context

- "INSIDE" INDIVIDUALS
  Pupils; Teachers; Administrators; Non-Professional Staff...
- "OUTSIDE" INDIVIDUALS
  Parents; Peers; Heroes; Authorities; Muckrakers; Policemen; Bookies; Junkies...
- "OUTSIDE" INSTITUTIONS
  - LOCAL GOVERNMENT: *Board of Selectmen or City Council; School Board; Superintendent of Schools; Recreation Commission; Park Department...*
  - STATE GOVERNMENT
    - BOARD OF EDUCATION: *Bureaus of: Curriculum and Institutions; Administration and Personnel; Research and Development; School Facilities and Services; State and Federal Assistance to Schools...*
    - BOARD OF HIGHER EDUCATION
    - ADVISORY COUNCILS...
  - FEDERAL GOVERNMENT
    - CONGRESS: *Elementary and Secondary Education Act; Selective Service Act...*
    - SUPREME COURT: *School Desegregation Decision of 1954...*
    - EXECUTIVE BRANCH: *Department of Health, Education, and Welfare; U.S. Office of Education; Department of Defense; National Science Foundation...*
  - MASS MEDIA
    - PUBLICATIONS: *Newspapers; Books; Comic Books...*
    - TELEVISION: *Commercial; Public; Educational; Instructional...*
    - OTHER MEDIA: *Movies; Radio; Records...*
  - PROFESSIONAL AND OTHER ASSOCIATIONS
    - INSTITUTIONAL GROUPINGS: *National School Boards Association; National Education Association; National Association of Secondary School Principals; National Association of Independent Schools; American Federation of Teachers; American Association of University Professors...*

- PROFESSIONAL AND OTHER ASSOCIATIONS (cont.)
  - FIELD-OF-STUDY GROUPINGS: *American Association of Physics Teachers; American Physical Society; American Mathematical Association; Association for Computing Machinery; American Association for the Advancement of Science ...*
- COLLEGES AND UNIVERSITIES: *Teachers' Colleges; Graduate Schools of Education; Arts and Sciences Faculties; Junior Colleges; Business Schools; Research or Curriculum Development Institutes or Projects ...*
- OTHER ELEMENTARY AND SECONDARY SCHOOLS: *Parochial Schools; Private Schools; Experimental and Model Schools ...*
- INDUSTRY AND COMMERCE
  - AS EMPLOYER OF SCHOOL GRADUATES
  - AS AGENT OF EDUCATION AND TRAINING
  - THE EDUCATIONAL INDUSTRY
    - TESTING INDUSTRY: *College Entrance Examination Board, Educational Testing Service; Science Research Associates ...*
    - EDUCATIONAL MEDIA AND MATERIALS: *Raytheon; RCA; IBM; General Learning; Education Development Corporation ...*
    - SYSTEMS INDUSTRY: *System Development Corporation; Lockheed; Litton Industries ...*
- FOUNDATIONS: *Ford; Carnegie ...*
- CHURCHES: *Parochial Schools; Religious Organizations ...*
- CERTIFICATION AND ACCREDITATION AGENCIES: *State Boards; North Central Association of Schools and Colleges ...*
- SPECIAL INTEREST GROUPS: *CORE; Urban League; Neighborhood Associations; American Legion; Parent-Teacher Associations; John Birch Society ...*
- INFORMAL EDUCATIONAL SYSTEMS: *Boy Scouts; 4-H Clubs; Religious Organizations; Summer Camps; Welfare Agencies; Peace Corps; Armed Services ...*

reform. While this is common knowledge, it may not be the *whole* truth.

James Becker, director of one of the U.S. Office of Education's regional laboratories, for example, states emphatically that "it is only possible to believe that the cities' public schools are, on purpose, no better than the people who control money and power have wanted them to be. True, there have always been enough school superintendents and principals who have been willing to accept the constraints imposed upon them, but it would be a gross error to assume that it has ever been, or is now, within the power of professional educators to make school systems much different from what their boards of control and those who control them decide. Educators do not make basic educational policy."[5] To the extent that Becker is right, the education establishment is obviously not the sole obstacle to change. External pressures for reform may be merely bread-and-circus politics, lip service paid to change that masks a real preference for the status quo.

The gloomy tenor of considerations of the immediate consequences of even the most superficial analysis seems to have escaped the attention of many enthusiastic advocates of technological innovation. If change is either unwanted or resisted, new technology alone cannot produce it.

On the other hand, whenever society has wished to change itself, the educational process has come to mind as an agent of social change. Systems analysis has helped us realize that because the schools are now tethered by many strings, they find it hard to change themselves, hence still harder to induce change in society. Although systems analysis offers no magic, it can further help to lead us from this realization to the acquisition of sufficient knowledge about the strings — what they are made of, how they are interconnected, who pulls them, how much they can stretch, and so on — to provide, first, understanding and, second, mechanisms for turning toward agreed-upon and explicitly defined goals.

The present tools of formal systems analysis work best on well-defined, simple, concrete models involving quantifiable concepts, measurable data, and, above all, thoroughly understood theoretical structures which adequately reflect reality. Some models having these qualities can indeed be isolated from the buzzing, blooming confusion of the educational world. Unfortunately, whether macroscopic or microscopic, the models available nowadays do not adequately depict the essentials of educational technology.

There is much literature on economic models for education. To the extent that it is relevant at all, it deals with such macroscopic concepts as total enrollments and spending levels. The introduction of technology into the schools is clearly related to available funds. Preliminary analysis, however, suggested the need for a finer-grained picture of fund flow to explain why ES '70's "rapid escalation of federal research funds for education," however *necessary,* is not *sufficient* to produce the desired "return on investment," especially when much of this "research" is mislabeled and turns out to be premature application.

Intelligent macromodelers understand the limitations of their models. In the concluding paragraphs of their paper, "Educational Models, Manpower, Planning and Control," P. Alper and his associates point out the dangers of treating educational decision sequences as if they were precisely like the input sequences controlling an industrial system. "In other words," they say, "the term 'controller' as used by control engineers is somewhat misleading with regard to educational planning. A controller generally produces the control sequence which is directly applied upon a plant, but some of the decision sequences emanating from the central decision-maker may in fact be markedly re-interpreted or even ignored. The central decision-maker is often a 'suggester' rather than a 'controller.' " The concluding paragraph of their paper then begins: "This brief outline of some of the difficulties of implementing an educational control system will be sufficient to illustrate that there are many differences between the control of a socio-economic process and the control of an industrial process and these differences do not favour the control of the former. There can, however, be no doubt of the need to understand the educational system better and to develop the power to make it more successfully respond to the demands placed upon it."[6] In subsequent chapters I shall examine both the system and the demands made of it in terms calculated to shed light on this control problem.

The microscopic realm is exemplified by the extensive literature on the psychology of learning. One might expect the psychology of learning to help explain not how the educational system is controlled, but how it best can reach its educational objectives. Pending much further progress, this expectation is disappointed. For example, a study conducted "to enable the Navy to gain more practical applications from the research it sponsors"[7] pointed to the inadequacy of microscopic studies by describing the limited impact on educational and training technology of the psychology of learning.

Robert R. Mackie and Paul R. Christensen, the authors of that study, concluded that just "a very small percentage of findings from learning research is useful, in any direct sense, for the improvement of training or educational practices . . . . Many learning research studies," they state, "simply are not translatable because the stimulus (or task) conditions employed by the researcher bear no determinable relationship to stimuli (or tasks) outside the laboratory."[8] Explicit quantitative analysis thus does not take kindly to transplantation from laboratory to schoolroom.

Nonetheless, some aspects of school systems and particularly of their national environment are best understood through appeal to aggregate quantitative data. Noting that the United States now has approximately 27,000 independent public school districts with 1,700,000 teachers, 42.6 million pupils, and a budget of $27.8 billion should make it clear that there is a difference between doing something about *a* school and doing something about *schools:* one dollar easily administered by any of us to any one favorite pupil becomes $42.6 million to be supplied by whom and applied how and for what ends to which of 42.6 million pupils throughout the country.

The local setting, however, is best appreciated partly undressed, since the sights, sounds, and smells of the real classroom are easily hidden by a statistical cloak. Anecdotes from direct observation have great value. Direct observations of the classroom have been attacked as merely sentimental or sensational, epithets frequently applied to the reporting in *Up the Down Staircase* or *The Blackboard Jungle.* My field studies have, however, convinced me of the verisimilitude of *Up the Down Staircase* and thus of its value as evidence. School people come by this conviction naturally. No teacher that I have met has disagreed with the following words of Robert Schaefer, the dean of Columbia University's Teachers

College: "In general, one finds more compelling accounts of satisfaction and frustrations in teaching from the literary record. Bel Kaufman's current best seller, *Up the Down Staircase,* and Evan Hunter's overly sensational but still persuasive *The Blackboard Jungle,* for example, convey a greater sense of reality about teaching in urban schools than anything research has yet produced."[9]

In *Equality of Educational Opportunity,* that monumental statistical study commonly called the Coleman Report, James Coleman makes a further case for observation by pointing out what statistics can miss: "The school environment of a child consists of many elements, ranging from the desk he sits at to the child who sits next to him, and including the teacher who stands at the front of his class. A statistical survey can give only fragmentary evidence of this environment."[10]

The soundness of this warning is evident in Coleman's own report. Tables 1 and 2 are presented here to illustrate what may be learned from such statistical studies and to contrast this with the findings of informal field reports. In Table 1 the question that somehow elicited the data tabulated in the same table inquires about the presence of fixed or portable language laboratory equipment but asks nothing about whether it is used and if so, how. The assumption that possession implies use is built into the question. It might therefore seem justifiable to conclude that language instruction has already made great strides, especially in western metropolitan areas. On the other hand, those who prefer to think that not nearly enough has yet been done for language study might point to the contrast between the data of Table 1 and those of Table 2, which suggest that nearly every pupil in the United States comes into contact with power tools.

The necessity for distinguishing between possession and use before either conclusion is drawn emerges clearly from my observation of the shop in the Pack School of Small City (Appendix A, p. 253). Such observations ring true in any institution. If the principal of the Pack School participated in

TABLE 1. Presence of language laboratories

Question 13n. Does your school have a foreign language laboratory with sound equipment?

Answers   a. Yes, with equipment installed in a fixed location.
            b. Yes, with portable equipment.
            c. Courses are taught without laboratory.
            d. We offer no courses in foreign language.

Percentage of students[a] in schools answering yes

	N	W(N)	W
United States	49	58	56
Non-Metropolitan Areas			
North and West	32	36	24
South	17	22	32
Southwest	38	36	19
Metropolitan Areas			
Northeast	47	80	79
Midwest	68	48	57
South	48	65	72
Southwest	69	90	97
West	95	94	80

Source: James S. Coleman, *Equality of Educational Opportunity,* U.S. Department of Health, Education, and Welfare, Office of Education (Washington, D.C.: Government Printing Office, 1966). The question appears in the principal questionnaire on p. 660; the tabulation of percentages is excerpted from Table 2.21.8, p. 73. Coleman does not explain how the percentages were derived from responses to the question.
[a]N, Negroes; W(N), "whites in the same counties as Negroes"; W, whites.

the Coleman survey he doubtlessly could, without the slightest twinge of conscience, have answered yes to question 13j of the principal questionnaire as reproduced in Table 2. And yet, as the account of Small City schools shows, the shop teacher

TABLE 2. Presence of power tools

Question 13j. Does your school have a shop with power tools?
Answers   a. Yes
b. No

Percentage of students[a] in schools answering yes		
	N	W(N)	W
United States	89	95	96
Non-Metropolitan Areas			
North and West	97	96	96
South	85	92	90
Southwest	88	93	91
Metropolitan Areas			
Northeast	67	95	97
Midwest	99	100	100
South	89	91	90
Southwest	92	100	97
West	100	100	100

Source: James S. Coleman, *Equality of Educational Opportunity*, U.S. Department of Health, Education, and Welfare, Office of Education (Washington, D.C.: Government Printing Office, 1966). The question appears in the principal questionnaire on p. 659; the tabulation of percentages is excerpted from Table 2.21.8, p. 73.
[a]N, Negroes; W(N), "whites in the same counties as Negroes"; W, whites.

there had been waiting eighteen months for his impressive array of tools to be attached to a power source. This illustrates in very concrete terms why, as Coleman said, "a statistical survey can give only a fragmentary evidence of this environment" and why, therefore, additional evidence is essential.

Having been struck on the one hand by the enormous gap between national policy pronouncements and their local effects and, on the other hand, by the lack of realism of local experiments laying claim to national implementation without regard to the effects of changing from small to large scale, I believe that a confrontation of the national view with intermediate universes of discourse, with people in them, discoursing, is important to an understanding of any form of technology.

1.3 THE NATIONAL SETTING: A SKETCH

The world of budgets with such household figures as $500 per year per pupil or homeowner taxes of $400 to $1,000 a year is part of a bigger world. To look at educational questions on a national scale is to magnify such figures with six or seven following zeros or, in scientific jargon, to shift scale by six or seven orders of magnitude.

The growth of the school system — in number of schools, teachers, expenditures, and so forth — is based in the first instance on the number of young people to be educated. As of 1967, children between the ages of five and seventeen made up more than one fourth of the population of the United States, compared to one fifth in 1950.[11] The number of public secondary schools in the country increased from approximately 25,000 in 1950 to 26,000 in 1964, while the number of students in these schools increased from 5,700,000 to 11,400,000 in the same period. At the same time, the number of students and schools in the non-public sector was growing

TABLE 3. National expenditures for public elementary and secondary schools (dollars)[a]

Expenditures	Year						
	1950	1958	1960	1962	1964	1967	1975
Total (10^9)	5.8	13.6	15.6	18.3	21.4	27.8	34.9
Capital outlay (10^9)	1.0	2.8	2.7	2.9	2.9	3.6	3.5
Capital outlay per pupil	40	83	75	76	70	85	75
Average salary, total instructional staff	3000	4700	5400	5800	6200	7100	8400
Operating expense per pupil	209	341	375	419	461	529	679
Number of pupils in average daily attendance (10^6)	25.1	33.6	36.1	38.2	41.0	42.6	46.5

Sources: "44.6 Million Pupils in Schools at Record $27.8-Billion Cost," *New York Times*, Jan. 2, 1967, p. 16. U.S. Congress, Joint Economic Committee, Subcommittee on Economic Progress (hearings of June 6, 10, and 13, 1966), *Technology in Education* (Washington, D.C.: Government Printing Office, 1966), p. 213. U.S. Department of Commerce, Bureau of the Census, *Statistical Abstract of the United States, 1965* (Washington, D.C.: Government Printing Office, 1965), p. 16. U.S. Department of Health, Education, and Welfare, Office of Education, *Projections of Educational Statistics to 1975-76* (Washington, D.C.: Government Printing Office, 1966), pp. 70, 75-77. The U.S. Office of Education arrived at its projections for 1975 by adding $1 billion to the trend figures in order to account for increased Federal spending (U.S. Dept. of Commerce, Bureau of the Census, *Statistical Abstract of the United States 1966*, p. 119). In deriving the per-pupil expenditure, $25 was added to include the effects of the Elementary and Secondary Education Act.

[a] All figures are in current dollars for the year except for 1975 projections, where 1965-66 dollars are used.

at an even more rapid rate: the number of non-public secondary schools was 3,300 in 1950 and climbed to 4,400 in 1964, while enrollments increased from 572,000 to 1,400,000.[12]

This period of growth was also a period of administrative consolidation. The number of school districts declined from 100,000 in 1945-46 to less than 27,000 in 1965-66.[13] In the 1960's there were more students per school and more schools per district than in the 1950's.

These changes naturally required a larger number of teachers. The total number of classroom teachers for public elementary and secondary schools was 914,000 in 1950 and 1,628,000 by 1964.[14] During this period, the overall teacher-pupil ratio dropped from 1:27 to 1:25.

Expenditures for maintaining our nation's public elementary and secondary schools and the kinds of expenditures projected for the future are summarized in Table 3. Note that the two great periods of growth in spending for education were after Sputnik (1957) and after the passage of the Elementary and Secondary Education Act (1965). The estimates in Table 3 take account of the impact of federal government spending on education, an impact which should not be minimized, at least in financial terms. In 1964-65, before the passage of the Elementary and Secondary Education Act (ESEA), the federal government was paying 4.3 percent of the total expenditure for public elementary and secondary schools. By 1966-67, the federal government's share had risen to 8.1 percent of the total—or almost double the proportion spent prior to this legislation.[15]

The increases projected for enrollment at all levels of education will necessarily place additional burdens on the educational system. Leonard Lecht has estimated that "providing the same quality of education [at all levels, public and private] as in 1962, with teachers' salaries, class sizes, and facilities per student at their 1962 levels, would mean raising spending for education in 1975 to almost $40 billion [in 1962 dollars]."[16] This $40 billion estimate is conservatively low, since it does not include "the increase in educational expenditures expected to occur because of rural-urban population shifts."[17] Nevertheless, the total expenditure projected by the U.S. Office of Education for public and private education at *all* levels in 1975 is clearly sufficient at least to maintain the status quo by a safe margin: it is $63.9 billion in 1965-66 dollars or $60.2 billion when converted into 1962 dollars.[18]

Lecht has further estimated that attaining the relatively modest objectives of increasing the ratio of enrollment to population, adding more and better paid teachers, and building an adequate modern plant for the *entire* educational system (including higher education) would cost $82 billion (in 1962 dollars)[19] in 1975.[20] Yet the U.S. Office of Education estimates that only $60.2 billion will be available. Taking public and private elementary and secondary schools only, Lecht estimates that to reach these modest objectives would require an expenditure of $54 billion in 1975.[21] The U.S. Office of Education projections indicate that there will not be that much available; the estimated total expenditure figure for public and private elementary and secondary schools in 1975 is $39.5 billion in 1965-66 dollars,[22] which is the equivalent of $37.2 billion in 1962 dollars.

Lecht's $54 billion estimate of what the elementary and secondary schools of 1975 will need to attain his modest objectives amounts to a per-pupil expenditure of approximately $1,000, since there will be an estimated 53.6 million pupils in public and private elementary and secondary schools in 1975.[23] Of these 53.6 million pupils, 46.5 million (see Table 3) will be in the public schools. Hence, using the rough average of $1,000 per pupil, the amount required for the public elementary and secondary schools alone would be $46.5 billion. The projection for 1975 is only $34.9 billion in 1965-66 dollars ($32.9 billion in 1962 dollars) or $679 per pupil (Table 3). Projected resources thus fall quite short of meeting even modest objectives. My assumption of equal expenditures by public and private schools in estimating $1,000 per pupil does not affect this conclusion. Private school expenditures ranging from $500 to $1,500 per pupil correspond to a range from $1,040 to $940 for public schools. The projected $679 is well below that range.

Table 4 shows defense and education spending in relation to the Gross National Product — current and projected. Comparing these two sets of figures is interesting in several respects. First we note that both are a decreasing percentage of the Gross National Product. Second, if we look at projections to 1975, we note that the total defense expenditures budgeted under hypothetical partial disarmament would, if diverted entirely to elementary and secondary education, double the budget for these levels of education. Perhaps one should say "*merely* double." Because the federal government currently contributes only 8.1 percent of the total cost of public elementary and secondary education, the use of federal funds to double the total expenditure level would really amount to a ten-fold increase over present levels of federal expenditure for this sector of education. Looking at it this way and taking into account the problems of convincing Congress that expenditure in any category should be multiplied by ten, one realizes that "Let's turn the whole defense budget into education" is rash talk indeed.

TABLE 4. Defense and education spending as related to GNP – current and projected

Budget item	Year			
	1966 (actual)	1967 (estimated)	1975 (projected)	
			High Defense	Partial disarmament
GNP (10⁹ dollars)	712	762.5	981[a]	
Defense spending:				
Dollars (10⁹)	57.7	70.2	67.5[a]	39[a]
Percent of GNP	8	9	6.9	4
Public elementary and secondary education spending:				
Dollars (10⁹)	26.1	27.8	32.9[b]	
Percent of GNP	3.6	3.6	3.3	

Sources: U.S. Bureau of the Budget, *The Budget in Brief. Fiscal Year 1968* (Washington, D.C.: Government Printing Office, 1968), p. 97; "44.6 Million Pupils in Schools at Record $27.8–Billion Cost," *New York Times*, Jan. 2, 1967, p. 16; Leonard A. Lecht, *Goals, Priorities, and Dollars: The Next Decade* (New York: The Free Press, 1966), p. 199; U.S. Department of Health, Education, and Welfare, Office of Education, *Projections of Educational Statistics to 1975-76.* (Washington, D.C.: Government Printing Office, 1966), pp. 68, 70.   [a]In 1962 dollars.   [b]Estimate from Table 3 converted to 1962 dollars.

Yet, curiously enough, if we shift focus from the national view to the household picture, the same proposal looks tame. Doubling the total education budget looks staggering on the national scale, but on a per-pupil scale it means something so simple-looking as changing a cost of $2.80 per day into $5.60 a day. Even so, there is evidence that school systems now operating at a budgetary level of $1,000 per pupil per year do not necessarily show radical differences from those near the national average of $500 per pupil. For example, the city of New York spent $960.38 per pupil in 1965-66.[24] A recent study characterized the result as "a static, internalized, isolated system which has been unable to respond to vastly changing needs and demands."[25] The doubling of budgets, while perhaps an essential condition for progress, is therefore not a sufficient condition.

It therefore seems clear that the amount of money currently projected to be available in 1975 is enough only to maintain the status quo and to go a little beyond it, but not enough to revolutionize education profoundly even if money were all it took to do so. The realization that this is so may account for the disorderly conduct of the market in educational futures. There is no breaking out of a circle where money can only follow accomplishment and accomplishment requires money, other than by projecting an image of future accomplishment so realistic and so vivid as to seem only just beyond grasp, perhaps just by the amount of the budget increase requested.

1.4 THE LOCAL SETTING: A SKETCH

My visit to Small City (Appendix A) provided firsthand, anecdotal information on two urban schools. For more formal data on finance and other matters, I turned to a detailed study of the schools of Watertown, Massachusetts, by the staff and students of the Harvard Graduate School of Education, entitled *Watertown: The Education of Its Children.*[26]

In 1964-65, the current expenditure for each of the 6,500 children in Watertown's public schools was $504,[27] compared to the national average of $484.[28] Budget and salary data for Watertown schools in 1965 and 1966 are shown in Tables 5-7 and Figure 3. Watertown's 1966 equalized school tax rate was $14.55 per thousand dollars of property assessed on an equalized basis.[29] The equalized tax rate for all municipal functions came to $30.90,[30] which meant that just under half of the local taxes were being collected to support the community's public schools. Median annual family income in 1960 was $7,003,[31] as compared to the national median annual family income in that year of $5,625.[32]

Table 5 reveals a characteristic feature of current school budgets, namely that salaries are far and away the largest single expense. It is therefore understandable that there should be great incentive toward holding the line on salaries, either by keeping the staff small and salaries low or by increasing the productivity of teachers. In terms of the future this desire manifests itself in the widespread hope that technology will do for schools what it has done in other sectors of our economy: increase production without increasing costs through the substitution of machinery for staff or at least through the addition of machinery that might obviate the need for additional staff.

The dominant role of salaries is often overlooked by educational market analysts, who mistake a total budget for funds to be freely allocated. Actually, however, relatively little of a typical school budget can be easily shifted to new categories. Teachers and principals are often blamed for reluctance to change. However, unless change is *willed* and *paid for* by the school board and the community, teachers and principals have little leeway.

Like corporate balance sheets or any other reporting document, school budgets are cast in stylized forms determined in part by historical accident, in part by the desire to inform, and

TABLE 5. Operating budget for Watertown public schools, 1966

Administration		$75,632
Instruction		
Salaries:[a]	2,689,936	
Books and supplies:	100,000	
Library books:	10,500	
	2,800,436	2,800,436
Other school services[b]		119,633
Operation and maintenance of plant		368,094
Fixed charges[c]		4,500
Community services[d]		1,000
Acquisition of fixed assets[e]		6,000
Program with other districts[f]		25,000
		$3,400,295

Source: Office of the Superintendent of Schools, Watertown, Massachusetts, 1966. The actual expenditures for the year are reported in *Annual Reports— 1966* (Watertown, Mass.: Watertown Stationers & Printers, 1967), p. 238.

[a] Includes salaries of principals, guidance counselors, athletic coaches, teachers, department heads, specialists (e.g., reading), and principals' clerks.

[b] Attendance offices, social worker, pupil health services, (e.g., school nurses), bussing, and athletic supplies.

[c] Athletic insurance.

[d] Scouts, etc.

[e] New equipment (unspecified, but probably non-instructional).

[f] Cost of participation in the regional trade school.

in part by the desire to conceal. For instance, the way funds are spread under the headings "administration" and "instruction" in Table 5 might be intended to suggest unusually low administrative overhead to avoid all the pejorative connotations "overhead" has for the lay public. The categories required in reports to the state (Table 6) reveal something of

TABLE 6. Expenditures in certain categories, Watertown public schools, 1965

Supervision	$49,649
Principals	209,291
Teaching	1,988,025
Textbooks	27,187
Library	17,429
Audiovisual	11,408
Guidance	88,341
Psychological	977
Educational TV	0
	$2,392,307[a]
1965 total enrollment	6,583
Per-pupil expenditures	
Textbooks	$4.10
Audiovisual	$1.73

Source: Data from Commonwealth of Massachusetts, *Annual Report of the Department of Education for the Year Ending June 30, 1965* (Public Document 2M-6-66-943139), pp. 11, 202-203, 211.

[a]The operating budget total for 1965 was $3,076,100, compared to $3,400,295 in 1966 (Table 5).

the extent to which administrative duties, like those carried out by principals and supervisors, are lumped under salaries in Table 5. Table 5 also lumps books and supplies together while the state requires that textbooks be listed separately.

Because Table 5 and Table 6 apply to two different years, exact matches are not to be expected, but both the similarities and the gross disparities are revealing. The data in Table 6, for example, enable us to infer an annual expenditure per child of approximately $4 for textbooks. In most public school systems, Watertown included, teachers are forbidden to ask the pupils to purchase supplementary materials on their own. This figure is therefore a *ceiling;* like those for teachers' salaries, it is useful as a yardstick for measuring the cost of technological products.

One way in which Watertown and indeed the Commonwealth of Massachusetts seems deviant is the low level of state and federal support to local schools (see Fig. 3). One might, as

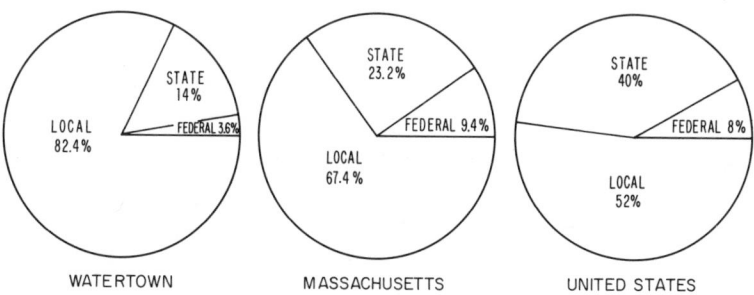

FIGURE 3. School Money Sources for Watertown, Massachusetts, and the United States

a consequence, expect Watertown to be somewhat more conservative financially than localities where the course which money flows from source to sink is not quite so short. However, since I do not draw conclusions which critically depend on the balance between local, state, and federal funding for schools, this atypicality does not reduce the value of the Watertown example.

Watertown School Department teacher salary schedules are shown in Table 7. This schedule is fairly representative, both in form and in content, of salary schedules throughout the American public school systems. The salary levels are low compared to those in occupations related to educational technology (see Table 10, p. 199). Although both are increasing, the gap is likely to remain.

Anyone familiar with the skyrocketing of salaries for technical specialists in the last few years will appreciate the significance of this disparity. It is well known that teachers leave school systems to find better-paying jobs elsewhere. However, having the better-paying jobs intrude into the structure of the school system itself adds new dimensions to the problem of setting teachers' salaries.

TABLE 7. Annual teachers' salaries in Watertown, 1967

| Salary step | Academic degree | | | |
	Bachelors	Masters	Masters plus 15 credits	Masters plus 30 credits
1	$5,600	$6,100	$6,350	$6,600
2	6,000	6,500	6,750	7,000
3	6,400	6,900	7,150	7,400
4	6,800	7,300	7,550	7,800
5	7,200	7,700	7,950	8,200
6	7,600	8,100	8,350	8,600
7	8,000	8,500	8,750	9,000
8	8,400	8,900	9,150	9,400
9	8,800	9,300	9,550	9,800
10	9,200	9,700	9,950	10,200

Source: Office of the Superintendent of Schools, Watertown, Massachusetts, October 25, 1967.

Finally, a word about physical possibilities. Classes in Watertown's schools ranged in size from about 25 to 35 students. In grades seven through twelve, nearly all teachers handle five such classes per day. The effective teaching "load" of most teachers is therefore about 125-150 students *per day*. Simple calculation reveals that, during a six-hour school day, the maximum amount of time a teacher can spend working individually with each pupil in each subject is about two to three minutes. It is not surprising, under these conditions, that mass production should prevail over "individualized" teaching. Emphasis on the goal of individualization is therefore quite understandable.

Another bit of minor arithmetic is useful for perspective. We have already noted that per-pupil annual expenditures in Watertown are approximately $500. Given 180 school days in the year we find that it costs $2.80 *a day* to keep a child in the Watertown schools. A recent survey of the cost of service through hook-up to some of the currently available commercial time-sharing systems (see Table 9, p. 193) describes a range of $24 to $43 *per hour*.[33] The meaning of such figures is analyzed further in Chapter 5.

Some forms of modern technology cannot be used properly without adequate space and other amenities. Books, for instance, need library storage space, and cataloging and librarians for keeping track of their whereabouts.

The oldest of Watertown's public school buildings was built in 1907. Of the eleven school buildings in use in 1967, four were built over fifty years ago, five over thirty-five years ago, and only two in the last decade. All of these buildings are characterized by an architectural inflexibility (for example, nearly all interior walls are load-bearing) which would make it very difficult to adapt these buildings to the unproved but potentially less rigid patterns of team teaching, non-graded individual study, instructional television, computer-aided instruction (CAI), and so forth. One elementary school, designed to accommodate 800 pupils, has just been built. This building, of cinder block faced with brick, is a virtual replica of the building constructed in 1907. If structural inflexibility indeed entails functional or educational rigidity, the new building is no better suited for change than the old.

2 Educational Technology: The People and the Institutions

2.1 GOALS STATED

What is a reproductive system, if it be not a system for reproduction. — *Samuel Butler,* Erewhon*

Statements about educational goals cannot be appreciated without knowing or at least guessing why they were made. Consider the following specimen:

> Your education has been planned and geared to arm and prepare you to function as mature and thinking citizens capable of shouldering the burdens and responsibilities which a thriving democracy imposes. It is through you and others like you that the forward march of democracy, spurred and fortified by a thorough and well-rounded education, will move on to greater triumphs and victories. We have no doubt that our aims and efforts in this direction will bear fruit and achieve the goals and objectives set forth, for in the miniature democracy of our school you are proving yourselves worthy and deserving of our trust and expectations.[1]

*New York: E. P. Dutton, 1917, p. 239.

The words are those of Maxwell E. Clarke, the principal of Bel Kaufman's fictional but altogether "real" Calvin Coolidge High School; the purpose is exhortation.

It would be foolish to condemn the statement as mere vacuity. Ritual formulae, whether in circulars, opening-day speeches, prayers, Fourth of July or campaign oratory, are too prevalent throughout time and across cultures to be dismissed as worthless. Saying that Maxwell Clarke's rhetoric is no guideline for explicit and quantitative systems analysis is not condemning it but merely judging it unsuited for a specific purpose, much as one might reject an automobile as a means for crossing the ocean.

A statement drawn from a best-selling novel rather than from a scholarly work might readily be dismissed as an amusing parody. Surely the real-life officials responsible for our public schools must make more explicit and sharper statements of purpose.

Consider, however, the official statement of educational philosophy of Watertown's senior high school shown in Figure 4. Obviously townspeople will respond to elected officials and professional staff offering "the best possible educational opportunities" and meeting "the special needs of the community" more favorably than if the *stated* policy were to get by with the least budget that's enough to keep the kids off the streets and to assure reelection. Everyone is also for individuality.

The rhetoric of this statement is therefore entirely in keeping with the rigors of local politics. It is irrelevant to carp about the absence from this statement of anything that obviously lends itself to maximization by explicit quantitative analysis. It is, however, worthwhile asking what relation the stated goals have to reality. If the two are close, then the statements have not only their undeniable political value, but they may also be taken at face value in guiding systems analysis. If, however, reality is at variance with the words, one

FIGURE 4. "Statement of Philosophy," Watertown High School, 1966

We who are responsible for the program of studies at Watertown High School believe:

that the comprehensive high school in America should offer the best possible educational opportunities for all students of secondary school age.

that each school must plan its program to meet the special needs of the community it serves.

that the program of studies must provide a meaningful sequence of subjects for each student according to his needs, abilities, and objectives including a core of common learning for all students that should assure an adequate base of general education.

that counseling services must be provided that will achieve the best matching of student need, ability, and objectives with an educational program.

that students must be encouraged to work to their capacity and elect a program of subjects that will challenge this capacity.

that students should be encouraged to participate broadly in the curricular and extra-curricular offerings of the school insofar as they are able to profit from this participation.

that each student is an individual and his individuality must be respected and strengthened, but, as he is a member of society, he must come to respect and understand his responsibilities as a member of his school and out-of-school groups.

that in and beyond the formal education program each student must be encouraged to understand the importance of good manners and ethical conduct in all his school and out-of-school life.

---

may expect to find in education the confusion and discomfort attending the simultaneous keeping of two sets of intellectual books. As we shall see, there is indeed a sharp break between rhetoric and reality, with interesting political and technological repercussions.

2.2 GOALS REALIZED

When in Miss Lewis' class a pupil finds it necessary to visit the men's room he is often denied that priviledge. —Sophomore

Mild Bladder symptoms (This is an occupational disease: there is simply no time to go to the bathroom!)—Teacher —*Bel Kaufman,* Up the Down Staircase*

Individuality is a recurrent theme in educational planning. The Watertown statement of educational philosophy in Figure 4 reflects this prevalent concern. The statement about providing a meaningful sequence for each student according to his needs, the declaration in favor of counseling services, and the encouraging of students to work to their capacity are three out of the eight paragraphs which strongly emphasize individuality. A fourth statement, while emphasizing that each student is an individual and that his individuality must be respected and strengthened, balances this against the responsibilities of the individual to society. Rhetorically, individuality is clearly In. What of reality?

The evidence makes plain, for example, that a relatively ancient form of technology, and one which in principle lends itself very well to individualization, the book, is still far from

*Englewood Cliffs, New Jersey: Prentice-Hall, 1964, pp. 180, 243.

being effectively assimilated in contemporary schools. Witness the following:

My dear Miss Barrett,

I am forced to cancel the library lesson you had planned for your 3rd term students in connection with their study of mythology. Sending them here six at a time creates havoc and disorder. They have already misplaced *The Golden Age of Greece* and have put Bullfinch on the Zoology shelf, besides talking. Two of your students took out books indiscriminately, that had nothing to do with the assignment. I cannot allow them the facilities of the school library until they learn the proper respect for the printed page.

Sincerely,

Charlotte Wolf, Librarian[2]

Nearly every sentence of this quotation evokes some major aspect of educational policy or of information science. Take, for example, "sending them here six at a time creates havoc and disorder" and juxtapose "scheduling" and "discipline." Misplacing the *Golden Age of Greece* evokes "information retrieval." How strange the notion of taking out "books indiscriminately, that had nothing to do with the assignment" rings next to "independent study." The Harvard report on Watertown says much the same thing but so much more soberly and dully that the point might well be missed.

But perhaps the library is only an adjunct to teaching and Watertown's goals are really met in the classroom. Recall that "the program of studies must provide a meaningful sequence of subjects for each student according to his needs, abilities, and objectives" and that "students must be encouraged to work to their own capacities." The following extract from

Watertown: The Education of Its Children illustrates its
authors' perception of the rift between rhetoric and reality:

> There is some excellent teaching taking place in the
> Watertown English classes, but the better teaching appears
> to occur most often in the upper divisions of each grade.
> Consequently, the students with the greatest need for
> skilled teaching are unlikely to receive it in Watertown. The
> majority of the language classes observed were drill lessons
> in grammar and usage and were often based upon work
> sheets or text book exercises.
>
> . . .
>
> The present program for noncollege-bound students is dis-
> criminatory, dull, and largely irrelevant to them as in-
> dividuals. It seems primarily to reaffirm their feelings of
> incompetence and to bind them to their division level.
>
> . . .
>
> The Study Staff noted that the prevailing teaching model is
> teacher-centered. The teacher selects the lesson and directs
> the whole class in a formalized drill, exercise, note-taking,
> or question and response procedure. The emphasis seems to
> be on covering and memorizing information. In addition,
> there is very little variety in the pattern of teaching.
>
> . . .
>
> Classes are usually, if not always, taught as if they were
> comprised of students all in equal need of each lesson; that
> is, the great individual differences in the "homogeneous"
> group are unrecognized. No formal diagnosis or pretesting
> program seems to be employed by classroom teachers at any
> level in any aspect of the English course, and no modifica-
> tions of the work assigned seem to be made for individuals
> or groups within the class.

Like the diagnosis, the proposed remedies reflect prevalent
fashion: "Apparently the possibilities of such teaching modes

as individualized or programmed instruction, team teaching, and grouping within the class have not been explored."[3] Perhaps the problems of teaching English are just not fashionable, and all will go well once the new remedies are applied. The humanities are indeed the last to be touched by the wave of reform that produced the New Math, the New Physics, the New Chemistry, and the New Biology. Perhaps it is in the more "innovative" realms that we may find a closer correspondence between goal statements and actuality. A cursory glance might suggest that this is so, but a closer look reveals many unresolved contradictions.

According to Uri Haber-Schaim, "The PSSC course in physics is used *in its entirety* [emphasis added] by more than half the high school students taking physics in the United States,"[4] but data compiled by the competing Harvard Project Physics showed the following:

Enrollments in public high school science by type of course 1964-65

Physics, total	526,200
Traditional physics	384,700
PSSC	99,900
Advanced physics	41,600[5]

For the same time period, the Physical Science Study Committee (PSSC) itself claims "5000 teachers and 200,000 students"[6] or somewhat less than half the students. Contributing to the confusion, James Bryant Conant, in *The Comprehensive High School,* asks a question subject to the same confusion between "availability" and "use" as Coleman's question about power tools and language laboratories:

Is physics offered?
If so, is any type of "new or advanced" physics available?
(For example, PSSC)

On the basis of responses to this question he concludes that "about half of all the schools responding have adopted the new physics, about half the new chemistry, and over a half (64.9%) one of the new biology courses. Thus the evidence is *conclusive* [emphasis added] that those in charge of curricula development in at least half the schools in our category are alert to innovations and have adopted them."[7]

Shifting focus from the national scene as depicted by "adoption" statistics to the local scene (Watertown) as depicted by anecdote or observation is helpful in sharpening the contrast between claims and reality: "Grades 10 through 12 offer traditional courses in biology, physical science, chemistry, and physics. Although the newer science texts are used in some courses, these new approaches are offered in name only. Lack of space, equipment, and time forces the science department to teach content-oriented courses rather than to use the laboratory approach recommended in all of the new curriculum materials."[8]

That the use of new approaches "in name only" is not merely a local phenomenon is shown by the following comment from a report to the Committee on Labor and Public Welfare of the United States Senate: "It is curious to note how the educational community changes its words but not its deeds; thus, 'learning by doing,' is replaced by 'learning through discovery,' the 'discovery method,' or the 'problem solving method' by 'injury' [sic]. Yet observations will show that in the majority of high schools, teachers of science lecture 80 percent of the class time, and that the laboratory time is given over to 'doing experiments' with equipment laid out in advance, hence, the results are postulated in advance. Yet teachers and administrators will assure the observer that the new curriculums (PSSC, CHEMS, BSCS, and the like) are being used and 'inquiry' is the mode of instruction."[9]

Some zealous advocates of modern educational technology will dismiss all the "new curriculums" as merely not radical enough. Introducing new technological devices will, we are assured, induce such an upheaval in the schools that true individualization will become possible.

The most glistening mark of educational technology in Watertown High School is the language laboratory. Contemporary advertising continues to use expressions like "tailored to individual students' progress" or "progress of all students on an individual basis" in describing language laboratories. Contrast this waffling with the statement of Watertown High School's language laboratory procedures shown in Figure 5.

The notes for laboratory assistants in Figure 6 reinforce the primacy of discipline over intellect or action. The technological basis for this effect will be explored at greater length in Chapter 4. In Section 2.5 I shall inquire further into why intellectual questions are not always primary in the minds of teachers. The account of my visit to Small City (Appendix A) rounds out the context.

In any case, the distance between the belief "that each student is an individual" and the practical insistence that "no one is an individual in the laboratory" is a measure of the gulf between statements of educational goals and reality. How do the principal actors perceive goals and reality? The next three sections are addressed to this question.

FIGURE 5. Watertown Language Laboratory Procedures, 1966

1. The equipment in the laboratory is not like ordinary tape recorders. The principles involved are quite different. *Please do not ask unnecessary questions about its operation* [emphasis added].
2. You will be assigned a booth for the year. Always report to your own assigned booth.
3. No books, pencils, pens, papers, pocketbooks are to be taken to the booths. People assigned to the first row will leave their belongings on the bookcase at the left front of the room under the windows. Those assigned to rows B through E will leave their materials in the bookcase under the blackboard at the opposite side of the room. Take only yourself to the booth.
4. You will stand quietly behind the chair at your booth until the teacher asks you to sit. Then sit in as close to the desk as possible.
5. *No one is an individual in the laboratory* [emphasis added]. Do nothing and touch nothing until instructions are given by the teacher. Then listen carefully and follow directions exactly.
6. If you find anything out of order in your booth, report it to your teacher immediately. This is very expensive equipment. You must take pride in it by giving it the best of care.
7. Remember—this is not a miracle machine. The better you concentrate as you listen, the more you will get out of the material broadcast to you.
8. You must leave the booth in perfect order with all equipment replaced to its original position.
9. Be sure to place your chair under the desk before you leave.
10. You will be dismissed one row at a time to avoid confusion. Please do not talk until you are in the corridor. If you cooperate, you will learn as well as enjoy your work in the laboratory.
Good luck to you!

FIGURE 6. Notes for Watertown Language Laboratory Assistants, 1966

1. Keep watching the students all the time.
   a. By standing in the middle of the lab on the window side you can see most of the lab.
   b. Walk along the rows to make sure all arms are folded; politely but firmly ask the students to do this.
2. Check all the equipment.
   a. Make sure students follow instructions.
   b. Report all problems at once to the teacher in charge.
   c. Do not switch any headphones. Have students move to an empty booth if they have a broken headset or any other mechanical difficulty. Students must sign out when changing booths.
3. It is your responsibility to make sure that no damage is done and all problems are reported during your period.
4. You must be present at every assigned period. If not present, you will be reported absent.
5. If the teacher does not show up during the assigned time, check to see if the teacher has forgotten to come.
6. Before the lab classes arrive, put on the correct tape for that teacher and period. The tape schedule for each teacher is posted on the bulletin board in the lab.
7. Remind the teacher when the time for the lab period is over.

2.3 THE VIEW FROM OLYMPUS

We are the hollow men
We are the stuffed men
Leaning together
Headpiece filled with straw. Alas!
Our dried voices, when
We whisper together
Are quiet and meaningless
As wind in dry grass
Or rats' feet over broken glass
In our dry cellar — T. S. Eliot, "The Hollow Men"*

Education is discussed at the most varied levels and in the most varied languages. By examining the agenda of the National Seminars on Innovation held in Hawaii in July 1967, we see yet another facet of the perception of educational goals. These seminars were sponsored jointly by the U.S. Office of Education and I|D|E|A, an organization engagingly described as "The Action-Oriented Division of The Charles F. Kettering Foundation."

Figure 7 is a reproduction of the title page of the seminar program. This reproduction cannot do full justice to the thickness and feel of the magnificent paper on which the title page was printed. Only direct tactile sensation could drive home the contrast between that paper and the pulp newsprint through which school children tear while scratching out their exercises with cheap gritty pencils supplied by cheap gritty school boards.

*From *Collected Poems, 1909-1962* by T. S. Eliot; copyright 1936 by Harcourt, Brace & World, Inc.; copyright © 1963, 1964 by T. S. Eliot. Reprinted by permission of the publishers.

THREE NATIONAL SEMINARS ON INNOVATION

Seminar A
July 2-9, 1967

Seminar B
July 9-16, 1967

Seminar C
July 16-23, 1967

SPONSORED BY
I|D|E|A, The Action-Oriented Division of
The Charles F. Kettering Foundation
&
The United States Office of Education

FIGURE 7. Program Title Page, "Three National Seminars on Innovation," Honolulu, 1967

In contrast to the teachers' cringing concern for the defacement of excessively vulnerable laboratory equipment, we find management enticed into something described cabalistically as I³, whose quasi-mystical functions are described in Figure 8. The programs provided ritual relief from the boredom of formal presentations...

Conferees Assemble in I³ Groups

... and formal presentations on boredom ...

"The War on Boredom"

The keynote of *innovation,* rung through many changes on the most varied institutional instruments, sounded ad nauseam throughout the three seminars...

The Real World of *Innovation*
> Title III Project Presentation

Are Today's Educational *Innovations* Worthwhile?
> Associate Secretary, National Association of Secondary Principals

The Role of Technology in Educational *Innovation*
> Director, Instructional Systems Development, IBM

Changed Roles for Teachers and Principals that Today's Educational *Innovations* Require
> Associate Secretary, National Association of Secondary Principals

First I|D|E|A *Innovation* Session
> Conference Participants

Innovation Dissemination
> Director, *Innovation Dissemination,* I|D|E|A

Suggestions for Improvement of *Dissemination of Innovation*

|I|D|E|A|

I|D|E|A is a new division of the Charles F. Kettering Foundation charged with the responsibility of assisting school administrators, teachers, and lay groups with plans for school improvement in order that the schools may keep abreast of a rapidly changing world.

I|D|E|A's activities include: (1) a laboratory for research and a league of cooperating schools to test new developments in the research laboratory, (2) a network of 36 demonstration schools, (3) a publication service which publishes newsletters and Occasional Papers on new and timely issues in education and, (4) a Materials Dissemination Center which is developing new curriculum material for the schools.

PACE

PACE, Projects to Advance Creativity in Education, is a nationwide program for educational innovation. Created under the auspices of title III, of the Elementary and Secondary Education Act of 1965, and directed by the Division of Plans and Supplementary Centers, Bureau of Elementary and Secondary Education, U. S. Office of Education, PACE aims toward improvement of education through support of innovative and exemplary educational programming. During its two brief years of operation, PACE has brought the opportunity to think and act creatively to hundreds of schools, school districts, and educational personnel. It has made it possible for children to participate in programs applying research to the classroom in the form of innovative endeavors ranging from computer assisted instruction to children's performing arts.

Involvement — Identity — Innovation
I3 Group

Involvement in thinking about ideas in concepts that are presented at the Seminars and in designing new approaches to the improvement of one or more facets of the education program . . .

Identity with persons having common interests and concerns, persons from throughout the nation who are working as school district superintendents, school principals, PACE projects directors, state department of education personnel, and members of the staff of the U. S. Office of Education . . .

Innovation in terms of the "intellectual input" "to be absorbed" and "reacted" to by the persons INVOLVED; INNOVATION in terms of the "creative output" to merge from the group and each of its unique individual members . . .

This is an I3 GROUP

It is a group having three major functions: (1) to react to new ideas presented by Seminar speakers; to place these ideas into the framework of an educational interest area; to determine the worth and implications of each idea in terms of the interest area under consideration; to inquire about questions that arise as a result of group deliberations, (2) to analyse a PACE project, improving its purposes, procedures and processes in light of the new knowledge acquired at the Seminars, and, (3) to prepare a listing of ideas for "new" educational developments, these ideas to be recommended to PACE and I|D|E|A for consideration as the focus of possible future programs.

To give as well as receive ideas . . .
To stimulate as well as be stimulated . . .
To teach as well as to learn . . .

THIS WILL BE THE ROLE OF AN I3 GROUP

FIGURE 8. The I³ Group

I³ Group Session
To *Disseminate* or Not to *Disseminate*
    Director, Center for Coordinated Education, University of
    California, Santa Barbara

... before rising to official crescendoes ...

National Stratagem for *Innovation*
    Deputy Commissioner of Education
Innovation as a Way of Life
    U. S. Commissioner of Education

The theme of *innovation* comes through so loud and clear
one might be led to believe that novelty is all that matters, that
older notions of quality or improvement have lost relevance.
There were, however, some cautionary notes ...

"The Need for Educational Assessment"

... somber diversions ...

    Boat Tour of Pearl Harbor and a Visit to Punchbowl
    The United States National Cemetery of the Pacific

... the tinkling of educational devices ...

    Computer Assisted Instruction (RCA)
    8 mm Cartridge Loading Projector (Fairchild)
    Video Tape Recorders (Ampex)
    Talking Typewriter (Responsive Environment Corpora-
    tion)
    Micro-transparencies (National Cash Register)
    Computer Assisted Instruction (IBM)

... some interdisciplinary chords ...

The Chemistry of Learning
Humanistic Technology

... and the climactic Rain Dance ...

Listing of New Areas of Development for Consideration by
I|D|E|A and the U.S.O.E.
I³ Group Session
The Future of Federal Programs in Education
Chairman of the House of Representatives Education
Committee

The other-worldly aura of such goings-on is not accidental.
What is expected of catch words like *innovation* may be
inferred from *Science and the Air Force,* an official history
written by Nick A. Komons and published by the United
States Air Force. As Daniel S. Greenberg has pointed out in
Science, this history "candidly tells the bizarre story of the 15-
year struggle to establish and maintain a basic research
program in the nation's most technologically dependent
military service."[10]

This history is replete with illuminating observations, like
that attributed to General James McCormack, then director of
Research and Development, Headquarters USAF, who "made
it clear that the AFOSR [Air Force Office of Scientific
Research] could not hope to get any money unless it accepted
a certain amount of semantic perversion in its programming... Basic research and applied research were dropped

101

from the programming idiom, replaced in turn by exploratory research and supporting research."[11] The games the Air Force played with labels are reminiscent of the Hawaiian Rain Dance. We learn there "arose such categories as electronics, materials, propulsion, and what have you. The more practical a category sounded, the better." Komons goes on: "The effort worked. AFOSR talked of applications, and the Bureau of the Budget loosened the purse strings."[12]

An administrator of the Air Force Office of Scientific Research is quoted as cracking: "We sold them the sizzle, not the steak."[13] General Thomas S. Power, who became head of the Air Research and Development Command in 1954 and later led the Strategic Air Command, is quoted in a 1956 memorandum as describing his feelings about the techniques that were being used to speed the growth of the Office of Scientific Research in the following words: "You can't tell and sell the public and the world on these things in such a way that they believe that this is just sky blue thinking." As Komons summarizes other statements in that memorandum, "AFOSR had to be 'truthfully deceitful' about its program so as to 'coat' it with a look of practicality."[14] The language, in short, is fund-oriented.

Although the time for similar official candor in what Tom Lehrer calls the "ed biz" is not yet here, the available evidence points to the same phenomenon at work. Talking about the dream education profession of tomorrow, Arthur Wirth says: "A difference of a new magnitude might emerge. The profession would eschew like the plague its old habits of premature promising or selling. A new breed of teachers would fly under the banner of those who are committed to generating and testing responsible ideas. They would enjoy the successes without being embarrassed or apologetic for tries that failed. They would operate from enough self-respect and self-assurance to let their critics know that this was the way of inquiry—and that any other way was shabby and unacceptable."[15]

In a setting where no one, including the universities, remains outside the system, where, through the medium of the budget mechanism, the pursuit of truth has become inextricably linked to the pursuit of social objectives, the risks of individual or group self-delusion rise in proportion to the need for persuading others, particularly nonspecialists. The partners in the educational enterprise seem bound, in David Riesman's words, to be "like all professionals faced with troublesome clients, duplicitous in finding the semantics by which all comers can be fended off."[16]

The dissemination of exhortations, promises, or policy statements that emerge from Olympus with some subtlety and with full consciousness of their exhortative character lends them a solidity and inviolability matching that of the Emperor's New Clothes. Myth becomes reality; scientism perverts science. We shall see that good intentions disguised by semantic perversion become the gospel of the rank and file, whose literal interpretation of the word is often grotesque. Truthful deceit by publishers or industrial folk leads to a mindless but massive application of shoddy devices to the wrong idea, often to an idea antithetical to the original intentions. Economy moves by Congress suffer a similar fate in their descent to the workaday world. The Schools of Education stand by dumbfounded or acquiescent.

2.4 THE VIEW FROM HADES

Between the conception
And the creation
Between the emotion
And the response
Falls the Shadow — *T. S. Eliot, "The Hollow Men"**

What happens when a Hawaiian seed falls on uninspired clay? Some details about one project will give an answer. One hopes that the case is extreme, for it is a paradigm of the bizarre consequences of confusing ritual rain dancing with science.

The story can be told in part through excerpts from the journal *Educational Technology*. In June of 1967, *Educational Technology* reported the following about a project supported by the U.S. Office of Education in Saginaw, Michigan:

INNOVATORS NEED SUPPORT — An article in this magazine early this year told of plans by administrators of the Saginaw Township Community Schools, Michigan, to put into operation a computer based demonstration school. Their proposal to the U.S. Office of Education for INDI-COM, Individual Communications System, was most ambitious.

In an application dated January 15 of this year, the school officials asked for funds beyond a planning grant, stating that "By June 30, 1967, the Planning Grant will expire, but its presence will have brought the Saginaw Township staff and community at large to a high pitch of interest and involvement."

Unfortunately, dreams of the project's sponsors have

---

*From *Collected Poems, 1909-1962* by T. S. Eliot; copyright 1936 by Harcourt, Brace & World, Inc.; copyright © 1963, 1964 by T. S. Eliot. Reprinted by permission of the publishers.

vanished. The cause of the demise of the demonstration
school in Saginaw Township is, according to a recent
announcement by the superintendent of schools, a shift in
sentiment on the part of the local school board—resulting
from a board election which placed several new members
into power. The new board came in and the project went
out, and that is the end of it for Saginaw Township, "high
pitch of interest" and all.

This educational debacle is instructive. As this publication has stressed on numerous occasions, local political
considerations are most important in all school improvement efforts, to some degree in all nations but in the United
States especially. *I do not know why the Saginaw project
was vetoed; perhaps there were valid reasons, perhaps not*
[emphasis added]. The important point about this is to
demonstrate that all persons pushing innovations in education at the local level had better make sure that public
support is carefully cultivated."[17]

That public support is necessary for innovation is obvious.
The suspicion that the local school board merely played
politics is well-founded. We may well believe that the
proposal for INDICOM was most ambitious. But what is
meant by a "computer based demonstration school"?

A form letter about the school board's action, dated April 17,
1967, and circulated by William A. Rodgers, Director,
Research Services, and Coordinator Title III "ESEA" in
Saginaw, tells us a tiny bit more and links the effort to the
Hawaiian Rain Dance:

> The proposal met the critical appraisal given proposals of
> this magnitude by the USOE and would have been operated
> by us next year but the Board of Education voted to
> withdraw the application! The details which led to this step
> by the Board are too complex to concern you with at this

time and indeed probably could not correctly be analyzed anyhow.

Because of the soundness of the proposal a substitute school system was sought to operate the program. The school system selected is Waterford, Michigan. The Waterford Board of Education has already gratefully accepted the responsibility, for carrying the program on and is destined to become listed in the annuals of educational history . . .

The ideas contained in the proposal were felt by the Dissemination Office of Title III, to be of value to the educational establishment at large and we served as a visiting PACE Fellows, to prepare a publication entitled "Towards a Computer Based Instructional System" which will be released this summer at the National Conference on Innovation to be held in Hawaii [emphasis added].

Politics and not substance is still the major theme of a letter to the editor published by *Educational Technology* in August 1967. Lawrence M. Gariglio, administrative assistant, Saginaw Township Community Schools, said:

To the Editor:

I noted with interest your article "An Independent Voice" dated June 30, 1967, and appreciate what you had to say. I thought perhaps you would be interested, because this is an important area, in many of the after-effects of our board's action in withdrawing the proposal entitled "INDICOM."

The community and board of education were informed by every means possible about the project during the planning of the project. It is all now a matter of past history, but when you get right down to it the blame falls on the shoulders of a school board who refused to believe the professionals working on the project and preferred to listen to the few people in the community who did not want their children taught via computers.

Regardless of how it was presented to them they refused

to believe and quite frankly still refuse to believe that what we were really talking about was a complete revamping of curriculum to meet the individual needs of students. The computer was only one of many tools to be used to help individualize the educational process. The fault of the administration was not being forceful enough with the board of education to at least allow the project to function and prove itself.

It is true that innovation needs public support, but our work in this area was directly responsible for the approval of at least six other grants through the U.S. Office of Education in this area, the biggest being New York City under Title III.

Our project was deemed by the U.S. Office in Washington and the Department of Education in Lansing as being one so important to the educational society that they took our district's name off the proposal and granted it to Waterford Township School District just north of Detroit. The grant was formally approved and the project will go ahead, so innovation and the planning for these innovations has not been completely lost.

Dr. William A. Rodgers, Project Director, as well as other members of the project staff carry with them to their new positions in other districts valuable information and knowledge gained as a result of this project. *The project was disseminated to well over 500 people doing similar work throughout the United States* [emphasis added].

A publication was written as a result of a PACE Fellowship that will receive distribution of over 3,000, so I think that the $93,800 spent by the United States Government for planning was a valuable investment to the improvement of education in the United States . . .[18]

We get to marrow in the following excerpt from *Toward a Computer Based Instruction System* by Rodgers and Gariglio, prepared pursuant to grant number OEG-3-6-000802-1477 from the U. S. Office of Education: "That the *individualization of instruction* is highly regarded as a worthy objective by the educational establishment is without question: public and private schools, industrial apprenticeships, maintenance training, armed services educational programs and the software world of the publishing companies present ample proof of that assertion. Yet, full implementation has been hampered because of the lack of technology precise enough to complete the job. At this writing it is still not precise enough to do the complete job but it is certainly clear, for anyone who has surveyed the field, that it will be precise very shortly. Such a prediction can almost be guaranteed."[19] Such is one reflection, at the working level, of the ES '70 assumption that "various elements of the educational process . . . have recently been examined by researchers and found to be important additions to current practice."

Rodgers' own expression of this assumption follows, nakedly revealing the seductive power of absurdity in full formalized attire:

A Curriculum Model

Let us assume for a moment that man's main drive is to understand the world in which he lives. Let us also assume that the world exists as a set of complex relationships. Then it behooves man if he is to understand the world in which he finds himself to decipher what these relationships might be.

Along the lines of Rene Descartes he begins to reason: (1) man relates to himself and other men as an individual, (2) man relates to other men in groups, (3) man relates to the elements, and (4) man relates to the unknown. This model of man's relationship to the World or Universe might be written Symbolically as $f(x) = y$ where y refers to the situation man finds himself whenever x takes any of the patterns cited in this paragraph. Let:

x = 1 stand for man vs. man or (Psychological Sciences)
x = 2 stand for man vs. society or (Sociological Sciences)
x = 3 stand for man vs. nature or (Natural Sciences)
x = 4 stand for man vs. super nature or (Philosophical Sciences)

Let us further classify man's place in the world as academic or non-academic and postulate that whenever x = 3 or 4 that y is academic and whenever x = 1 or 2 that y is non-academic. With this schema we can define the objectives of the school as being academic or non-academic. Furthermore, when f (1 or 2) = y then the "concomitant-affective" objectives of the school are realized in the categories of values, appreciations or attitudes. When f (3 or 4) = y then the cognitive objectives of the school form a hierarchy of skills, facts, principles, generalizations, and concepts.

Obviously any such schema is wide open to criticism from many viewpoints and we would be the first to say so. Yet the description serves the useful purpose of describing a continuous curricula K-12, for the subject matter of the natural and philosophical sciences rather than the discontinuous "grade-level" curricula now in use. In other words instead of having arithmetic, algebra II, plain and solid geometry, etc., we will have mathematics K-12. Even the 12 will not be binding for some pupils but is merely a landmark for the subject matter specialists and curricula writers.

When the curricula objectives for f (3 and 4) = y are programmed successfully the attention can be turned to directly teaching the f (1 and 2) = y objectives. Right now some of all of man's relationships with the world are being included as objectives of the curricula but more by coincidence than by design. *This paper calls for a total systems design to the curricula* [emphasis added].[20]

Rodgers' conclusion reveals how close he is to an important addition to current practice: "When such a design is planned, and implemented, then perhaps a theory of instruction such as that presented here can be disseminated."[21]

Unfortunately, this theory of instruction has already been disseminated all too well, as evidenced, for example, by the following letter addressed to me. Except for omitting the letterhead of a Midwestern school district and the name of its author, a "Specialist in Curriculum Research and Development," the letter has been reproduced verbatim:

> We are interested in the continuous curricula (K-12) that has been described as "A Curriculum Model" on pages 15-17 of the PACE publication *Toward a Computer Based Instruction System*. Although the most sophisticated model may not yet be developed, we would be interested in finding out what you are currently using.
>
> It is our intention to develop a program from some arbitrary package of concepts which have been sequentially arranged. Naturally we are also interested in the testing materials that are being used to assess pupil progress.
>
> Our school system is exclusively an elementary district with approximately 7,500 children (K-6).
>
> Thank you for your consideration.

Thus do the echoes of Hawaiian dances reverberate through the land. School districts which would describe themselves as average, finding themselves caught in the frenzy of well-intentioned prods toward innovation, succeed merely in using the unaccustomed medium of the innovative lingo to gush forth with pale echoes of good intentions and all too few vestiges of common sense.

My critique of the drum beating for innovation, total systems analysis, information dissemination of educational innovations,[22] and so on, should not be mistaken for a defense of a status quo imposed by ignorant or bigoted local school boards. The local attitudes evident in the Saginaw episode and reflected by some members of Congress hardly deserve cheers. Yet if, as Gariglio suggests in his letter, the professionals want to be believed, they have an obligation not to build their claims entirely on mumbo-jumbo. The problems of education are too complex for amateurish panaceas, too serious to be clouded by semantic perversion, truthful deceit and, ultimately, self-delusion.

The pioneering efforts of Congress and of the U.S. Office of Education, through Title III and other legislation, to stimulate improvement of elementary and secondary education deserve the strongest praise and support. *It is most unfortunate that a prevailing innovative orthodoxy has channeled these efforts into a single mold.* To fit this mold, every proposal must twist its intentions into an accepted but meaningless verbiage. *Toward a Computer Based Instruction System* typifies the resulting widespread perversion of the original good intentions.

2.5 THE PEOPLE IN THE SCHOOLS

Who are the teachers and administrators at the receiving end of artificial dissemination? Whose hands and minds participate in realizing the value of new technology for pupils? George Bernard Shaw's characterization of teachers ("Those who can, do; those who can't, teach") is rather sharper than most presentations. Still, the mass media when favorable — Miss Barrett in *Up the Down Staircase,* Sir in "To Sir, With Love," Mr. Peepers, or Our Miss Brooks — do emphasize skills designed to "win affection rather than to win respect for professional attainments."[23]

The status of the teacher as a professional is particularly precarious. New York City recruiting brochures paint a glowing picture of the teacher's professionalism, of the opportunities for professional development, and of the personal relationship between administrative staff and teachers:

> The administrative staff is composed of men and women with a modern outlook. They realize the value of creativity in teaching, encourage innovation and new approaches, and understand the need for academic freedom within a professional atmosphere. But even more important, they know that the most effective teaching will result where the teacher is recognized as an individual and is given the opportunity to make full use of his abilities and specialties. The personal relationship established between the administration and the teachers has promoted the progress of education both in the schoolroom and at the level of professional development.[24]

The picture painted by the report of the mayor's Advisory Panel on Decentralization in the New York City Schools, commonly called the Bundy Report, is altogether different:

> New York City teachers are isolated at the end of a long chain of command. They are not consulted regularly, if at all, about curriculum, or classroom surroundings, or the criteria on which colleagues, to say nothing of supervisors, are chosen. Initiative and innovation, if not discouraged, are administratively difficult because of the uniformity imposed perforce by a highly centralized system. Furthermore, the Panel has it on the word of teachers who appear to be dedicated to their profession that in too many schools teachers are fearful. They are said to be subject to overt and subtle reprisals (including, ironically, assignment to difficult classes) for any criticism of the school. The way to avoid

reprisals, as one teacher put it, "is to take all directives from the supervisors at face value and never question, criticize, suggest, or file grievances."[25]

It may be one of the tragedies of the present system that the talents of these professionals are not given full rein. The minutiae and bureaucratic distractions that prevent the teacher from concentrating on teaching are eloquently portrayed in the pages of *Up the Down Staircase:*

"But I am busiest outside of my teaching classes. Do you know any other business or profession where highly-skilled specialists are required to tally numbers, alphabetize cards, put notices into mailboxes, and patrol the lunchroom?"[26]

"Trouble is," Paul smiled his most charming smile, "a teacher has to be so many things at the same time: actor, policeman, scholar, jailer, parent, inspector, referee, friend, psychiatrist, accountant, judge and jury, guide and mentor, wielder of minds, keeper of records, and grand master of the Delaney Book."[27]

Whatever innovative talents a teacher may have go unrecognized in the contemporary classroom. Teachers are rewarded for taking accurate attendance records, keeping their classrooms neat and quiet and their own mouths shut outside the classroom. As David T. Bazelon sums it all up: "The school as an institution has many procedures which undercut the status of the teachers . . . they are rewarded for longevity and not for success in the classroom."[28]

If the teachers seem unduly bogged down in alphabetizing attendance cards and patrolling the lunchroom, the administrators are often similarly distracted. There is a

displacement of educational goals by disciplinary actions and efforts at control of behavior . . . A large proportion of administrative . . . energy is consumed simply in maintaining control . . . the principal indicated that one of the charms of his job was the unpredictability of his day: epileptic fits; boys suspended from class; boys skipping classes and wandering over to other schools, being held there and being brought back by the police . . . That very morning, the normal start of the principal's day was livened by his need to deal with two boys who had had a serious fight in the school bus on the way to school.[29]

Otherwise unable to influence their environment, teachers have turned to unions for better conditions and higher pay. The demands of the teachers' strikes reflect more blue-collar concern for job security, more human concern for physical security than professionalism. As one teacher put it, when queried about his reasons for joining the union: "I'm covered by Lloyd's of London for $100,000 in case I clobber one of the kids."[30] Innovation understandably fades before self-preservation.

Teachers have neither been trained for nor allowed to play a role in school improvements. As indicated in the Bundy Report, teachers are rarely consulted in matters of educational development. In the "new" curriculum efforts, teachers were rarely used as anything but tinkers. Those who were drawn in were judged aberrant by their colleagues and went unrewarded by their superiors. This prejudice against educators is evident even in the higher ranks. A well-known professor of science education privately complained to me that one needs a Zacharias, a Holton, or a Seaborg to head up a large curriculum-development effort in science because professional educators are unknown to the National Science Foundation and, in any case, have had little experience with multimillion-dollar efforts.

In fact the innovators have been relatively indifferent to the plight of teachers. The thrust of the new curricula was to draw in "subject matter specialists" and "scientists in the field" and to make the materials as "teacher-proof" as possible. The drive toward teacher-proofing is understandable, for efforts to inform teachers and to continue their own education on the job have not met with much success. We have the following terse testimony of an official of the National Education Association concerning professional development: "Inservice teacher training is the slum of American education."[31]

Moreover, where good refresher courses or specialized training courses have been set up, informal conversations with responsible teachers and administrators suggest that following an initial wave of enthusiasm for sending teachers to these courses administrators have grown increasingly reluctant to do so. The simple reason is that summer institutes and the like, when well conducted, prepare teachers for jobs outside education. They are subsequently lured away by higher salaries and better working conditions. School administrators are thus driven to keeping their teachers barefoot and pregnant in order to keep them from running off with a new lover.

It seems obvious that if teachers know little about or are only mildly interested in a particular tool or technique then this tool or technique will not enjoy widespread use. On my trip to Small City I encountered evidence of this phenomenon. Overhead projectors were introduced into a brand new high school to meet the emergency created by the failure to install undelivered blackboards. These projectors remained even after the blackboards came, but older teachers who had complained all along that they needed a pilot's license to use these gadgets, promptly abandoned their use. Although I was told that the younger teachers had been enthusiastic about the new devices, I saw no evidence of anyone using them in any classroom.

As long as the stereotype portrayed by Philip Jackson in *The Teacher and The Machine* is believed by technologists and educators alike, it is unlikely that technology will ever be enthusiastically greeted in the schools:

> If there is one thing the teacher, particularly the female teacher, is not, it is an engineer. Indeed, it is difficult to think of two world views further apart than those symbolized by the Golden Rule on the one hand and the slide rule on the other. The one calls to mind adjectives such as romantic, warm, tender-minded, naive; the other calls to mind adjectives such as realistic, cold, tough-minded, efficient. One is essentially feminine, the other masculine. These two lists of adjectives undoubtedly exaggerate the real differences to be found between these two groups, but they do give us pause when we consider the likelihood of increasing the dialogue between the tender-minded teachers and the tough-minded technicians. To say that they do not speak the same language is a gross understatement.[32]

As we shall see in Chapter 4, the technicians have done little toward learning their necessary ally's language. They have done still less toward endowing processes and devices with the quality I have described through the metaphor of "transparency." As another designer has put it: "To be completely successful, the work of the telephone components designer must be completely unnoticed by the customer. For him, the telephone is merely an extension of his senses, his oral link to people some distance away."[33]

3 Educational Technology:
The Processes

3.1 WHY INDIVIDUALIZATION AND WHAT IS IT?

Current educational talk and writing is all for *individualization of instruction*. Even steel companies, or at least their ad men, profess a belief in this "ultimate dream" (see Fig. 9).

In spite of or perhaps because of an obscure but tantalizing meaning, individualized instruction nowadays gets held up to the public as a panacea. Newspapers seize eagerly on official pronouncements on the subject. The following remarks on the Individually Prescribed Instruction project (IPI) at the Oakleaf School in Pittsburgh were attributed by the *Boston Globe* to Louis Bright, formerly Associate Commissioner of Education for Research, to explain why federal officials are so sold on individualization. Bright was said to claim that "youngsters of all ability levels would learn more. And they would enjoy school far more, thus reducing discipline problems." We shall see in Section 3.4 that *whether* they would learn more and *what* they would learn more of is by no means clear.

Next, the article states that "there would be no need for compensatory education for deprived children, on which the

117

Federal government now is spending $1 billion of its $4 billion annual education budget." The implication of net dollars savings is, however, highly questionable, as we shall see in Chapters 4 and 5.

We are then told that "the dropout problem would largely be licked." Perhaps the dropout rate might be reduced somewhat if pupils were indeed to find school more relevant and enjoyable. As for teachers, they "would cease being mere dispensers of information and would be free to tutor students individually and encourage youngsters to think and to express themselves." But, in current experiments, I observed both teachers and pupils behaving like robots. The claim that "parents could take children out of school for vacations any time during the year without disrupting their learning process,"[1] is pure nonsense for the foreseeable future.

These remarks do illustrate the several types of reasoning that account for the high fashion of individualization: reasoning about individuals, reasoning about social goals, and reasoning about educational technology.

The first concerns the individual himself. Many psychologists now publicly agree that there are individual differences in learning capabilities, although teachers and the public are slower to see this point. John I. Goodlad conducted a survey in which over 10,000 parents and teachers were asked to indicate their knowledge of academic variability among fourth-graders. He reported that "in answer to the question, 'What percentage of a fourth-grade class is at grade-level?' respondents select from five choices: less than 20 per cent, 20 to 40 per cent, 40 to 60 per cent, 60 to 80 per cent, 80 to 100 per cent. Although the first is the correct response, the answers for all groups queried spread out in a bell-shaped curve peaking slightly to left of

He is learning to read from a computer. Someday a single computer will give individual instruction to scores of students — in a dozen subjects at the same time.

(The steels are ready whenever you are)

The computer will very probably revolutionize teaching — and learning — within a decade. It is already happening in its early stages.

Computerized instruction can practically (and pleasurably) allow each student to learn more, faster, but always at his own pace. Individualized instruction, the ultimate dream of effective education, is well within the range of possibility. And, by spurring students to think experimentally, computers may eventually spark imaginative, independent thinking.

Computerized education will require huge tonnages of steel. In addition to computers themselves, this method of education will necessitate construction of new buildings, special communication systems, new steel furniture, movable interior steel walls and partitions. Required will be improved sheet and bar steels, and untold miles of highly dependable steel pipe and tubing.

Republic Steel has anticipated the steel needs of the future. New mills, new processes, and intensified re-

search and development will assure that the new weight-saving, more durable steels will be ready when needed.

At this moment, the long reach of steel from Republic is probing into every area where man's imagination needs it — from schoolroom to satellite, from the heartbeat of man to the drumbeat of defense. Republic Steel Corporation, Cleveland, Ohio 44101.

You Can Take the Pulse of Progress at

REPUBLIC STEEL

CLEVELAND, OHIO 44101

FIGURE 9. Republic Steel and Individualized Instruction

119

center. Obviously, there is much to do in merely teaching the facts of individual differences to persons who deal with individuals every day."[2] Still, it is considered reasonable to assume that different learning and teaching techniques, perhaps even different goals, are best for different individuals. A search begins for means to these ends.

The second type of reasoning emphasizes social goals or problems. It stems either from a belief that the needs of society are not well met by education or from a conviction that education does not serve equally well the interests of various groups in our society. Thus, for example, the needs of the gifted child drew much attention in the early post-Sputnik period when a need was felt for leadership in a variety of technological races; the Great Society bore down particularly on the needs of what are described euphemistically as "disadvantaged" children. Whatever the goals of education, projected teacher shortages, both in quantity and quality, suggest a need for alternative ways of teaching and learning. Hence interest grows in the use of materials for self-instruction or of mass media. How the choice of means affects the individual becomes a lively question.

Finally, technology itself presents new means that seek their proper ends. In principle, "classical" programmed instruction in the manner of S. L. Pressey or B. F. Skinner allows each student to move at his own pace. It came into vogue as *the* way to self-instruction without expensive individual human tutors. It is now recognized as one of many possible tools of instruction. More recently, others saw in the computer and its flexible branching capability an especially powerful new tool for adapting instruction precisely to the needs and the capabilities of the individual.

Technologists frequently proclaim that if only educators would specify precisely what they want, then technology could produce it. We shall see that this is asking a great deal of educators and of their goals; it is asking a great deal of our limited ability to tell when we've reached a goal; it neglects technical limitations; it dismisses the need for interaction more intimate than buying and selling; it begs many fundamental questions of social and financial policy.

What does individualization really mean? Current thinking on that question is both varied and confused: "During the past decade, the term 'individualizing instruction' has become a watchword with educational reformers. Two recent year-books of educational organizations have had this term as title ... Oddly, both volumes were written as though everyone knows what individualization means since neither of them offers a working definition of the term. In point of fact, there is great confusion."[3]

The cynic might be tempted to dismiss individualization as a fad without deeper significance than Detroit's customizing, namely taking a mass-produced object and stamping it with gold initials or heaping chrome on fins to give the illusion of individual tailoring. This is the sense in which computer programs greet you with "Good morning, Johnny" by filling in the blank in "Good Morning, – – –" with the name you had to give to identify yourself to the machine in the first place. This is more genteel than 'Do not fold, spindle, or mutilate!' "Hey you!" or "Good to see you, 367-A-45096," but just as superficial, even when randomly selected variations heighten the effect of spontaneity.

In spite of such sophomoric games, one can discern more serious issues behind the huckstering of the exploiters and the confusion of the scholars. One's interpretation of individualization must necessarily vary depending on whether he is relating this concept to the goals of education, to the process of education, or to the learner. Failure to sort out these three aspects of the educational system accounts for much of the great confusion. It will therefore prove helpful to distinguish between universal and particular goals, mass-produced and custom-tailored processes, and grouped and lone learners. Making these distinctions, and defining the complementary technical factors described in Section 4.2 begins the necessary task of producing effective guidelines for matching educational goals with the people, the processes, and the devices of educational technology.

Goals of education may be either universal or particular. For example, we now accept in principle the goal of universal literacy, and we would like to reach it in practice. We do not, however, insist that every adult American play the violin. IQ-tests and the College Board examinations establish de facto national standards. On the other hand, we do not insist that everyone pass the examinations required of certified public accountants, airline pilots, or barbers.

The balance between uniformity and deviation has deep social consequences. In his 1949 Inglis Lecture, *The Cultivation of Idiosyncrasy,* Harold Benjamin emphasized one aspect of the political consequences of this balance by asking explicitly a question "which a democratic society may ignore only at its deadly peril. The question is double-barreled:

1. How much uniformity does this society need for safety?

2. How much deviation does this society require for progress?"[4]

The choice of balance also has economic consequences. To

the extent that goals are universal and, especially, to the extent that they are specific, explicit, and operationally defined, the economies of scale and the efficiencies of mass production may be realized. The mass production of individuals wedded to a brand of soap or capable of cleaning and reassembling a rifle is routine. To the extent that goals are particular or vague, mass production seems unattractive or ineffective.

The *processes* of education may be either forms of mass production or varieties of custom tailoring. This distinction applies independently to the creation of a process and to its application. A book, for example, may be created by mass production for the sake of low cost. It may, however, either be read aloud to a large captive group or else selected by an individual and read privately in whole or in part as he sees fit. A lecture may be created ad hoc by a professor or produced at some institute for widespread use. It may be delivered live in an auditorium or televised to a nation-wide audience.

The choice of process can also be independent of the choice of goals. A prescribed textbook serves universal goals, a printed blank diary particular ones. A lecture may express the idiosyncracies of a professor or the official views of a ruling party. An individual tutor can serve either to tailor the presentation of universal, specific, and operationally defined goals, as in assisting his pupil in cramming for a specific national test, or else to tailor a discussion with his pupil to suit both their idiosyncrasies.

The means of mass production are economically interesting only on a scale that is at least substantial if not universal. Hiring a large hall for a lecture pays off only if there is a large audience, and sales in at least the thousands are needed to break even on most books. The live lecture requires grouping of its audience for economy's sake. The videotaped lecture or the book can reach a large audience of isolated individuals and still be economical. In general, because information technology has made possible an increasing independence of creation and application, the quality, the time, the place, and the rate of learning can be individually tailored to varying degrees even though the goal may be rigidly prescribed and the processes created by mass production.

The *learner* is always, quite obviously, an individual. He may, of course, be doing his learning in a group or alone. This choice is nearly independent of educational goals that are not intrinsically socializing goals. Obviously, no individual can learn to get along with a group if he has no group to get along with. There is, however, greater latitude in grouping when the individual is learning, for example, reading or arithmetic. Given the book or television as prior social creations, grouping is not an essential matter, but rather a hotly debated question of economy, convenience, and effectiveness mixed with questions of socialization.

To the extent that a group is homogeneous in every quality that matters, the distinction between universal and particular goals loses that much force and mass production for the group becomes more nearly equivalent to tailoring for its individual members. Conversely, both distinctions are sharpened for more diversified groups.

Applying the foregoing distinctions will explain much of the ferment and confusion found rallying around the flag of individualization as a consequence of our society's urgent desire to reach at once several conflicting objectives. The schools are now being asked to do custom tailoring economically for diversified groups while aiming at both universal and particular educational goals: Technology is exciting because, as we shall see in Chapter 5, it promises to let us do just that.

The nature of the gap between promise and real possibility must be understood if progress is to be made toward satisfying society. Otherwise, my conclusion that educational technology can now be little more than a placebo for the ailing educational organism will be interpreted as a denial of its potential value, and hence as an unwitting reinforcement of the conservative argument against further investment for "inconsequential" returns.

3.2 CAN INDIVIDUALIZATION WORK?

What schools are asked to do is primarily a matter of political choice. *How* they might or might not do it is amenable to systems analysis. What are the technological consequences of asking the schools to do custom tailoring economically in diversified groups while aiming at both universal and particular goals?

We ask the schools to group their students because handling a class of 25 to 40 in lockstep, more or less uniformly at one time and in one place, has seemed cheaper and easier than other alternatives. Were the groups homogeneous in some ideal sense, meeting this request would not significantly affect the choice of goals or processes.

By asking schools to deal with diversified groups for important social reasons, we add to the difficulties that inevitably arise from the failure to achieve ideal homogeneity even when one tries hard to get it. The choice of diversity rather than homogeneity is primarily a social and political choice. Technology enters the decision-making process through its effect on the range and the relative advantages and disadvantages of alternatives.

The problems of scheduling in time and space provide a useful example of the questions that spring up when individual differences must be accounted for. Analysis of this example illustrates how technology influences the answers to policy questions.

Given a diversified group and the conclusions of psychologists about individual differences in learning, the alternatives range from strait-jacketing the pupils and let the psychologists be damned, through attempts to preserve something of a group in time and space while allowing some individual variations, on toward some nominal grouping for administrative control with individual activities otherwise freely spread in time and space.

Ample illustrations of the prevalent first choice are given in Chapters 1 and 2. The second choice is demonstrated in well-run classrooms in many schools, and in experiments such as those with so-called Individually Prescribed Instruction (IPI), which are described in Section 3.4. The third choice is a goal of such experimental schools as Melbourne and Nova High Schools in Florida. It is the normal mode in the best American colleges and universities, and in some European ones. In our best colleges, being a member of the class of 19XX means little as far as choice of courses is concerned, although the courses themselves are designed for groups in which homogeneity is presumed to be enhanced by the self-selection of the students who join. Being grouped as a third- or fourth-year graduate student means still less, because the advanced graduate student most often works alone with his professor.

Some advocates of various forms of individualization play

down the seriousness of scheduling and other administrative problems: "Schools considering nongrading seem to worry unduly over the administrative problem which they fear will develop when the curriculum becomes unhooked, disassembled, and fluid, letting students move from one phase to a higher one at frequent intervals."[5]

Nonetheless, various experiments have indicated that worries about the viability of individualization are, in fact, well-founded even under very carefully controlled conditions. IPI, as well as experiments in computer-aided instruction, for example, has set itself universal educational goals and envisages mass production in the creation and the dissemination of the process. Especially in the earlier and more advanced of these experiments the application of the process is tailored exclusively to variation in individual rate of learning. Serious problems arise even under such careful limitations. These may be partially overcome, as Melbourne and Nova High Schools have done through heroic efforts in sheltered habitats. Adaptation to the prevalent habitats is, however, another matter.

Patrick Suppes of Stanford University has found that when students are given the opportunity to progress at will "the rate at which the brightest children advance may be five to ten times faster than that of the slowest children."[6] Although he began one experiment with a group of students "very homogeneous in initial measures of ability (IQ range from 122 to 156, with a mean of 137.5)," after a year and a half the spread was "almost two years."[7]

To gain insight into the effects of such a spread without the hazards and expenses involved in fiddling with real children in real schools, some investigators have turned to computer simulation studies. A study led by John Cogswell at the System Development Corporation (SDC) included the simulation of an individualized ninth-grade algebra course:

> The simulation was based on data that represented actual students in the operating school. The passage of the students through the course, receiving instruction individually and in small groups, being tested, getting help from the teacher, and being referred to the counselor, was simulated entirely on the machine. The results led to the conclusion that the school's procedure for grouping students was both inefficient and impractical. It appeared inefficient because of the time a student had to spend waiting for a group to form, and impractical because as students spread out over time the number of groups increased and the size of each group decreased. Demand for instructors soon exceeded their available time and students were spending too much time in non-productive waiting. These conclusions were subsequently verified in the school being simulated.[8]

The study further points out that two schools in different parts of the country which had independently experimented with a continuous progress plan for four years "independently decided to place their slowest students back in a lockstep group plan . . . Although [this] administrative decision may be justified by the explanation that the slow students are not suited to the plan, the simulated data indicate that the resources and the organizational plan have become increasingly unsuited to the slow students."[9] Thus serious difficulties appear even within the narrow confines of rate tailoring. Many forces tend to drive efforts back toward lockstep grouping.

One might be tempted to shrug these problems off with "it's all a matter of scheduling, which computers could easily do."

Let us therefore take a closer look at the logistics problems that arise. One of the most pressing matters is how to handle enough sufficiently accurate information to keep track of the students and resources. One reason why the lockstep system has persisted for so long may be that it minimizes information-processing problems. Students progress in unison; they are given identical assignments and they take tests simultaneously. With rate tailoring, on the other hand, each student may be working at any one time at a point in the curriculum different from every other student's, even if every student is working through the very same curriculum. Each student's status must therefore be tracked individually. To complicate the matter still further, the records must be kept in "real time"; namely *at any time*, not just weekly or by marking periods, the student's status as a learner must always be available to the decision-maker, whether a computer or a human guidance counselor.

An effective monitoring device and evaluation scheme must be built in, because otherwise it would be impossible to know when to schedule a student for, say, extra help. Extrapolation from the SDC simulation suggests that "with a population of 900 students, there would be from 30 to 40 changes between courses and about 300 mastery tests daily."[10] In a simulation of 10 students in a French course, demands on equipment were seen to change "within a 20 minute period from a demand state for 10 computer terminals to a demand state for five different teachers."[11]

The scheduling device must also keep track of the available instructional resources. Keeping an accurate, real-time list of teachers, rooms, and media is a major inventory-control problem at the edge of the state of the computer art (Chapter

5). Because there is not an inexhaustible supply of equipment, priorities must be set and the coordinator (or computer scheduler) must have effective resource-matching techniques. Unless many units of each resource are made available, and the costs of instruction correspondingly increased, competition will arise sooner or later. The result, as described above by the SDC study, is likely to be a relapse into lockstep.

Even if the problems of logistics could be solved, the need would remain for staff that can effectively and happily shrug off the lockstep habit. As Glen Heathers points out, neglect of staffing is perilous: "Perhaps the greatest weakness of these ambitious change projects lies in their lack of intensive programs of staff education that would enable teachers to change their instructional practices to meet the requirements of the innovations."[12] What is needed to do so? What is expected of the teacher under rate-tailored systems? Some of the flavor of these expectations is conveyed by Figure 10, which describes what is expected of teachers under the IPI process.

Having adopted rate-tailored instructional practices, the teacher must not only know his students, but he must also transmit information about them to other teachers. What kind of information does one need to make scheduling decisions? What is a meaningful way in which to express someone's competence as a learner? Suppes comments, "Indeed, there are so many questions about performance that can be asked, that teachers, administrators and supervisors are in danger of being swamped by more summary information than they can possibly digest. We are only in the process of learning what summaries are most useful from the pedagogical standpoint."[13]

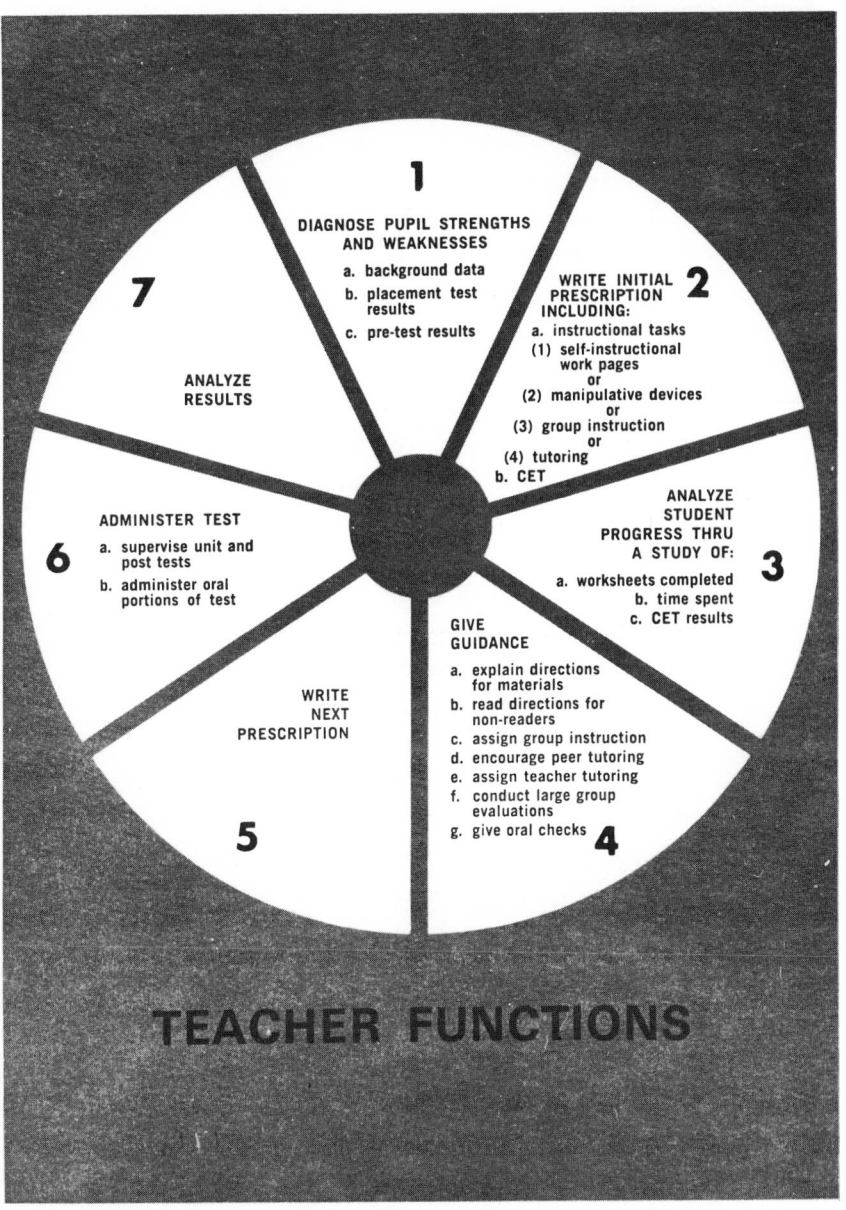

TEACHER FUNCTIONS

FIGURE 10. Teacher Functions in the Individually Prescribed Curriculum

Even if these communication problems could be overcome, the system would still make extraordinary demands on the teacher. "The point," says R. L. Bright about IPI after predicting universal individualization within ten years, "is that a student's question may be on any unit of any subject in the entire elementary curriculum and beyond."[14] The problems this situation raises have led to attempts to make curricula "teacher-proof" and to make machines take over where people fail.

Scheduling, logistics, and personnel are not the only problems. Rate-tailored instruction also meets with community resistance. Pressures to conform range from the desire of the pupil to stay with his age group to the insistence of parents that their kids be treated like everyone else. Joan's parents complain because Susan, in the same class, has a different book. The problem is compounded if Susan's book is more advanced and therefore more prestigious. This problem can be agonizing, as I found out in visiting a "special class" in Small City (Appendix A): "We discussed the textbook with him and he pointed out that the boys regarded the use of a fifth-grade textbook as a great stigma; he therefore supplied them with junior-high books to carry around in the halls and in the cafeteria, so that they could avoid losing face with their age peers."[15]

The viability of individualization, even in the restricted sense of rate tailoring, thus depends on every aspect of the educational enterprise. Unless the whole changes, the viability of isolated mutations is dubious. We shall see this clearly by using the distinctions made in Section 3.1 to classify and to discuss the fitness and the viability of some specimens of individualization.

The prevalent mode of public elementary and secondary education aims primarily at universal goals. Its processes are created primarily by mass production. They are applied uniformly to groups selected primarily for homogeneity of chronological age. This is the system which individualization aims to reform.

Technological devices suitable to some degree at least for tailored application of educational processes are available in the elementary and secondary schools, but, typically, they have failed to yield any tailoring. As we have seen in Section 2.2, there are various types of failures.

In principle, books readily lend themselves to tailoring through the availability of multiple copies for individual use and the ease of selecting a particular book and choosing particular passages in it. In practice, school libraries are scarce, cramped, and inaccessible to their intended users, the children.

Audiovisual aids have been in vogue for some time. But we hear, "I had brought my own phonograph to school (no one could find the Requisition Forms for 'Audio-Visual Aids' — that's the name for the school record player.)"[16] Language laboratories are touted as aids to tailoring but the laboratory assistants are told to "put on the correct tape for that teacher and period" (p. 95) and, to underline the point, students are told that "no one is an individual in the laboratory" (p. 94).

As for some of the other currently fashionable instructional processes, "Apparently the possibilities of such teaching modes as individualized or programmed instruction, team teaching and grouping within the class have not been explored" (p. 90). Where they have been, the theory has often not worked out in practice: "Team teaching has too often become 'turn teaching' — 'I'll teach today and it's your turn tomorrow'."[17]

If, as the ES '70 planners claimed, "various elements of the educational process . . . have recently been examined by researchers and judged to be important additions to current practice," then the failures of the prevalent mode might be ascribed simply to institutional resistance to change. Exhortations from Hawaii, money, and other inducements might then prod or shame institutions into getting with it.

What elements of the educational process have been examined? Are they important additions to current practice? Some examples of processes are presented in the remainder of this chapter. The influence of devices is then analyzed in subsequent chapters.

3.3 EXPERIMENTS IN INDIVIDUALIZATION AS INDEPENDENCE AND CREATIVITY

In 1961, J. Lloyd Trump proposed a plan for changing the conditions of the schools, beginning with the observation, "Schools that experiment with independent study find it difficult to stimulate even the most able students to do truly creative, independent work . . . Teachers' assignments have left little room . . . for the exercise of initiative . . . What was supposed to be independent study looked quite similar to the homework that usually occurs."[18]

The Melbourne High School in Florida boasts of being the first to implement the Trump Plan. B. Frank Brown, the principal of Melbourne High, sharpens Trump's idea as follows: "Individual study refers to short-term, directed learning; independent study refers to self-directed, long-term study."[19] In individual study, "students do research. They experiment. They examine. They read. They investigate. They consider evidence . . . Assignments . . . are definite, but they are always open-ended, allowing the student to escape forward."[20] In independent study, on the other hand, the student "organizes and directs his own learning experiences . . . [The main requirement for admission is that the student] be willing to drive toward the fulfillment of dimly perceived capacities."[21]

Individual study, as Brown defines it, seems to aim at universal goals through the rate-tailored application of mass-produced processes with, presumably, no more reliance on grouping than may be necessary for socialization and mutual stimulation. In independent study, the creation and the application of the process are both presumably tailored by the learner himself.

Distinct from both individual and independent study is Melbourne High's Quest Plan. This curriculum component is designed "to foster and expand traits of curiosity and imagination . . . A student may spend from one to three hours a day in quest."[22] The key to the Quest Plan is apparently the substitution of particular for universal goals, but with a curious requirement, presumably intended to enable evaluation of the student's work: "The Quest Phase is designed to let curious students be creative *with definite objectives,* or to permit students to pursue work in more depth than is possible . . . in the regular classroom."[23] Although creativity is assumed to be a logical consequence of an individualized environment, Brown never mentions just *what* a definite objective of creativity might be or just *how* the student is to be creative.

The question is indeed worrisome. Some objectives of

Behavior of Mealworms,[24] a unit produced by the Elementary Science Study of the Education Development Center (EDC), are described by the statement that the unit "stimulates children to ask questions about the observable behavior of an unfamiliar animal and then directs them to ways of *finding answers for themselves* [emphasis added]."[25] In the terms of Section 3.1, the application of the learning process is presumably to be tailored by the learner himself.

As soon as it is granted, however, this license begins to be revoked bit by bit. To explore the question "How can mealworms follow walls?" the teacher's guide suggests that "building a variety of 'mealworm walls' is another worthwhile activity. *The idea can be introduced by the teacher* [emphasis added] if it does not evolve naturally."[26] Here, once again, albeit on a higher plane, is the deus ex machina of lockstep, ready to descend at the slightest pressure of convenience and economy, or at the least sign of failure to "cover" what's to be covered. Restrictions then blossom quickly and choke the learner's tailoring: "Often the array of materials leads some children to make elaborate structures *with little apparent purpose* [emphasis added]. Walk around and ask, 'Why are you making your wall that way?' *Perhaps materials should be limited so there is no opportunity to construct more than is necessary* [emphasis added]."[27]

Clearly learner tailoring makes it tough for teachers. Consider the plight of a teacher who has boned up exclusively on crabs, and faces the following situation reported by John Goodlad: "the writer remembers only too vividly visiting a classroom using—thankfully, only beginning to use—the materials of a new project in elementary-school science. Arriving a few minutes before the class was scheduled to begin, he almost tripped over a cluster of excited children examining a handsome box turtle."[28] The teacher's reaction is predictable: "Said the teacher, 'Now, children, put away the turtle. We're going to have our science lesson.' The lesson was on crabs!"[29]

The problems of learner tailoring are not new. Nor are they restricted to major issues such as "developing creativity." The usual dreary college laboratory experiment in which the student listlessly manipulates preset apparatus to take predictable readings supporting a foregone conclusion is a poor image of living science. The original experiment, which perhaps earned somebody a Nobel Prize, was a far more exciting adventure, the outcome of which, if predictable at all, was foreseen only in hunches and hopes. Is it reasonable to expect that the flavor of years of research can be conveyed in a three-hour lab followed by hours of formal "write-up"? What are viable alternatives?

Attempts to find them have so far yielded only partial answers under unique, sheltered conditions. Nova High School, which espouses goals like those of Melbourne, is a case in point. It has attracted much attention for its innovations in physical plant, its wide variety of hardware devices and its motto, worthy of Cyrano de Bergerac, *Love, learning and laughter.*

This school is the offspring of one man, Stuart Synnestvedt, working within the unique power structure in Broward County, Florida. The community structure is based on retirement fortunes eager to provide a technical base for new industries, to supplement tourism, and to attract children and grandchildren to a sunny paradise now shunned for lack of good schools. Students are admitted from anywhere in the county.

Selection criteria include "a willingness to work diligently and attend school regularly."[30] No free bus transportation is provided; parents must either chauffeur their children or pay for bus service. The racially integrated result is a school serving the children of highly-motivated middle- and upper-class parents.

Innovative jargon is abundant. The day begins with Ad Com (administrative communication) which—fancy name, same old thing—is known elsewhere as "homeroom." The schedule is organized in thirty-minute mods (modules) usually paired to yield old-fashioned sixty-minute periods. Libraries, I mean Resource Centers, are beautiful and stocked not only with books but also with a variety of microfilm readers and printing devices (which I did not see in use). I observed happy burbling in these libraries, yet great concentration. Above all, the shelves were open and the librarians friendly. Teacher Aide rooms and nearby carrels for teachers were busy, with teachers and teacher aides (secretaries) writing, typing, mimeographing, and collating.

One product of this effort is the Learning Activity Package, intended to "initiate the possibility of individual progress and in general, student responsibility in learning."[31] Typically, however, teachers admit that most student activities are teacher-supervised, with groups of twenty or so pupils per class. One English teacher pointed out that she and her three team colleagues found it hard to give individual attention to each student in six groups of twenty, especially so in the case of the slower children. As a consequence, they reorganized some of their groups into subgroups *according to ability.* TV was rarely used, the teacher said, but she had just gone with her colleagues to the school's TV studio to make a tape of introductory material to present to each of the six groups, feeling that her team should not have to take the time to repeat the same stuff six times viva voce.

The school has adopted a kind of just-plain-folks protective coloration. Special privileges, like clerical help for teachers, make it a target of less-favored school personnel. The staff is instructed not to compare scores or brag. As a sun-tanned echo of the Bronx High School of Science, Nova is an island of quality and wealth in a sea of mediocrity and poverty (Florida stands forty-sixth among the states in expenditure per pupil). Reproducing Nova successfully elsewhere without the shelter of the special motives, the politics, and the wealth of Broward County seems improbable.

Have the conditions described by Trump really changed? Are these experiments already the important additions to current practice assumed by ES '70, or still only fascinating, worthwhile, but incomplete experiments?

The capacity for truly creative, independent work is vital to our society. Such work can be messy, expensive, and time-consuming. Our present schools are organized for neatness, low budgets, and time compression. That can be changed. But still, one cannot sensibly argue that a student should personally recapitulate the intellectual history of mankind in every detail in every subject. Moreover, even the most creative individuals must learn some of their society's arbitrary conventions or be doomed to being ignored as cranks. So must the least creative, or be doomed to helplessness. Much sugar may coat the pill, but in the last analysis learning that red means *stop* and green means *go* or that the plural of "man" is "men" is rote and can be nothing more.

Creation and rote are the extremes of a structure whose

shape is scarcely discernible, but whose elements supply the stuff of education. The extreme advocates of creation have a hard lot. Those who can, do; but those who can't, can hardly even teach; how can anyone describe the unknown? Shifting the ground from creation to creativity improves the odds slightly but the priceless and essential payoff is still remote and uncertain. It certainly does not yet lend itself to explicit quantitative analysis. Measurable results come easier with rote. It's easy to say that one wants to teach that "red" means *stop* and, when the job's done, there's immediately something almost tangible and certainly useful to show off.

Debates on the role of creative independent work in formal educational institutions and on how much time can be effectively devoted to such work in conventional school settings will be with us for a long time. Neither the question nor the answers are clear even for Ph.D. programs in university departments, or professional programs in schools of law or medicine. Meanwhile, nothing justifies pushing the schools or letting them lapse entirely in either direction.

3.4 AN EXPERIMENT IN INDIVIDUALIZED MASS PRODUCTION

Individually Prescribed Instruction (IPI) is an experiment in reaching *measurable* universal goals through mass-produced processes with tailored application. To set up educational goals so as to know when you've got there is widely and wisely advocated, but measurement is not easy, as noted by John Goodlad: "The difficulty with this laudable goal of providing for continuous progress is that there must be an identifiable 'something' that progresses."[32] This thought is amplified by

Theodore Sizer: "Educators talk 'goals' ad nauseam; but they rarely cast these goals in any form that is measurable and, even when they have done this, they feel that careful assessment is often a prick to their pride and somehow un-American."[33]

The failure to cast goals in measurable form and to assess results carefully is often nothing more than self-defense by threatened institutions, but more of it is plain ignorance. Where assessment is done, it is based all too often on pathetic faith in the illusory objectivity of statistical manipulation by incompetent hands. S. S. Stevens has recently noted how common "scientific decision" by statistical calculation has become, especially in education. From 1948 to 1962, while the proportion of articles in six psychological journals based on statistical inferences increased from 56 percent to 91 percent, the proportion in the *Journal of Educational Psychology* rose from 36 to 100 percent.[34]

Robert Glaser, the director of the University of Pittsburgh's Learning Research and Development Center, where IPI was born, sets great store in *behaviorally defined objectives*, seeking to cast goals "in terms of observable competence and the conditions under which it is to be exercised."[35] The search is difficult. About such aspects of human behavior as complex reasoning and open-endedness, Glaser can say only that if these are desirable, they *must* be recognized—which is easy enough—and measurable—which does not necessarily follow from the wish. Thus he is driven to lament that we have been forced "to settle for what can be easily expressed and measured."[36]

Figures 11 and 12 show samples of expressed behavioral objectives in reading and elementary arithmetic. No harm need ensue from multiple-choice questions like "Why did the

	level C	**level D**
NUMERATION	1. Reads, writes numerals 1-200. Sequence from any starting point. 2. Supplies number 1 more, or less, or in between — 1 to 200. 3. Skip counts 2's, 5's, 10's to 200.	1. Reads, writes to 1,000. Any point. 2. Skip counts, by 3's, 4's from any point. 3. (a) Identifies and reads decimal fractions to hundredths. (b) Converts decimal numbers to fractions and other forms. (c) Fills in missing simple decimals.
PLACE VALUE	1. Identifies place value of the units, 10's, 100's to 200. Indicates >, <. 2. Writes numbers, columns 100's, 10's, units.	1. Identifies units, 10's, 100's 1000's. Uses >, <. Writes number before, after to 1,000. 2. Writes numerals, expanded notation, to 1,000. Regroups, renames. 3. Uses number families, bridging, to work addition, subtraction problems. 4. (a) Gives place value of decimal fractions in fractional or other form. (b) Makes place value chart.
ADDITION	1. Use of associative principle. 2. Adds 2 numbers — sum of 20. 3. Sums of 2 or 3 numbers, no carrying. 4. Uses >, <, =. Equations, 2 step, combining add-subtract. 5. Works · column addition — 3 or more addends, sums to 20.	1. Demonstrates mastery, sums thru 20. 2. Does column addition — no carrying. 3. Finds missing addends — 3 single digits. 4. Uses words, sum, addend — labels part. 5. Adds, carrying to 10's using 2 digit numerals, 2 or more addends. 6. Adds, carrying to 10's, 100's, using 3 digit numerals, 2 or more addends. 7. Adds, carry 10's, 100's, using 3 digit numerals, 2 or more addends. 8. Finds sums, column addition. Using 2 or more addends of 1 digit.
SUBTRACTION	1. Subt. problems — numbers to 18. 2. Subt. 2 digit — no borrowing. 3. Finds missing addend — 2 single digits.	1. Mastery subtraction facts, numbers to 20. 2. Subtraction no borrowing — 3 or more digits. 3. Subtraction borrowing 10's place — 2 digits. 4. Subtraction borrowing 10's, 100's — 3 digits. 5. Subtraction borrowing 10's, 100's — 3 digits.

FIGURE 11. Behavioral Objectives in Arithmetic

author write this book?" (Fig. 12) so long as "this book" is not confused with the works of Shakespeare or Newton.

And so, the educator is trapped. If he responds *exclusively* to the pressures for measurement and assessment, he becomes the "pedagogical plainsman" whom Harold Benjamin scornfully describes as "continually constructing curricula, sorting

Level C

Evaluative Comprehension

Skill	Example	Method
2. Write a short description of a picture, telling what is seen.	2. Look at the picture. Who are making a snowman? <u>**Two children**</u> Is it cold out? <u>**yes**</u> Write about the picture.	Individual worksheets
3. Draw a picture that illustrates an event in a story read aloud by the teacher or read silently in a book.	3. Go to the Learning Center. Get <u>Where the Wild Things Are</u>. Read the story. Draw a picture of Max and the Wild Things dancing in the moonlight.	Individual worksheets Discs
4. Select correct answers from a worksheet to questions that examine understanding of the author's purpose.	4. Get <u>You Can Plant Flowers</u> from the Learning Center. Read the book. Put an X̄ in the box beside the right answer. Why did the author write this book? 1. ☐ To make us laugh about flowers. 2. ☐ To help us learn about bees. 3. ☒ To help us learn about planting flowers.	Individual worksheets

FIGURE 12. Behavioral Objectives in Reading

subjects, fussing over facts, determining the significance of dates, tampering with time allotments, and computing percentages of sacredness."[37] If he responds *exclusively* to the siren song of "creativity, inquiry, etc.," he gets mired in his own platitudes under the guns of Goodlad and Sizer. Our existing schools result from an unhappy balance of these opposing pressures.

IPI has chosen to tailor primarily for variations in rate of progress, recognizing this factor to be but one of many recognized individual differences: "The project's concern for the individualization of rates of progression should not be taken as a judgment that this represents an attack on the most important aspect of individual differences. It represents a decision to make a rather intensive study of a school program which concentrates on this one aspect. Other aspects such as differences in interests and in other personal qualities may be equally important or even more important, but this project, at least for the present, will concern itself largely with the differentiation of rates."[38]

With the goals thus narrowed, measurement of progress can be defined by tests of the pupil's mastery of subject matter as captured in the form of behavioral objectives like those of Figures 11 and 12. Tests "are measures of achievement in the various units and objectives, with some further indices of the rate at which a student has been achieving mastery and the amount of practice and review he has required. Little use is made, at present, of measures of general intelligence or aptitude which have seemed difficult to relate to instructional decisions in the elementary school. From the placement tests no measures are obtained of subtle aspects of learning style, but perhaps reliable measures of this can be found."[39]

Some of these tests are integrated with the course material. They "are seen as part of instruction, and the students look forward to them because they get immediate information about whether they need additional work in a unit or can move on to new work. The overall philosophy of this built-in testing program is that at any point in time the student's performance is so monitored that a detailed assessment is available of his performance and progress."[40]

The pupil passes from one curriculum unit to the next upon reaching "a posttest mastery criterion of 85%."[41] He then obtains a "prescription sheet" (see Fig. 13) for the next unit. These sheets identify each skill a pupil is to learn and the worksheets or other materials he is to use. The pupils themselves then assemble worksheets from available files or pull a record from a shelf and take it to an unoccupied record player.

Although Glaser wisely warns that "the setting of a criterion level . . . is an experimental question which needs investigating,"[42] this caution has quickly been lost sight of. Professional and public discussions now accept 85 percent with the same mindless reverence they already accord to the 95 percent confidence level of statistical tests. Further subtle but vital questions are thus forgotten: "Do different units and differing students require a uniform level of proficiency? If too high a criterion is set, a student can spend too much time mastering fine points of one unit, while he might be beginning the next. A bright student might begin to learn multiplication while still becoming proficient in the fundamentals of addition and subtraction, and in this way develop a richer concept of addition; another student may require more detailed mastery of fundamentals before he moves on. The questions involved seem more complex than we had originally supposed."[43]

As far as the teacher is concerned, she is dispensing medicine supplied by others, with a crude thermometer as her main official guide. The clerical tyranny of the "prescription" has replaced the clerical tyranny of the Delaney book. The students' independence in filling out their prescriptions is the independence of file clerks. The logistics of this clerical enterprise is not trivial: "The accumulation and maintenance

Name _____ Class __4__ Page __1__ MASTERY Pull

Level __E__ Unit __MULTIPLICATION__ 1-4-5-6-7-9-10

			Unit Tests			
		Pre		Post		
		1	2	1	2	3	4

					Unit Tests					
Begin	5/20	173		Score	90	49		86				
End	6/6	183		%		54		96				
Days Worked		11		Date	5/16			6/6				

#	Date Pres.	Pres. Init.	Page No.	Skill No.	Items	Score	Date	Sc's Init.	Part 1 Items	Part 1 %	Part 2 Items	Part 2 %	Sc's Init.
1	5-20	J.J.	E 156	1	42	39	5/23	d.s.					
			157		15	15	5/23	d.s.					
			159		24	24	5/23	d.s.					
			160				5/24	d.S.	16	14	88	3	3	100
5	5/24	m.m.	E 174	4	5	5	5/24						
			175		25	25	5/24						
			177		19	19	5/24						
			180		19	18	5/24						
			193				6/1	G.M.	20	20	100	5	1	20
10	6/1	J.J	E 194	5	8	8	6/1	d.s.					
			195		10	10	6/1	d.s.					
			199				6/1	I.L.	15	15	100	2	2	100
	6/2	J.J.	E 213	6			6/2	I.L.	14	14	100	4	4	100
	6/3	J.J.	E 251	7			6/3	G.M.	4	4	100	6	6	100
15	6/4	J.J.	E 261	9			6/4	G.M.	12	12	100	4	4	100
	6/5	J.J.	E 281	10			6/5	G.M.	15	15	100			
			TAKE 1st Post Test										
20													

FIGURE 13. Individually Prescribed Instruction "Prescription Sheet"

146

of the day-to-day records required for individualized instruction is a sizable enterprise for a school. In the initial years of the Oakleaf project, we have been accomplishing this by hand. Each teacher has the assistance of an aide for individualized classes, and there is a data-processing room with a staff of clerks who receive information from teachers and teacher assistants, process it, and return it to the classroom."[44] Let us pause to reflect that these circulating nuggets of information are as genuine as the 85 percent criterion level.

The clerical burden and automatic behavior currently imposed by IPI leads its developers to look forward to the use of computer technology. Says James Becker, Director of Research for Better Schools, a regional educational laboratory financed by the U.S. Office of Education, and responsible for "disseminating" IPI: "Perhaps an over exaggerated definition of IPI would be to state that it is the utilization of humans to simulate in a manual paper mode that which can be accomplished by the computer and the best of our automated technology."[45]

I have observed that under their clerical burden, the teachers tend to act like unresponsive machines. Even in Oakleaf High School, the showcase of IPI, I found that the teacher aides who grade tests were instructed to "keep poker faces, *smiling* poker faces." I found this Orwellian touch chilling, however necessary it might be today to keep the peace between unionized professionals and non-union subprofessionals.

There is no denying the observation that children at Oakleaf and McAnnulty, another IPI school in Pittsburgh, were well disciplined though freely moving about, happy, and eager. On the other hand, they could frequently be observed marking time with a hand or a flag raised, waiting for the teacher to answer a question or for their turn to have tests scored by teacher aides, just as children mark time in ordinary schools.

The children are happy and eager, but what are they learning? They are learning about that valuable but restricted range of human knowledge and attitudes that can be mechanically expressed and measured. Without other forms of education, they may grow up under the dangerous illusion that there always exists a correct answer to every question.

The claim has been made for IPI that many students are performing two to four grade levels above the norms for their age, [46] but what does this buy them? They move on into a high school where the principal systematically disperses them among conventional classes to avoid clannishness. No longitudinal studies of the long-term benefits of IPI have been made, but the odds are that any effects will rapidly disappear in the deliberate leveling of the high school environment. As far as current practice is concerned, the usual relapse into lockstep has merely been postponed.

The positive value of the IPI experiment is undeniable. It is, however, altogether unwarranted to look at IPI and the like as the immediate answer to every school maiden's prayer. In the first place, IPI cannot simply be wafted into other schools by the wave of a magic wand and be counted on to meet the expectations of its developers. The difference between heroic dedicated efforts in a laboratory environment and hostility or indifference in ordinary social and administrative habitats is the difference between survival and living death. Intensive and protracted engineering efforts are essential to prepare a laboratory product for survival in the field (see Section 4.4). Much special attention to administrative practices, teacher training, and organization of materials was necessary to make IPI work in schools like Oakleaf and McAnnulty where I observed it.

In the second place, the latest available information indicates that IPI costs from $37 to $115 a year more per pupil than current practices.[47] Nevertheless, R. Louis Bright has predicted "that within another ten years almost the entire academic portion of instruction will be on an individualized basis in most schools."[48] As a consequence of rain dancing about innovation dissemination, experimental application of IPI has escalated from 23 schools[49] to 88 and "already 1,000 school districts have asked to become part of IPI."[50]

If the aim is truly experimentation and not just bread and circus, this course of action is absurd. Extending the experiment into the high schools fed by 23 schools would make far more sense than spreading it to 88 or 1,000 schools to create the illusion of change, when change in elementary school is almost certain to be wiped out in high school. *By diverting resources into "dissemination," the pressures for quickie curealls threaten to stop further progress while imposing on pupils and taxpayers yet another change in form without change in substance.*

IPI has made progress toward reaching *measurable* universal educational goals, through processes created by mass production and applied by mass production with rate tailoring to pupils grouped by the level of their posttest scores rather than by their chronological age. It is an experiment and valuable as such. It is not yet an important addition to current practice. As its originators and disseminators are first to stress, many complex questions of abstruse theory and of workaday practice still remain unanswered.

IPI shows promise as an intelligent and bold experiment pointing toward significant and valuable improvements in *one* of the ingredients in the educational mix. As a process which an industrial engineer might call mass production to narrow specifications with rigid quality control, it lends itself to those essential though limited aspects of education which can be effectively mechanized. The words "mass production" are taboo to many, owing perhaps to the fact that important aspects of education either cannot or *should not* be mass produced. This fact should not preclude the application of well-designed mass-production and quality-control techniques where they make sense and when they are ready. The choice of mix is a policy matter which technology should not be permitted to settle by default. Caveat emptor.

3.5 AN EXPERIMENT IN TAILORING

Some further perspective is gained by looking at an experiment in which the process is created by custom tailoring and applied through an ingenious combination of tailoring and mass production. The goals are prescribed but, since they apply to a group self-selected for homogeneity, the distinction between the universal and the particular is less important than otherwise. Learning takes place through a combination of lone and group activities. The setting is an elementary college course in biology at Purdue University.

Published materials about this experiment are inauspicious, filled as they are with the usual cant: "Emphasis on student learning rather than on the mechanisms of teaching is the basis of the integrated experience approach. It involves the teacher identifying as clearly as possible those responses, attitudes, concepts, ideas and manipulatory skills to be achieved by the student and then designing a multi-faceted, multi-sensory approach which will enable the student to direct his own activity to attain these objectives. The program of learning is organized in such a way that students can proceed at their own pace."[51]

In 1962, faced with a jump in enrollment from 380 to 480 in his biology course, Professor Samuel Postlethwait decided to develop something he has since labeled the "audio-tutorial approach." The result I observed is a harmonious, balanced mix of human and technological resources applied under Postlethwait's expert and energetic leadership by one full-time instructor, a secretary, and a pack of enthusiastic graduate and advanced undergraduate assistants. The effort is backed up by such research resources of a large university as a greenhouse and a film-production facility and their staffs.

Weekly "laboratory" sessions (in the jargon: Independent Study Sessions or ISS) are the core of the course. Each student is guided through the week's material by a pre-recorded tape, available at each of thirty-two carrels in the laboratory. In the course of his work, the student may be asked to read from textbook, study guide, or journal material provided at the carrel; he may observe or manipulate materials at his carrel or at one large central table; he may use appropriate instruments set about the laboratory. A workbook is supplied for use in recording observations; film loops are provided to show dynamic phenomena, such as the growth of a seedling toward the light, or to develop spatial visualization, as by presenting a series of microscopic sections to reveal three-dimensional structure. There is indeed no doting on any single device or process, but rather an attempt to use each to its best advantage.

Postlethwait carefully, if intuitively, spells out objectives, following the old-time rhetorical rule of telling the students what you're going to tell them, telling them, then telling them what they've been told.

The independent study sessions are supplemented by "general assembly sessions" (GAS, an unfortunate acronym) given over to visiting lecturers, general announcements, special movies, and the like. In addition, "integrated quiz sessions" (IQS, a better one) bring together all students eight at a time with a staff member. First each student is asked to deliver an oral explanation of some aspect of the week's laboratory, and then a written quiz is given.

The differences between Postlethwait's carefully engineered environment and other attempts at tailoring are illuminating. Few college settings can compare with it. Most elementary and secondary schools are on another planet. The ready availability of graduate students and research resources is one of the obvious points of difference between the colleges and the lower schools. The differences affecting scheduling merit more detailed examination.

Laboratory scheduling is a combination of weekly lockstep with free-for-all rate tailoring within the week. A different set-up is provided each week. The student who misses a week has had it. Within the week, however, the student may come to the laboratory whenever and as often as he wishes, possibly not at all if he feels confident enough. Thus, the dispersion phenomena noted in Section 3.2 are bounded within each week. The nightmarish logistics of supplying any student of what grew to be a class of 600 any set-up at any time is forestalled.

The laboratory is open daily from 7:30 A.M. to 10:30 P.M., a schedule that would be revolutionary in the schools. Saturdays and Sundays are reserved for tear-down and set-up. Predictably, pile-ups tend to occur as Friday afternoon approaches, especially at the beginning of the semester before students have had enough time to understand the situation and adapt to it. The measures taken to encourage adaptation are interesting. First, sixteen of the carrels are always left available on a first-come, first-served basis, and sign-up sheets are provided for the remaining sixteen, so that planning and impulse are balanced. This much depends on assumptions about student maturity and responsibility not commonly made and perhaps not tenable in the lower schools. Second, the whole course is scheduled through clever parasitism on the Purdue registrar's computerized scheduling system.

In the registrar's conventional terms, Postlethwait's course calls for scheduling one lecture hour per week, one recitation hour, two laboratories, and two hours-by-arrangement. The first lecture session is a GAS and it is announced that there will be few of these, but that the time should be kept open. Recitation is replaced by IQS. The remaining nominally scheduled hours are available for threatening the students. They know they *could* be compelled to be present at the laboratory at precisely the scheduled times without either official conflict or overflow, since the computer scheduling is based on a nominal class size of thirty-two, or precisely the laboratory capacity.

Other forms of application tailoring are used beside rate tailoring. The graduate students are always about, largely unencumbered by policing and clerking. In splendid contrast with the Watertown rules described in Figure 5, Postlethwait's Rule No. 2 for the 7:30 A.M. staff is: "Make coffee!" The room next to the laboratory has reference books, a blackboard, a large table with chairs, ashtrays, a coffee urn, and a pile of doughnuts with a cashbox. Many schools scarcely provide such facilities for their teachers. Both students and staff participate in bull sessions, discussions, and information exchanges. All is not mechanical perfection in this microcosm; witness an amusing by-play between some students entering the room and the people clumped around the blackboard in animated discussion: "Where did you get the chalk?" "We stole it, we stole some" was the cheerful reply. Adaptability is as characteristic of this environment as it is uncommon in the schools.

The course is created by custom tailoring and it continuously evolves. The different graduate students who are responsible for laboratory set-ups in different weeks vie for the approbation of their supervisors, their peers, and their students. Postlethwait records the weekly tape, but he insists — and the assistants confirm it — that he is strongly influenced by his staff. He prepares his tapes as if talking to one student and considers poorest those tapes where he becomes enamored with his own voice and falls down on frequent, direct student involvement. He speaks wrathfully of people who use tapes simply as lecture surrogates, stating that students could read either lecture notes or textbooks directly and much more quickly and effectively. He insists that tapes be erased at the end of the week, avoiding obsolescence.

The tape in use at the time of my visit reveals something of the Postlethwait style of tailoring. It began: "Hello there, this is Bio 108. Say, did you read about Dr. Kornberg's research released about December 15, 1967? This is a very important piece of research, and as a student interested in science I assumed you might be interested in the truth about what is going on here, 'cause the papers gave this quite a build-up, almost embarrassing build-up, so I have duplicated a couple of articles from *Science* magazine for us to discuss a couple of minutes and for you to read later. So . . . will you pick up the article, the one entitled 'The Synthesis of DNA and How They Spread the Good News,' will you pick it up please." There followed thirty seconds of music to give time to pick up the materials laid out in the carrel. Postlethwait then interpreted the significance of Kornberg's work, asking the student to turn to page 81 of the study guide before beginning a brief discussion of the relation of Kornberg's results to earlier lessons on cell division, DNA replication, and so forth. Later he said it was time to turn to the lesson for the week and began a review of several types of plants.

Although scripts of the tapes and other materials produced for the course are distributed commercially, Postlethwait states that he does not attempt to record tapes for export, feeling that to do so would bind both him and the recipients to inappropriate modes of expression and yield unsatisfactory results. Avoiding rigid packaging and teacher-proofing transfers major responsibility for resources and for flexibility to the recipient. The implications of this policy are clear from Figure 14, a statement of necessaries set down by disciples at Golden West College after a semester's trial of the Postlethwait system. From the point of view of the public elementary and secondary schools, even these minimal conditions for viability are Utopian. But they are not sufficient for effectiveness. The keystone is Postlethwait and his enthusiastic crew. Where comparable talents can be mustered, comparable results may be expected. Where not, the results might well be inferior to those obtainable through conscientious teacher-proofing. In this respect, therefore, higher education, like military or industrial training programs, provides a better laboratory for educational technology than lower schools.

FIGURE 14. Necessities for Audio-Tutorial Approach, Golden West College

Total Administrative Commitment — The allotment of adequate budget and teacher time was necessary prior to proceeding with the initial steps.

Total Commitment of Faculty Involved — The establishment of the A-T program required a sincere desire, on the part of the faculty, to improve the technique of conveying information. It was also necessary to spend some time outside of the scheduled teaching assignment.

Adequate Office Equipment — A minimum of two type-writers, one dictating unit and one transcribing unit was required.

Competent Clerical and Lab Assistant Staff — Two full time student secretaries and one full time lab assistant were used during the summer development period. The same staff continued, on a part time basis, during the fall school term.

Minimum Supplies and Equipment — Supplies and equipment for student use in the program should be available at the time the program is written. Two of the most valuable items used were: the National Teaching Aids microslide viewers and slides; and single-concept, synchronized sound, 8mm movie projector and loop films.

Minimum Audio-Visual Preparation Materials — A large dry mount with adequate supplies; and drafting equipment for preparation of directive signs and charts used in the study carrels and on the demonstration tables.

Minimum Software Requirements — Appropriate workbooks were necessary for the particular course (a liberal arts, non-major, general biology course). A workbook was written concurrent with preparation of the programs.

Equipment and Staff for Maintenance of Program — The provision for "student proof" tape players and headphones (especially developed for A-T), sufficient supply of tapes, tape splicer, tape bulk eraser, film splicer, spare parts, demagnetizer for tape players; and tutors for laboratory supervision and lab assistant's time to clean recorder heads and prepare the lab daily were necessary.

4 Educational Technology: The Devices

4.1 THE SCOPE OF EDUCATIONAL DEVICES

No article of apparatus for the schoolroom is more indispensable than the blackboard . . . It is the TABLET for recording mental processes of the pupil . . . It is the MIRROR reflecting the workings, character and quality of the individual mind. It is the chief auxiliary of the teacher; the AIDE-DE-CAMP, the MONITOR, the GUIDE. — *Andrews and Company*, Illustrated Catalogue of School Merchandise, *Chicago, 1881*

There is a tendency nowadays to equate educational technology with inert *devices*, especially with such recent and glamorous products of electronics as television or computers. This attitude reflects neither common sense nor a systems point of view. Devices are only the kit of tools that people may use in a process to achieve some human end.

The kit includes physical devices, called "hardware" in the jargon. Hardware, as the *form* of tools, is useless without intellectual *content*, or "software," which animates the tools and gives them meaning, precisely in the way that meaningful printed words differentiate a book from a bound collection of blank pages. Significantly, such a collection has no English name of its own, but must be called a "blank book." The choice of tools appropriate to a purpose and their organization by and with people into a harmonious well-balanced process that fits the stated purpose is an important part of the job of systems designers. Defining the purpose is policy making and not systems design, although in practice means and ends are never independent of one another.

In this section, I shall merely list some tools as a reminder that there are educational devices other than TV or computers. But, first and foremost, responsible systems analysis must not neglect people. It is always simpler and, for some, more fun or more profitable to think exclusively of inert hardware. It should, however, go without saying that a system intended for human use should be adapted to people and not vice versa.

Among devices, the book is still paramount. Speaking of *the* book, like speaking of *the* computer, is misleading in several ways. There are, of course, good books and bad books. This is obvious to everyone, but *the* computer, being less familiar, seems to conjure up ideas of uniqueness, omnipotence, and idolatry. Moreover, books just don't happen. They are written, edited, composed, printed, shipped, bought, stored in libraries, reviewed, catalogued, circulated, read, and, sometimes, understood and absorbed. Comparable things must happen to computers, their contents, and their effects. We still have much to do to make the most of books: "It is sobering to realize that only about half of the elementary schools in the United States possess libraries of any kind and that most of the other half are woefully short of books for their libraries. There appears to be one level of discourse in education where we talk champagne and another where we drink half-beer."[1]

We must also remember blackboards and chalk or paper and pencil, since these humble media still cause administrative problems in the schools: "Why do you need so many paper-clips? Supplies are running low. All out of desk blotters. All out of rubber bands. All out of board erasers. No red pencils — only blue. Can let you have half envelope of chalk — all out of boxes. Chalk is not to be wasted. *No unauthorized students are to use it.*"[2] Perhaps this will look less prosaic if chalk, blackboard, and teacher are described collectively as a man-machine audiovisual aid system badly in need of optimization.

For the rest, a quick listing must suffice. Whole books can be and have been written about the technical details of each, yet the relation of any to the others remains obscure and at best vaguely intuited. There are laboratories and shops, tape recorders and language laboratories; flash cards, Cuisenaire rods, and the abacus; maps and globes, films (in reels, loops, and strips, of every gauge under the sun, talking and silent), games logical and games simulating, duplicating machines from Addressograph to Xerox, transparent ripple tanks and plastic women, computer simulation programs and Link trainers, overhead projectors and slide projectors, teaching machines straight and branched . . . Let us not forget the light switch in my own lecture room; I can never find it in the dark, after showing films or slides.

4.2 PROPERTIES OF EDUCATIONAL DEVICES

Significant properties of the goals of education, the processes, and the learners were defined in Section 3.1. To help continue with the task of matching these with significant technical factors, the latter must now be defined in turn. We may think here of devices in a broad sense, encompassing the people and the organizations serving as agents of education. *Novelty* and *glamor* are not the only properties of educational tools worthy of note or sufficient to make them valuable for teaching. What are the really important characteristics?

Cost and *value* are of obvious importance. Cost, especially if measured in dollars, is the more easily defined of the two, particularly if one is satisfied with purchase or rental of equipment as a true cost. Because, in many instances, such direct expenses are not adequate measures in themselves and because they can be amortized, presented, or hidden in many ways, depending on the purpose or the method of accounting, even this simplest variable presents some complexity. Value is naturally much harder to define because it, in turn, depends on goals. There is, therefore, a tendency to polarize values either toward the extreme of considering only dollar values, such as teachers' salaries or pupils' lifetime earnings, or else toward the assertion that everything human is priceless.

More purely technical factors must also be considered: flexibility, generality, scheduling, parallelism, amount, physical accessibility, reliability, maintenance, complexity, comfort, standardization, integration, and content. These factors are not logically independent of one another but merely sufficiently distinct to be usefully considered in isolation.

Flexibility or adaptability is the ability of man, machine, or organization to meet the needs of the moment. People have varying degrees of flexibility. Organizations that encourage individual initiative are more flexible than those that work solely by the book. Philip Jackson describes the flexibility of the blackboard as follows:

The blackboard is literally at the teacher's fingertips. He can write on it, draw on it, immediately erase what he has written, or preserve it for days. He can scrawl key words on it, produce a detailed diagram, or write out a series of essay questions. He can use the board himself, or ask his students to use it. He can place material on it in advance, or use it to capture the fleeting and ephemeral thoughts emerging from a discussion. Given this flexibility, it is no wonder the chalk-smudged sleeve has become the trademark of the teacher.[3]

Like many of the other characteristics, flexibility is relative. Brick walls, sliding partitions, and screens are increasingly flexible ways of dividing up room space, and the value of each depends on whether changes need to be made in decades, minutes, or seconds. The choice of partition naturally depends also on such other factors as cost, blocking of unwanted noise, fire retardation, and so forth.

Another factor closely related but not identical to flexibility is *generality*. We commonly tag people as generalists or specialists. A blank piece of paper and a blackboard have equal generality in that anything that can be written on one can be written on the other; they have great generality since most anything can be written on either. The blackboard, however, is clearly more flexible than paper in that it lends itself more readily to erasing one thing and replacing it by another.

Unless a resource is infinite or there is no demand for it, *scheduling* its use is necessary. People keep appointment calendars; libraries keep reservation lists for popular books.

Scheduling is closely related to what might be called *parallelism* or the simultaneous availability of multiple abstract or concrete instances of a given resource. In most classrooms, for example, paper is more parallel a resource than blackboard space in that it is quite easy to have each of thirty or forty students writing on his own sheet of paper at one time while perhaps only two or three students together can be accommodated at the blackboard. The teacher/pupil ratio is a measure of teacher parallelism.

The *amount* of a resource must also be taken into account. Amount is clearly distinct from parallelism. A committee of three examiners does not function in the same way as three individual tutors. Forty sheets of paper arranged in a single pad can be used by only one person at a time while forty loose sheets are easily distributed. A paper pad is of course quite flexible in this respect because there is little trouble in tearing off individual sheets. The contrast between a pad and a bound notebook should sharpen the distinction.

Physical accessibility is another important property. The ease of getting at a resource sometimes depends on administrative decisions, other times on physical constraints. A sheet of paper in the student's desk is clearly more accessible than one in the teacher's supply closet and that, in turn, is more easily gotten than one in the supply room in the basement. It is important to point out that even this simple observation hides behind it the whole mechanism of the supply flow from manufacturing to purchasing through inventory control to distribution. All these matters are of great scope and complexity in a school system. The school's one movie projector is, in most instances, stored in a place remote from the point of use. If demand is high there will, since parallelism is low, be a serious scheduling problem as well.

Reliability, or the ability to perform properly under normal conditions of use and abuse is a key factor. For the teacher reliability includes the ability to withstand insult or injury; for the film projector, resistance to repeated transportations with their attendant jarrings, joggings, and occasional droppings. Reliability is a problem with even the most modest of devices, as anyone who has had a piece of chalk break in his hand or who has cursed a skipping ball point pen will testify. It is not absent either from the most advanced marvels; as Patrick Suppes points out, "Whenever I have a captive audience I can't help preaching reliability. It's *the* sermon in computer-assisted instruction."[4]

Reliability and *maintenance* go hand in hand — even rocks are eroded by normal effects of wind, rain, and ice. People need vacations, organizations need fresh blood. Even a blackboard requires occasional refinishing. Maintenance may be preventive, as when students are asked to put covers on books; it may take place in the course of service, as when Scotch tape is applied to a torn page; or it may be necessary to repair damage at appropriate intervals, as when students are asked to clean up their books by erasing all marks before returning them to the stockroom at the end of a unit or a semester.

The *complexity* of a device must also be carefully considered because it affects not only the training required to use it but also the ease of continuing operation and use. Complexity is relative. To an illiterate, reading looks enormously and often insuperably complex. But, since we attach great value to reading and writing, corresponding effort is invested by most nations in training individuals to a point where these acts become second nature. In the absence of incentives for the same investment in training people to thread movie projectors, the projectors must be made more simply so that unmechanical people can operate them.

Comfort is an important characteristic. A congenial teacher is preferred to a sourpuss. People should feel at ease and comfortable with whatever device they are using. As pointed out in the preceding paragraph, complexity may or may not be uncomfortable depending on training and habituation.

Standardization is yet another facet of concern. The best three-by-four-inch slide is worthless to the owner of a two-by-two-inch projector. The most impressive investment in programs tailored specifically to one computer is worthless to the owner of another computer if that machine uses a different computer language. There is also *integration* or the ability of two media to work hand in glove. When the textbook speaks of experiments for which there is no equipment in the laboratory, there is no system.

Finally and most important is the question of *content.* Teachers of arithmetic should know arithmetic. A book of blank pages cannot be a textbook. A computer without programs is impressive but it is equally worthless.

4.3 A CASE STUDY: THE LANGUAGE LABORATORY

The inventor of such a machine must be a divine magician, he also believed, and the machine itself a living, intelligent organism which, as it was improved and articulated, paralleled human ontogeny. It became "an inspired bugger," "a cunning devil," and, after passing through a "sick child" stage, a "magnificent creature" ranking second only to man. What Clemens was expressing in personifications such as these was not only his hope for the machine but also his basic layman's ignorance, his credulity in the face of what seemed to him a divine mystery only because he knew hardly

anything about mechanics.—Justin Kaplan, Mr. Clemens and
Mark Twain*

The properties of educational devices described in Section 4.2
are not independent. They interact with one another in
complex and generally ill-understood ways. The interactions
take many forms. For example, maximizing reliability or
parallelism will tend to increase cost. This is obvious to any
two-car family. Conversely, fixing cost will constrain reliability and parallelism. This is obvious to any family aspiring to
own two cars on a one-car budget. Maximizing both flexibility
and simplicity is often troublesome since maximizing flexibility tends to entail some complexity, as in the difference
between cars with manual and automatic shifts.

The need to reconcile conflicting demands leads to what
systems analysts call "tradeoff studies" or the search for what
game theorists call "minimax solutions." In plain language
this means that when you can't have everything, you must try
to make the most of what you've got.

The choices between universal and particular goals, mass
production or tailored processes, and group or lone learning,
discussed in Section 3.1, are all influenced by technological
possibility and economic cost. Books are attractive devices
precisely because they can be effective and economical fairly
independently of these choices. As we shall see in Section 5.1,
computers *promise* to be attractive for the same reason:
tradeoffs are simpler when there are fewer constraints.

The language laboratory will serve to illustrate tradeoffs,
particularly between parallelism and cost. The aim is not to
design the best possible language laboratory but rather to

*New York: Simon and Schuster, 1966, p. 283.

display specific relationships that cannot be described effectively by clean-cut mathematical abstractions. Divorced from a concrete example, such an illustration would rapidly degenerate into the useless reiteration of vague principles. The language laboratory is used as an example because it is more readily intelligible to laymen than, say, a computer system and because good data are available. The general approach is equally applicable to other devices, such as books, computers, television, or film, or, for that matter, to any mixture of these that may be desired by those who advocate "the multi-media approach."

Figure 15 shows the layout of a typical thirty-booth language laboratory. Each booth or carrel has a tape recorder accepting tapes held neatly and permanently in protective

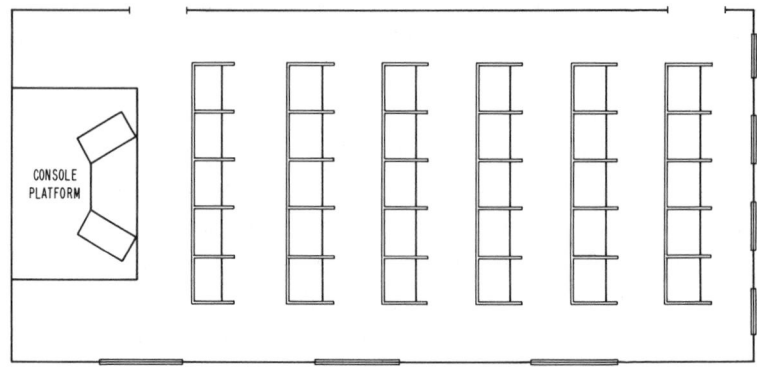

FIGURE 15. Layout of Typical Language Laboratory

cartridges. Each tape recorder is designed for two-channel operation: one channel may be used to record material from the master tape played by the teacher while the other is used to record student responses. In principle, therefore, rewinding and playing back such a tape enables the student or teacher to review a session by listening to the master tape and to the responses made by the student on the first go-around. Controls available to the student let him rewind, stop, play, or advance the tape. He may also choose between recording on both channels or reviewing what is recorded on them. Headphone jacks are provided and there is a microphone and a volume control.

The teacher's control console is on a raised platform at the front of the class. Although only five input devices are on hand, namely four tape recorders and one record player, the console is wired to take up to eleven independent inputs. Thirty rotary switches arranged in five rows of six each, corresponding to the layout of the student booths, let the teacher connect any one student position to any one of the five input channels. The equipment therefore allows up to five distinct transmissions to go on in parallel. Another set of switches, again one for each student station, lets the teacher listen to individual students at will. Her position has head-phones and a microphone, a switch to activate the micro-phone, and another selector switch to determine whether what she speaks into the microphone is broadcast to the whole class or only to an individual student.

Such an installation at Watertown High School costs $18,000 (see System 1 in Table 8). For the sake of comparison, this total capital outlay is also expressed as per-student capital outlay and as annual per-student expense for various amortization periods. What does the school expect to get for its money? What does it get?

I was told that the general aim of the Watertown language laboratory is to give the students more and better practice in speaking and in hearing a foreign language. Presumably, this means more than what they could get from a live teacher and better than what they could get from that teacher if she happened not to know the foreign language to be taught, a common situation owing to the shortage of qualified language teachers.

There is, however, some question as to the actual effects. Some language laboratory supervisors have told me that the laboratory is ideal for daydreaming by students accustomed to treating sounds from their ever-present transistor radios as mere background to other activities. Sharp monitoring by the

TABLE 8. Prices of three language laboratory configurations

System	Cost[a]
1. Watertown High School 30-station installation with 5 independent channels	$18,000
2. 30-station installation with 36 tape drives, 4 tracks each, providing 36 independent channels or 144 channels in locked groups of four	45,000
3. 30-station installation with 150 independent channels	200,000

Per-student expenses

		Annual outlay[b] for straight-line amortization over—			
System	Capital outlay in year of acquisition	5 yr.	10 yr.	20 yr.	50 yr.
1	$ 12.00	$ 2.40	$ 1.20	$ 0.60	$ 0.24
2	30.00	6.00	3.00	1.50	0.60
3	133.00	22.66	13.33	6.67	2.66

[a]Watertown figures are actual costs. The other figures are estimates from salesmen, who typically understate costs to help in closing a sale.

[b]These figures are conservatively based on a student population of 1500. The current student population of Watertown High School is 1390, and the capacity of the school building is 1150.

teacher could counteract this tendency, but teachers and supervisors agree that many teachers treat the language laboratory period as simply another study hall. After starting the transmission of the drills, these teachers sit at the master console, reading magazines or correcting papers, and only occasionally troubling to monitor those students who show obvious signs of not being hard at work. Teachers daydream too. One teacher said that "the main problem in the lab is the routine — it's monotonous." The students in the same school confirm this. They complain that lab periods are "always the same" and that what they do in the laboratory is only tangentially related to their regular class work.

Besides the obvious supplying of native speaker sounds, the other major attraction of the language laboratory is the favorite: *individualization.* As a Raytheon brochure advertising "<u>R</u>andom <u>A</u>ccess <u>T</u>eaching <u>E</u>quipment" of the type installed at Watertown puts it, "RATE systems are tailored to the individual students' progress, as each position permits the instructor to gauge the progress of all students on an individual basis. Therefore, the entire class is not limited to the learning capacity of the slowest members, thus permitting fast progress through any given area of instruction when possible."[5] This is not the way the equipment is actually used. In the Watertown High School, for example, I saw notes for laboratory assistants (see Fig. 6) stating that the laboratory is rigidly scheduled for mass application to a group, in spite of the fact that the system is capable of a fair measure of parallelism.

As previously noted, the system can run up to five separate programs at once. The lack of tailoring is therefore not due to equipment limitations: the problem is supporting logistics. It is difficult, according to both students and teachers, to pick materials relevant to what goes on in the classroom. The problem of multi-media integration, reflected in such time-worn complaints as "the reading in the textbook has nothing to do with the lectures," cannot be solved merely by introducing technology more elaborate than books. The point is simple: if it is hard to pick one set of tapes, it is still harder to pick five and to monitor the progress of students proceeding on five different tracks. The kind of freedom and effort embodied in Professor Postlethwait's biology course (Section 3.5) is necessary to realize this equipment's potential.

The system also makes it quite easy for teachers to observe student performance. The fact that there is an audible click in the student's headphone when the teacher switches in to listen to him is relevant or not according to one's view concerning privacy and fudging, and, in any case, can be designed in or out of the system at will. The inescapable fact remains that even an alert teacher can give each of 30 students at most 80 to 120 seconds of attention in a forty- to sixty-minute period. Consequently, private schools tend to design their language laboratories for 15 rather than for 30 students.

The common notion that introducing technology necessarily turns education from a labor-intensive to a capital-intensive activity is clearly not borne out in this case. Neither is the direct identification of installed equipment with effective use noted in Section 1.2.

Nonetheless, tailored application *is* possible even within the limitations of the equipment in the Watertown language laboratory. Because each student has a tape machine available right in his own carrel, there is no technical reason why he should not pick out any tape in the library, mount it on his tape recorder, and work away on his own. He cannot do so simply because there is no open tape library. Cost is surely not the only reason for this lack. The agonies of conventional libraries described in Section 2.2 suggest additional reasons.

In fact, the trend is away from open library use. The manufacturers of language laboratory equipment now provide student tape machines remote from student carrels as well as the usual remote master tape drives. Motivations seem clear-cut: the schools fear students will destroy equipment. Removing the tape drives to another room leaves only earphones, microphone, and carrel at the students' mercy. The manufacturers see greater profits in fancier gadgets. Typically, remote systems have dial-access equipment enabling students to dial up more than the maximum of eleven channels provided by the rotary-switch selection equipment of the Watertown system.

The cost of dial-access for 30 stations is $45,000 (see System 2 in Table 8). Manufacturers are apt to inflate parallelism by claiming 144 available channels. For the sake of lower cost, however, these are supplied by putting four tracks on each of only 36 independent tape drives. In reality, then, there can be no more than 36 independently timed processes; although four different programs may be recorded on the four channels of one drive, these four must proceed in strict synchronism. Such a system permits some measure of rate tailoring, retains obvious lockstep features, and exacerbates the problem of monitoring student performance.

Looking at how such a system operates at Oklahoma Christian College, we can see some marvels of *human* adaptability:

> The system provides two methods of playing recordings. Out of the 136 total programs, 36 are arranged to be used for scheduled programs so that those tapes in heavy demand

171

may be played at designated times. Thus a tape in English composition, which the teacher wishes students to hear on a Monday or Tuesday, may be scheduled as often as 10 or 12 times on each of those two days. A student, then, has ample opportunity to listen to this English tape at an hour when he has no class. He simply comes to his carrel at his choice of the hours the tape will be played, dials the number in his directory for the English lecture, and at the specified moment a time clock will start the machine. Should he be late, he will "join in progress" [note the euphemism] or he may select a later time. By using machines that play four tracks in one direction, four such scheduled programs may be played on one machine at the same hour. [Note the virtue made of necessity.] Nine machines, then, can accommodate the 36 programs which may be played at a particular hour. The other mode of operation allows for 100 of the 136 programs to start at the moment they are dialed. These programs, set up on 13 four-track and 24 two-track machines, are available at any time. This type of programing is for tapes not in heavy demand, for short programs that will soon be back at the beginning, or for programs that may be heard from the middle as well as from the beginning—shorthand dictation, for example.[6]

A recent graduate of Oklahoma Christian, now a student of mine, said that "if for some reason a student wishes to hear a lecture which is not currently assigned in the directory, there are some available free channels. All he has to do is go up to the control room and put in a request for the particular tape that he would like to listen to. And in ten to fifteen minutes usually he can go back down to his carrel and review a previous lecture or hear some material that is available in the tape library which has not been assigned for any course."[7]

All of this is still quite short of the degree of parallelism one normally expects of a good library. The Watertown High School library has seating capacity for only 64 of its 1500 students, although the American Association of School Libraries recommends seating capacity for at least 10 percent of the student body.[8] A 30-station installation capable of accessing 150 truly independent channels (Table 8, System 3) is therefore quite niggling by good book library standards. This is obvious if we equate the number of stations (30) with seats in the library and of channels (150) with books easily accessible rather than hidden in remote stacks and available only by request to the librarian. We see, unfortunately, a very sharp increase in cost, which is the typical consequence of even moderate demands for parallelism.

The capital outlay for 150 independent channels would have to be amortized over more than twenty years (see Table 8) to bring the annual per-student expense near Watertown's annual per-student textbook expenditure of $4.00. A similar comparison on an annual per-student capital outlay basis shows that the per-student capital cost of such a laboratory in the year of acquisition, $133, is roughly one and one-half times that of the national average annual capital outlay per pupil in 1967, $85. Even granting that equipment costs will in time decrease, we must remember that, whatever form of technology may be involved, costs rise steeply as the degree of rate tailoring and parallelism is increased.

4.4 RELIABILITY AND LEAD TIME

We have already seen that machinery is not necessarily used merely because it is available. The horrible fate of those who *try* to use it is one reason why.

Hard design lessons must be learned to make equipment that will stand up under the kind of use that seems normal in schools. The felt need to protect personnel, plant, and equipment has manifold unfortunate consequences in every kind of educational institution.

At one extreme, we find the Pack School (Appendix A) padlocking its auditorium for security. Watertown's fears for the safety of language laboratory equipment lead to such inanity as the instructions to pupils and assistants reproduced in Figures 5 and 6. A widely distributed industrial version of these same instructions shows an even greater preference for aversive control over positive reinforcement. The irrational petulance of the catalogue of Educational Electronics, Inc., a distributor for Raytheon language laboratory equipment, is reminiscent of Joseph Heller's *Catch-22:*

> 2.6 Talking to other students, lack of work, lack of attention, etc. should bring a warning to the students that a second offense could lead to their expulsion from the laboratory. For major offenses involving extended damage, students should be barred from periods ranging from two weeks to the balance of the year.
>
> .   .   .
>
> 2.12 Students should be held responsible for laboratory work even if they have been barred from the laboratory, and they should be tested on their laboratory work.[9]

Postlethwait devotes three pages of the instructions to his laboratory monitors to household remedies for common mishaps to tape players, movie projectors, and microscopes. Watertown teachers are constrained to logging failures for the next repairman's visit.

Not even the genteel Ivy League environment gives immunity. A colleague of mine reports an experience of fine irony (see Appendix B). He used a tape recorder coupled with a slide projector to teach undergraduates how to use key-punch machines. He found his recorded fifteen-minute narration, which was automatically synchronized with thirty slides, to be an effective teaching device. Unfortunately, it seems that he needed *another* slide lecture, of considerably greater length, to teach these students how to live with the slide projector. He soon became an expert in field repair of the machine and he and I both engaged in lengthy correspondence with the manufacturer inquiring about commissioned repairs, arranging appointments with sales representatives, and other time-consuming trivia.

Much of the glowingly advertised educational hardware and software is made by the same kind of companies and serviced by the same kind of servicemen that are responsible for your washing machine, your television set, your record player, your typewriter, and other relatively complex mass-produced items. This means that parts that "never break" will break on whatever you buy, that the operating manuals are revised far less often than the machinery is redesigned, that it is entirely possible that the machinery will spend as much time in the shop as at work, and that outlay for repairs can begin to approach the magnitude of capital outlay. In short, when the time, labor, cost, and frustration of using a device exceed some threshold, the device becomes useless. The account in Appendix B shows how bad things can get even for those kindly predisposed to machinery.

Other reliability problems may seem still more petty, unfit as subjects of lofty speculations or grand planning. Take knobs, for instance. Control knobs that are held on a shaft by a spring and therefore pull off with a little force are standard on many appliances designed for home, industrial, or military use. They are a clearcut invitation—if not necessarily to vandalism—to absent-minded but nonetheless destructive fiddling. Knobs are spring mounted for a simple reason: they are cheaper to install than knobs held by set screws, which need a screwing operation in addition to the pushing operation to attach them.

It took a while for manufacturers to learn that set-screw knobs are a must in school equipment. I have been told that the problems created by students bringing screwdrivers to the language laboratory are not as acute now as immediately after the knobs were installed. I suspect, however, that not even the Allen screw, which requires a special wrench, is safe from the student with a greater interest in tinkering than in language.

Perhaps the best example of common equipment that must be as reliable and as cheap as educational equipment is the telephone. This instrument is so widespread that it must lend itself to operation by practically anyone, under the most varied conditions, including frequent assault by vandals. Even the most innocent-looking engineering improvement of such a very stable system as the telephone can take major effort. Take, for example, the dial, which has been in continuous development for well over twenty-five years. A new dial, the so-called nine-type dial, is now in production by the Bell System to replace the seven-type dial now standard equipment on most telephones. The nine-type dial has slightly less noisy gears than the seven-type dial. The intent was to make a dial with more reliability and a longer life which was also less noisy and disturbing. This comparatively small change is the product of one and a half years of labor by three design engineers and of an expenditure of about $2 million for retooling the manufacturing plant. The difference between a laboratory prototype and a reliable instrument amenable to wide distribution under severe conditions of use must therefore be measured in large multiples of such human and dollar costs. When major organizational changes are entailed, the multiplier is still greater.

Telephone-like reliability at present telephone rates results from a peculiar constellation of circumstances, including long-term development, widespread use, near-monopoly operations under public regulation, a high degree of standardization, and mass production. To the extent that such conditions do not apply or are unacceptable in the educational context, the nature of the reliability tradeoff remains largely unexplored. It is clear, however, that when equipment is not intrinsically reliable, it is used either perversely or not at all.

Such problems only seem trivial. They are of *major* importance in making technology fulfill its promise of usefulness to education or to anything else. Important additions to current practice rarely spring full-grown from the laboratory. As Karl Deutsch pointed out, the "leadtimes from the first model to large scale application in private commercial inventions are of the order of magnitude of 15 years,"[10] although merely *adopting* wholesale and large-scale operations, as from another equally developed country, takes less time.

What is important here, however, is what Deutsch calls the "longitudinal" lead time of the pioneer. Going for the first time from laboratory to wholesale and large-scale operations often raises problems unsolvable except by some lucky breakthrough with devices or modes of organization. At the very least, protracted design and testing efforts may be necessary. The time lag between research findings and their implementation noted by ES '70 is therefore quite normal. It becomes distressing only when truthful deceit has confused research findings with important additions to current practice.

5 The Computer in Education

5.1 THE COMPUTER'S MUTED TRUMPET

If books are old-fashioned, tape recorders of limited scope, and well-trained people stubborn, militant, and scarce, where shall we turn? The answer seems simple when one listens to the trumpets of praise for computers.

Patrick Suppes leads off an article in the *Scientific American* as follows: "One can predict that in a few more years millions of school children will have access to what Philip of Macedon's son Alexander enjoyed as a royal prerogative: the personal services of a tutor as well-informed and responsive as Aristotle."[1] The individual tutor evidently stands for the epitome of tailoring the application of an educational process, however produced. As we have seen in Section 3.1, he may serve either universal or particular goals. Individual tutors offer learners many options between lone learning and group effort. Suppes claims the same for computers.

Computers can serve any goal. They are indifferent to how the processes they apply are created. The man-made programs that control computers can embody universal or particular goals; they can be mass-produced or hand-tailored on the spot. Computers can perform for either groups or lone individuals.

Stored-program technology endows any one computer with

great flexibility. It can accept and execute any properly prepared program. It is at least as general as a blackboard. Almost anything may be written into the computer once we have figured out what to write. Multiple access and communications techniques promise parallelism and easy physical accessibility. A computer is potentially an excellent tool for scheduling anything, including itself, provided we tell it how. Like good tutors who can marshal resources beyond their own, computers can marshal most other educational devices and make them perform at their command, provided we have told them what to command.

Learning to exploit such grand clerks takes time. Hence Suppes quickly admits, "The basis for this seemingly extravagant prediction is not apparent in many examinations of the computer's role in education today."[2] Later in the same article, the introductory trumpet is muted still further: "The instruction of large numbers of students at computer terminals will soon (if academic and industrial soothsayers are right) be one of the most important fields of application for computers ... although all these efforts, including ours at Stanford, are still in the developmental stage."[3.]

Troubles, as we shall see, arise from cost, amount, reliability, maintenance, complexity, comfort, standardization, integration, and content. In short, much longitudinal lead time is still between us and the realization even of glorified clerical functions. Hence, when the trumpet's sound reached the halls of Congress through the testimony of Donald Hornig, Director of the Office of Science and Technology in the Executive Office of the President of the United States, it was yet more muted: "I would add the promising field of computer-assisted instruction, which conceivably may make it possible some day for us to provide to each student some of the high quality individual attention that young Alexander received from Aristotle."[4.]

Others, less circumspect, show traces of the familiar semantic perversion. Speaking in fund-oriented tones they forecast that computer technology's "greatest benefits may come from its effect on culturally deprived children — the student population often of most concern to the central city school district." The same report, prepared by Technomics, Inc., for the Philadelphia school system, flatly states that: "*Computer Centered Learning* offers the first real opportunity for individualizing the educational experience of millions of children . . . As a direct teaching and learning tool, the computer offers the likelihood — over the next decade or two — of making learning an exciting and welcome experience for *every child* in the school system!"[6] The only stated qualification is revealing: "These revolutionary changes in the capability of educational systems will not come about without a great deal of effort, planning, and leadership."[7.]

5.2 COMPUTERS AND INDIVIDUALIZATION

Have experiments with computer-aided systems indeed yielded important additions to current educational practice? There is no denying that computers are becoming as valuable to the administration of education as they have become to the conduct of the routine clerical business of any other enterprise. But instruction and learning, not administration, are the primary purposes of school.

A computer is a serviceable tool for marshaling the stimulus-response-reinforcement contingencies which advocates of programmed instruction see as the essence of learning. Computers, serving as expensive page turners, have therefore been used to mimic programmed instruction texts. Deprived of the ability to skim, however, the learner may find himself more restricted than with the cheaper, conventional printed programmed material. Some claim that the advantage of a computer over simpler "teaching machines" lies in its capability for practically infinite branching. But the real bottleneck is our inability to foresee more than a very few of the most common possible learner responses.

Another advantage is seen in a computer's ability to handle responses constructed ad lib by the learner, rather than selected from preordained alternatives. Some capability to recognize misspelled words and to pick out preselected key words does exist, but has not been used to the fullness of its limited advantages. Responses to requests like "describe a relationship," "define a concept," or "explain how something works," are well beyond the realm of current computer capability. Recognizing arbitrary English sentences by computer is still beyond the frontier of either linguistic or computer science (see Prologue II). Scoring some of the Individually Prescribed Instruction (IPI) material in Figure 12 is thus beyond foreseeable computer abilities.

These facts have been disguised somewhat by spending much time, effort, and money on so-called "author languages" meant to allow the designers of drill-and-practice or tutorial systems to encode their material conveniently in palatable forms. Most of these languages elicit a question and the correct responses from the author. They then enable him to specify one or more wrong answers which trigger a return to the question, some cute response, or other branching action.

The following is a sample of one author's "dialogue" with a computer:

2. SPECIFY QUESTION.
WHO INVENTED THE ELECTRIC LIGHT?
3. SA.
A+THOMAS EDISON
B ALEXANDER BELL
4.SAT.
A F: THATS VERY GOOD B:3
B R: HE INVENTED THE TELEPHONE, TRY
AGAIN . . .[8]

Suppes has reported on extensive experiments with drill-and-practice in mathematics offered to pupils at individual teletypewriter terminals. As in IPI, the emphasis is on rate tailoring. Learning is not altogether by rote, but, since responses to exercises must lend themselves to evaluation by a computer, the replies as of now are restricted to multiple choice among very specific preordained answers. The learner is constrained to answer on the author's terms.

The student's response *is* evaluated immediately. His rate of progress through review exercises or problems of increasing difficulty is determined by the machine on the basis of evaluated responses. The harassing human bookeeping of IPI in its current state is therefore avoided, but some of its limited flexibility of response is also lost.

Suppes recognizes that "we do not yet have substantial evidence of the efficacy and efficiency of computer-assisted instruction of the sort that is often claimed."[9] In fact, the very techniques of evaluation are still being developed: "The problems of internal comparative evaluation have not yet received intensive consideration in our drill-and-practice program, nor as far as I know, in other areas of computer assisted instruction."[10.]

Intuition and anecdotal evidence do support the optimism necessary to continue experiments. Like myself and many others, Suppes has found that students rise to impressive levels of intensity and concentration while working at computer consoles. No one can say as yet how much of this is merely a consequence of the unusual attention students receive in experimental situations, a consequence well-known as "the Hawthorne effect." Moreover, the reliability and response-time of current computer systems still create problems. I shall return to these questions in Section 5.3.

As with the other rate-tailored processes I have examined, scheduling is a serious problem with computer systems. This problem is manageable with ten minutes a day of drill-and-practice experiments, but becomes more severe in more ambitious undertakings. The careful organization of Suppes' Stanford University–Brentwood School experiment illustrates this point. The experiment is intended to develop *tutorial* programs enabling a computer system to carry the main load of instruction in elementary mathematics.

The computerized classroom at Brentwood is in a separate, windowless building on the grounds of the Brentwood School. This building was financed with federal funds and is dedicated entirely to the experiment. The building includes a set of offices, a conventional machine room where the principal components of the computer are housed, and a classroom with carrels holding the individual computer-teaching terminals. There is also, immediately adjacent to the computerized classroom, a conventional classroom with low tables and chairs and a blackboard.

The description of the project issued to the public misleads in stating that "the Stanford-Brentwood Computer-Aided Instruction Laboratory is the first to be an *integral part* [emphasis added] of a public school," unless one appreciates the full significance of the qualification that it "is housed in a specially-built classroom/laboratory."[11] The significance becomes clear when one interprets the public explanation, which is couched as a catechism:

Q: How does the laboratory fit in the organization of the school?

A: The school sends children to the laboratory at regular periods each day. The children stay for a half-hour to study either reading or mathematics and at the close of the period return to their own classroom. For the first year, there will be eight half-hour periods per day.

Q: Will the classroom teachers go with their children to the CAI laboratory?

A: The laboratory can handle only 16 children at one time, so the classroom teacher ordinarily stays in her room, to work with the children who come to the laboratory during another period. The laboratory is always open to the teachers, and they frequently come to observe.

Being "an integral part of a public school" therefore means only that the facility is on the same plot of ground as the school and serves the same children. The laboratory essentially guarantees that the children who are delivered to it will be kept there for a full half-hour, come what may. This arrangement insulates the remainder of the school from possible schedule disruptions. The insulation is provided, among other things, by the conventional classroom adjacent to the computer-aided classroom: when the machine won't work, the children are taken into that room and taught or amused in conventional ways, until the guaranteed time period is up. It is therefore risky to generalize from this experimental set-up to arbitrary school environments.

How very sheltered this situation is in still other ways is revealed by additional questions and answers:

Q: Who operates the laboratory?
A: The laboratory is operated by the Institute. There are specially trained teachers and computer technicians on duty at all times during the school hours.
Q: Who supervises the children while they are in the laboratory?
A: The Institute's staff includes experienced, certified[12] elementary school teachers whose main job is to supervise the children and help them use the system.
Q: Do the teachers who will be in the laboratory need special training?
A: The laboratory teachers must know the curriculum material thoroughly and must also be trained to operate the CAI system.
Q: How long have you been developing curriculum materials for this project?
A: The Brentwood CAI Project began in June, 1964. However, personnel of the Institute have been involved in developing learning materials for younger children for over 10 years.

The *promise* of "revolutionary changes in the capability of educational systems"[13] is still just that. The required "effort, planning and leadership"[14] is nothing short of revolutionary.

5.3 SOME REALITIES OF COMPUTER TECHNOLOGY

Educational technologists today are making claims for a potential performance of computers *in the schools* that has yet to be realized in any *experimental* environment. For example, there is much talk about the value of computers in such administrative functions as scheduling.

Although classroom scheduling by computer is advertised as a fait accompli, this is true only in the rather limited sense of assigning students to conventional classroom groups and insuring that the number of groups matches the number of available teachers, and that these groups and teachers fit into available classrooms. The whole operation typically takes place once a term. Mechanizing this unpleasant and tedious task is clearly a worthwhile and useful accomplishment that deserves wider acceptance. Scheduling classes, however, is a far cry from keeping track of individual students week by week, day by day, hour by hour, or minute by minute, and matching them in turn with resources themselves parceled out in smaller packages than teachers per semester or rooms per semester. Packaging individual students is more complex than wrapping lamb chops at the supermarket meat counter.

Advocates who claim that all school record-keeping can be done by a computer point to the obvious value of having all grades, test results, and the like available to guidance counselors, teachers, and administrators. Unfortunately, experimenters all too often claim success in these areas after establishing, for example, a small file of occupational descriptions and a corresponding small file of student-interest profiles. Assuming the data mean something, the experimenter may well succeed in demonstrating on a pilot scale that a computer system can help students find out about their own interests and how to tailor their courses of study to satisfy these interests.

But time and again in the brief history of computers glowing experimental results have lost their meaning in the translation from pilot scale to useful operating size. For instance, quite aside from cost factors, scaling up a pilot venture into a file system containing descriptions of all possible occupations and, much worse yet, keeping such a file up to date with any degree of accuracy raises problems which, in spite of repeated claims to the contrary, are far from being solved, even by military, business, or industrial organizations. In almost every case on record, projects faced with problems of scaling up have either been abandoned or drastically curtailed, so as to produce files that can be organized in rigid formats with precisely defined content and rigorous updating disciplines.

In short, the design and the management of what the computing profession calls "large data bases" are very much at the frontier of today's capabilities. This is true enough of large complex files to be handled by what are now conventional batch-processing tape-file-manipulation procedures. It is doubled in spades for files (of any size) to be handled by multiple-access systems, which require either that many different files be accessible to many users or that the same file be accessible to many users and that access be a matter of seconds. When, in addition to records of a student's profile, and so forth, the computer is asked to store each student's answer to every test question for later review by a research team or individual teacher, the problem is magnified still further.

The major computer manufacturers now freely admit that they have consistently underestimated the difficulties to be overcome in developing complex systems. This admission after the fact is characteristic. As Ascher Opler has said: "The history of the development of computer hardware, software and applications has been characterized by (1) lateness, (2) rescheduling, (3) cliff-hanging finales, (4) substitutions of interim versions for the promised ones, (5) the substitution of a

'Phase 1' goal for the full goal, or (6) the on-time delivery of the promised system in a version whose quality and reliability were too poor to allow system usage."[15] Thus, in spite of much loose sociological talk about accelerated rates of change, Karl Deutsch's estimates of longitudinal lead times (Section 4.5) still apply. The prospect of schools making effective routine use of large data base systems within the next decade is therefore dim.

When we examine what *is* available, we see most of the problems already evident in language laboratories, among them problems of reliability, scheduling, parallelism, and cost. Computer devices for instruction have not yet been designed with any greater attention to the special reliability requirements of the schools than any of the devices discussed in Chapter 4. Indeed, they bring their own peculiar "minor" problems. Current experience with teletype terminals for computers suggests that tomorrow's maintenance logs will include entries about chewing gum in the mechanism. Owners of graphic-display terminals are learning that a deposit of ear wax interferes with the operation of light-pens. Since the grass always looks greener on the other side of the fence, we must put our faith in the biomolecular genetic engineers, who may have earless and therefore waxless pupils in their production line.

A computer-aided-instruction system can have one important advantage over central audio or television systems. The latter progress inexorably, by and large, and the student who has missed a piece of a French lesson is out of step with his class for the rest of the session. To the extent that the individual pacing and branching features of computer systems are successfully realized, this particular limitation need not

instruction in particular subjects at times not bound by the desires of every other school sharing the machine. Conclusions based on the foregoing rough-and-ready calculations are reinforced by a current estimate attributed to Allen B. Corderman, Director of RCA Instructional Systems, "that the equipment which RCA would release would be leased for about $50.00 a year per student."[16] Contrast this figure with Watertown's expenditure of $4.00 per student per year for all textbooks.

Lawrence Stolurow, looking at a variety of actual IBM systems based on the use of the obsolescent 1401 and a high utilization of 300 hours per month (or just 50 hours less than two shifts a day), arrives at a cost of roughly $7.50 per student hour for a terminal. Similarly basing his estimates on 300 hours per month of usage per terminal, he arrives at an estimate of $1.95 per terminal hour for the more modern IBM 1500 system. Such estimates are rather optimistic, for the assumption that terminals might be used over two shifts entails a revolutionary change in school hours. Stolurow relates this $1.95 figure per terminal hour to an estimate of $0.56 per student per hour for current *total* instructional costs, based on an average expenditure per student in public schools of $564 a year, 180 days of schooling, and approximately six hours per day.[17] On the same terms Watertown spends $500 per year, $500/180 = $2.80 per day, or $2.80/6 = $0.46 per hour. Stolurow's *optimistic* estimate therefore reflects a cost for *one terminal hour* amounting to four or five times what is currently being spent for *all instruction* per hour.

Stolurow's estimate is scarcely the most optimistic. Daniel Alpert and Donald Bitzer of the University of Illinois have given plausible estimates of a cost, for central equipment and terminal devices only, of roughly $0.25 per pupil per hour for a system yet to be designed to serve *4000* student terminals. Their Plato III system, a source of much valuable experimentation with hardware and software, now serves *20* student terminals.[18] Nor is Stolurow's estimate the most pessimistic: "the lease charges for an IBM 1500 system with 16 student terminals are in excess of $7,000 per month. This does not include personnel costs to operate the system or the cost of developing software for the system. Even assuming 100% utilization of each student station, the per pupil per hour cost would probably exceed $7-$8 over a period of time, which is far greater than 'conventional' instruction costs."[19]

That there is a long way to go toward any of these estimates is evident from the analysis of contemporary costs given in Table 9. All of these contemporary systems have storage and therefore parallelism limitations akin to those of the Brentwood Experiment.

Felix Kopstein's and Robert Seidel's study of the economics of computer-administered education corroborates the foregoing estimates for the short range. They estimate costs of hardware alone ranging from a high of $7.65 per student hour to a low of $1.20, the latter based on an eighteen-hour day, plus nine hours on Saturday.[20] An optimistic estimate based on a nonexistent 448-terminal system yields a range from $0.93 down to $0.16.

What of the longer range? Kopstein and Seidel wisely dare deal only with *"an estimation of how much CAI can be permitted to cost,"*[21] not with how much it might actually cost. The importance of taking into account *all* the factors described in Sections 3.1 and 4.2 in evaluating proposed systems is underlined by their caution that "if pluralism is allowed to

TABLE 9. Costs per hour of time-shared terminals

Cost items	Bolt Beranek & Newman	Dart-mouth	CEIR	Quik-tran	G.E., Valley Forge	Applied Logic	G.E., Schenectady
Redistributed overhead	$4.50	$4.50	$4.50	$4.50	$4.50	$4.50	$4.50
System support	5.00	5.00	5.00	5.00	5.00	5.00	5.00
Long distance calls	[a]	9.45	24.50	12.25	[b]	12.50	12.55
Terminal charge	2.00	2.00	2.00	4.50	2.00	2.00	2.00
Supplier's charge	12.50	8.80[c]	5.00	13.00	30.00	19.40[c]	17.20
Total cost per hour	$24.00	$29.75	$41.00	$39.25	$41.50	$43.50	$41.24

Source: Reprinted with permission from Thomas C. O'Sullivan, "Terminal Networks for Time Sharing," *Datamation*, 13 (July 1967), 39; published and copyrighted 1967 by F. D. Thompson Publications, Inc., 35 Mason St., Greenwich, Conn.

[a] Local calls only.
[b] Supplier provides foreign exchange lines in Boston, eliminating need for long distance calls.
[c] Assumes an average use of the Central Processing Unit (CPU) of 4 percent of hook-up time.

exist in instructional programing as it is in textbook writing, lecturing, and so forth, it is quite clear that the informational requirements will outstrip any sort of improvement that we could make in the instructional model, and thus cause CAI to be completely unfeasible and highly inefficient as a means of instruction."[22]

These words stand in sharp contrast to the claims of the Technomics study, which estimates that "for full implementation of the recommended centralized system the Philadelphia School District would, ten years from now, be spending almost 10% of its total income on computer systems"[23] that combine educational and administrative functions. The study then goes on to absorb the shock of this estimate by making one still more startling: "Though apparently large, this figure is not nearly as startling as it seems, since services provided by these systems would substantially decrease personnel requirements. In fact we estimate that in the area of management control, student records, and scheduling alone, *the decreased requirements for administrative and clerical personnel would virtually pay for the entire system* [emphasis added]."[24] As if this were not enough, still stronger claims are made: "However, it is in the area of computer-centered learning that the greatest economies would take place. It appears now that the computer as a teaching tool can double or even triple educational achievement by means of individualized instruction, computer monitoring of progress, stimulated motivation, individualized counseling, and on-going testing and evaluation of individual children. And this can occur at no additional cost or even at lessened costs per pupil."[25]

Consider what such estimates imply in the local and the

national setting. Watertown's 1966 budget is approximately $3,400,000 for 6,500 children (see Section 1.4). Ten percent of this, of course, is $340,000 or $52 per pupil. Since the current expenditure per pupil in Watertown's public schools is $500, and Leonard Lecht estimates (Section 1.3) that approximately $1,000 per pupil is necessary to meet his modest objectives for 1975, $52 per child now would be roughly $104 ten years hence.

Given the expected national enrollment of 46.5 million children, $104 per child translates into a national bill of nearly $5 billion. On the other hand, ten percent of the funds estimated to be available for elementary and secondary public education in 1975 is only $4 billion. This billion-dollar difference is consistent with Lecht's estimate of a deficit of $14 billion resulting from the difference between the $40 billion the Office of Education estimates will be available in 1975 and the $54 billion Lecht requires to fulfill his wish for better teacher salaries, improved plant, and so forth.

Whether 4 or 5 billion dollars is to be paid for computer systems is not significant. What is significant is the assumption that *net* personnel requirements will decrease; if it holds, then the 4 or 5 billion dollars for computers can indeed be diverted from other budget categories without net change in budget totals; moreover, the $14-billion deficit might even be reduced since personnel that are not needed demand neither raises nor plant improvements. If the prediction does not hold, and computer costs must be added to all others, the deficit to be fought for rises toward 18 or 19 billion dollars. The prediction, common enough, that computers reduce net personnel requirements must therefore be examined.

5.4 THE PERSONNEL TRADEOFF

Emphasis on merging administrative and educational functions on a single computer system is often motivated by the realization that, in the short term, the cost of computers dedicated entirely to educational use is prohibitive in any but experimental settings. The common reasoning is that administrators will want the machines for their own work or prestige and that educational users may then ride the coattails of the administration and participate in the economies of scale and high load factor. There are circumstances in which this reasoning is sound enough. The production of a weekly payroll and a weekly grade-sheet or "achievement summary,"—the former clearly administrative and the latter plausibly an educational tool—on one and the same machine is reasonable enough, provided that their deadlines do not coincide too closely.

But, as many computer centers of all kinds have found out to their despair, routine scheduled administrative work and unpredictable experimental work coexist only very uneasily at best, and quite often to the serious detriment of both. Where the demands of administrative data processing and education require the same facilities at precisely the same time, the argument is invariably won by whoever pays the bills. Finances permitting, the loser sets up an independent installation.

As for decreases in personnel requirements after such mergers, what evidence there is does not point to any. At best, the introduction of data-processing equipment in any kind of organization preserves the status quo or yields some slacking off in the *rate of personnel increase*. Actual figures are very hard to come by, for those one can find are usually the a priori estimates of promised savings made in the feasibility studies preceding installation.

No tradition of careful reporting after the fact seems to have been established, for obvious reasons. This is not to say that no advantages have ever accrued from installing automatic equipment. Frequently, the justification is a clear-cut ability to handle greater volumes of old-fashioned information or the ability to produce new reports, new modes of control, new systems for prediction that otherwise could not have been installed. My point is therefore not that there have been no real benefits. Rather, these benefits have hardly ever been measurable a posteriori in terms of the net dollar savings predicted a priori.

The importance of this last observation should not be minimized. For example, people in the Bell System are fond of explaining that, had automatic dialing and switching equipment not been introduced into the telephone network, there would not be today enough women in the United States to operate the manual switchboards that would be required for today's telephone system, which, of course, could not have materialized on its present scale without automatic switching. There may well be good reasons for introducing technology in the schools. There may even be savings through mass production. But there is no evidence at all for savings through personnel reduction or through the combination of administrative and educational functions.

This analogical reasoning is confirmed by the little evidence now available from actual experimental computer-aided instruction, evidence which fails to support the idea that no additional costs are necessary and cost reductions are possible. The teacher/pupil ratio is impressively more favorable in experimental situations than in real life. It is quite possible that this is merely an expected and quite reasonable consequence of early experimental status. Nevertheless, it points up the fact that there is no hard evidence whatsoever for a decrease in the number of teachers required per pupil. If such a decrease is to materialize it requires a transition from hand-tooled laboratory situations to mass-produced, institutionalized, and routine operations.

The development and the operation of computer systems require the services of a host of new specialists, such as computer programmers, curriculum planners, frame writers, artists, machine operators, and maintenance technicians, whose salaries are rarely included in rosy estimates of computer system costs. The salary scales for some specialists are shown in Table 10. They are to be contrasted with teachers' salary scales like that shown in Table 7 (p. 82) and with the projection for 1975 of an average salary for instructional staff of $8400 (Table 3, p. 72).

Heretofore, the teacher or prospective teacher could apply new-found skills only by abandoning the school system. The technical occupations which will invade the schools if all the daydreams materialize will, for the first time within the school system itself, confront teachers with individuals directly involved in the educational enterprise but already earning in 1967 salaries well above the teachers' salaries projected for 1975. Considering that about 80 percent of Watertown's $3.4-million budget for 1966 went into salaries, the consequences of a drive toward adjusting teachers' salaries to meet those of technical people without much more schooling than themselves, and often with less, beggar the imagination.

It may safely be assumed that costs *will* rise wherever

TABLE 10. Annual salaries in education industries

	Programming[a]				
	Established ranges		Actual salaries paid		
	Ave. low	Ave. high	Low	Medium	High
Manager of programming	$10,000	$14,000	$6,000	$11,100	$20,500
Lead programmer	8,600	11,500	5,400	10,000	15,600
Senior programmer	7,600	10,400	4,700	8,800	14,000
Junior programmer	6,200	8,300	3,300	7,000	11,400
Senior computer operator (Boston)	–	–	3,700	5,700	7,300

	Educational Films[b]
	Base salaries
Film editor	$12,700
Assistant	8,600
Apprentice	5,300
Cameraman	11,700
Assistant	10,000
Producer-director	21,000

	Educational Games[b]
	Starting salaries[c]
B.A.	$7,200
M.A.	8,400
Ph.D.	12,000

[a]*Source:* "1967 Report—EDP Jobs and Salaries," *Business Automation,* 14 (June 1967), 41. The *low actuals* seem quite divorced from reality on the Eastern Seaboard. The *medium actuals* are closer to my experience with starting salaries for college graduates. The range for manager of programming is more likely $15,000-$25,000.

[b]Data from trade sources.

[c]Increased at a rate of $50 per month per year of relevant experience.

computers are introduced. The timing of a transition from experiment to widespread addition to current practice thus must depend on evidence of rising *value*. The analysis of Sections 3.3-3.5 suggests that for a long time to come explicit quantitative determination of value will be biased toward the rote-learning end of the range of educational elements. The exercise of informed intuitive judgment about value therefore retains a paramount importance.

5.5 THE COMPUTER'S PROMISE

Were a computer's educational promise limited to page-turning, grand clerking, or gimmicky imitation of Miss Dove, fiscal misgivings might be well-founded at any price. Gargantuan clerical prowess can solve many vexing workaday problems, but it scarcely excites the imagination. More subtle qualities, however, make computers capable of profoundly affecting science and education by stretching human reason and intuition, much as telescopes or microscopes extend human vision. I suspect that the ultimate effects of this stretching will be as far-reaching as the effects of the invention of writing. In their scientific applications computers have been cast in two quite distinct but complementary roles: as instruments and as actors.

The computer's role as an instrument is by far the more clear-cut and firmly established of the two. The advance of science has been marked by a progressive and rapidly accelerating separation of observable phenomena from both common sensory experience and theoretically supported intuition. Anyone can make at least a qualitative comparison of the forces required to break a matchstick and a steel bar. Comparing the force needed to ionize a hydrogen atom with the force that binds the hydrogen nucleus together is much more indirect, because the chain from phenomenon to observation to interpretation is much longer. It is by restoring the immediacy of sensory experience and by sharpening intuition that computers are reshaping experimental analysis. Some examples of how this happens are given in Prologue II.

It is in their other role, however, as active participants in the development of scientific theories, as actors, that computers promise to have their most profound impact on science. A physical theory expressed in the static language of mathematics often becomes dynamic when it is rewritten as a computer program; one can explore its inner structure, confront it with experimental data and interpret its implications much more easily than when it is in static form. In disciplines where mathematics is not the prevailing mode of expression the language of computer programs serves increasingly as the language of science. Once more, illustrative examples may be found in Prologue II.

Computers used in this way, far from reducing the scientist to a passive bystander, reinforce the need for the creative human element in experimental science, if only because witless calculation is likely to be so voluminous as to be beyond the power of even the fastest computer. Human judgment and intuition must be injected at every stage to guide the computer in its search for a solution.

I have introduced the paradigm of the computer as instrument and as actor in terms of scientific research, where it has begun to prove its worth. It seems to apply to instruction and learning as well. The examples I shall use to illustrate this are drawn from my own recent experience with THE BRAIN.

(Why let the devil have all the good tunes? "THE BRAIN" is an acronym for The Harvard Experimental Basic Reckoning And Instructional Network.)

I chose mathematics as the experimental vehicle to permit the quickest possible passage to the desired study of *effects*. The coherent architecture of modern mathematics minimizes uncertainties about what is being taught or learned, albeit far from eliminating them. Computers being just that, the technical problems of fitting the tool to the task have proved bearable, though thorny and time-consuming. Finally, *applied* mathematics being a tool of many other disciplines, it opens a window toward wider vistas.

Let us look through a computer at some mathematical phenomena. To see the promised effects clearly, we'll assume transparency, as through clean well-fitted glasses, though in truth our present lenses distort, their frames chafe, and their price is high.

Let us assume the student knows that the equation $y = 2x$ describes number pairs (x, y) which, like $(1.5, 3)$, satisfy the equation. He knows that each (x, y) also defines a point in the plane described by the axes of Figure 16a. (Figure 16 and Figures 18-22 show photographs of what the student sees on his graphic-display terminal. These terminals are rather like TV screens, with one important difference. Using a keyboard or a special stylus, the student or the teacher can command a computer to construct and display an image on the screen.) What pattern — he might then ask himself — is formed by points which all satisfy the equation? Teacher or student might plot a few, as in Figure 16b. "As we began to plot points from the truth set for $y = 2x$," the experimental protocol reports, "the kids had no idea they would all lie on a straight line. Gradually they saw this pattern emerge and it looked very much like [Fig. 16b]. 'Hey, that's neat!' one of the girls said, and someone else said 'Look, they're all in a straight line!'"[26] And so they crossed Descartes' bridge from algebra to geometry.

Overkill? Perhaps. No one could advocate using so large a tool solely for so small a problem. Still, the glint of promise is there. The same lesson was "taught to the other half of the class the following day using the traditional methods of pencil, ruler and graph paper, and was not nearly as successful . . . The teacher spent most of the lesson having to correct mistakes the kids made on their own papers in plotting points from the truth table of $y = 2x$ [Figure 17 shows a paper retrieved from one of the students in this class]. Many of the kids were very slow to see the straight line pattern of all these points since, at this stage, it was impossible for them to distinguish incorrect reasoning or calculation from errors in graphing."[27]

The bridge crossed, the instrument grows more powerful. Approximating the area under a curve by a sequence of rectangles is an ancient procedure and, in the limit, defines the definite integral. Figure 18 shows how 6, 12, and 18 rectangles successively yield 6.1, 5.7, and 5.5 as approximation to $5.1 \doteq 2 + \pi$, the value of $\int_0^\pi (\sin x + 1) \, dx$.

The printed form of Figure 18, looking like similar textbook figures, cannot portray the excitement of observing convergence step by step, developing a feeling for rate of convergence, and examining the nature of convergence by handily exploring the behavior of inscribed rectangles, rectangles of varying width, with the given curve or with others, ad lib. A formal proof of convergence may then follow, supported by a deep intuitive grasp.

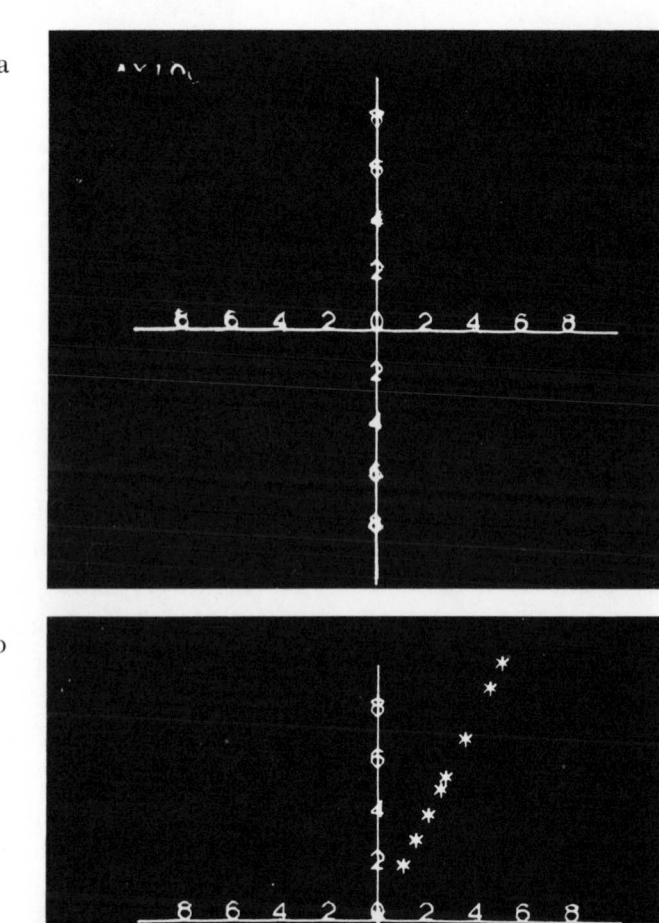

FIGURE 16. Crossing the Bridge between Algebra and Geometry

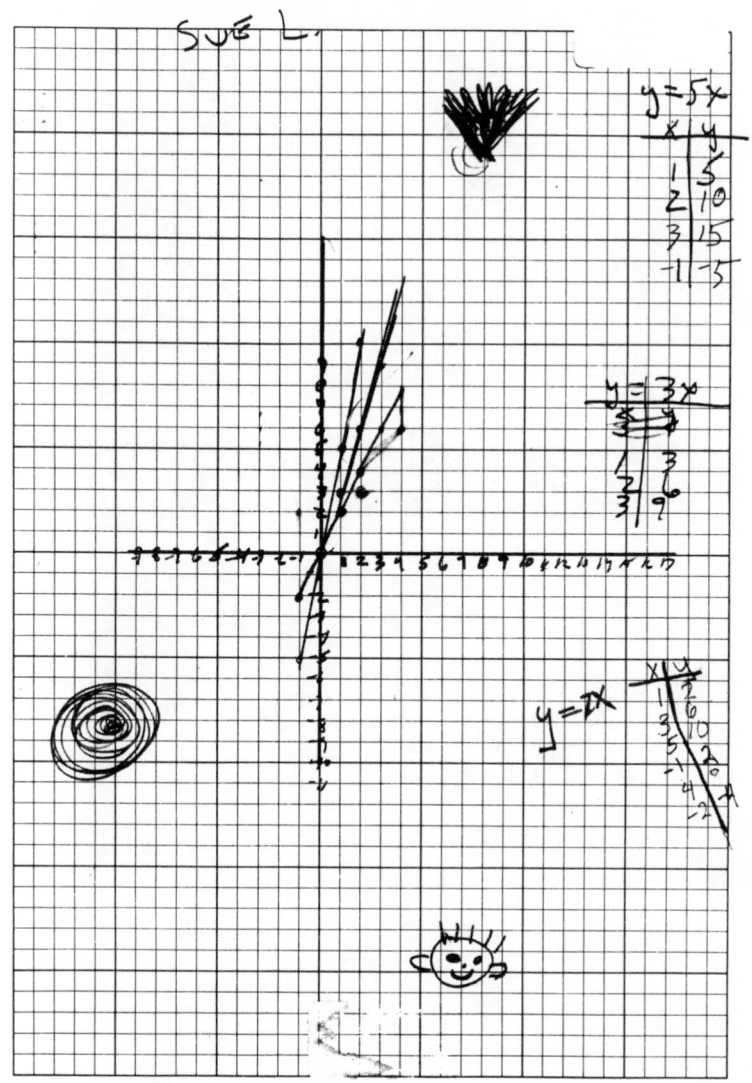

FIGURE 17. A View of the Bridge (without glasses)

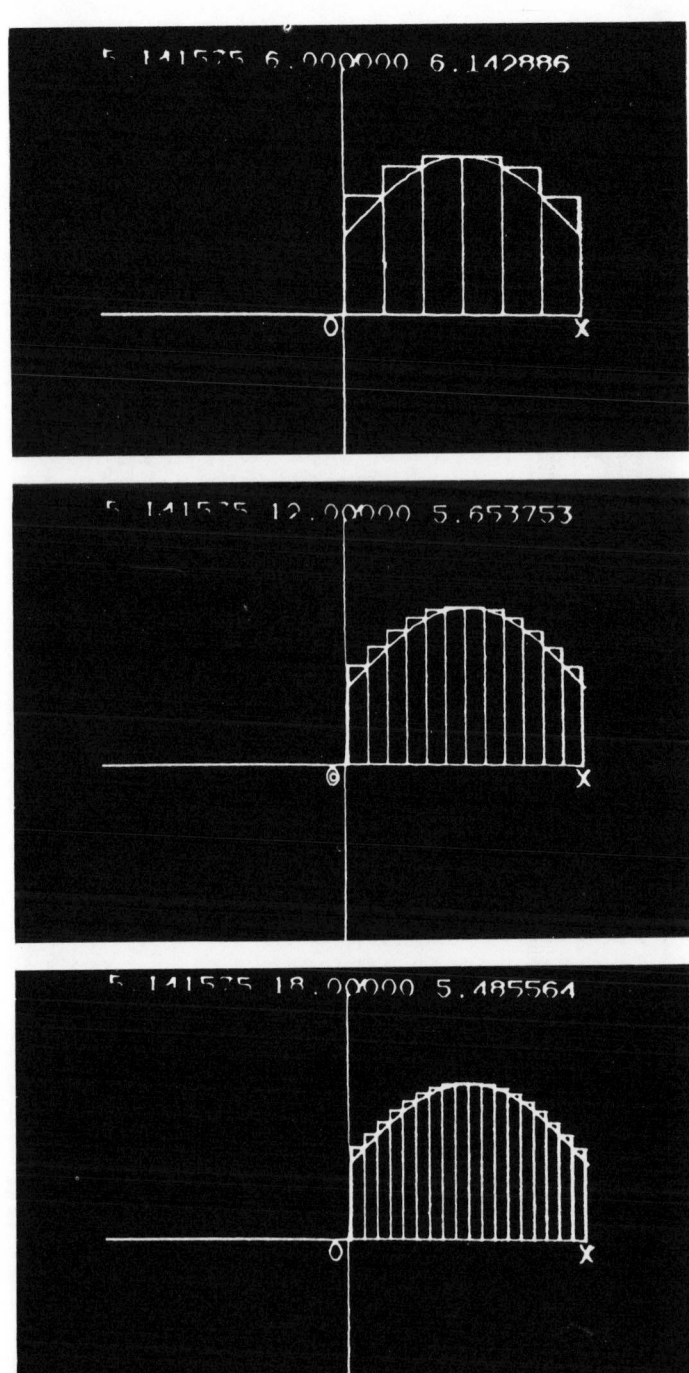

FIGURE 18. The Dynamics of Convergence to the
Definite Integral

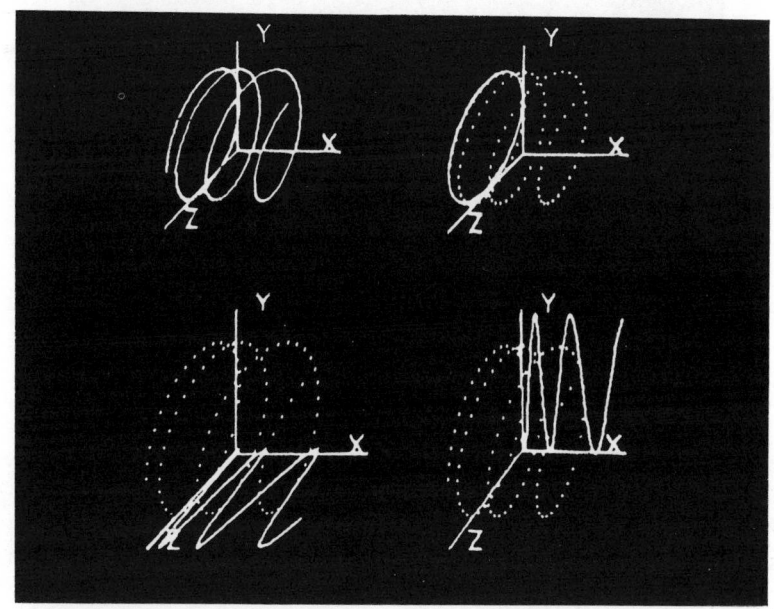

FIGURE 19. Spiral in Space

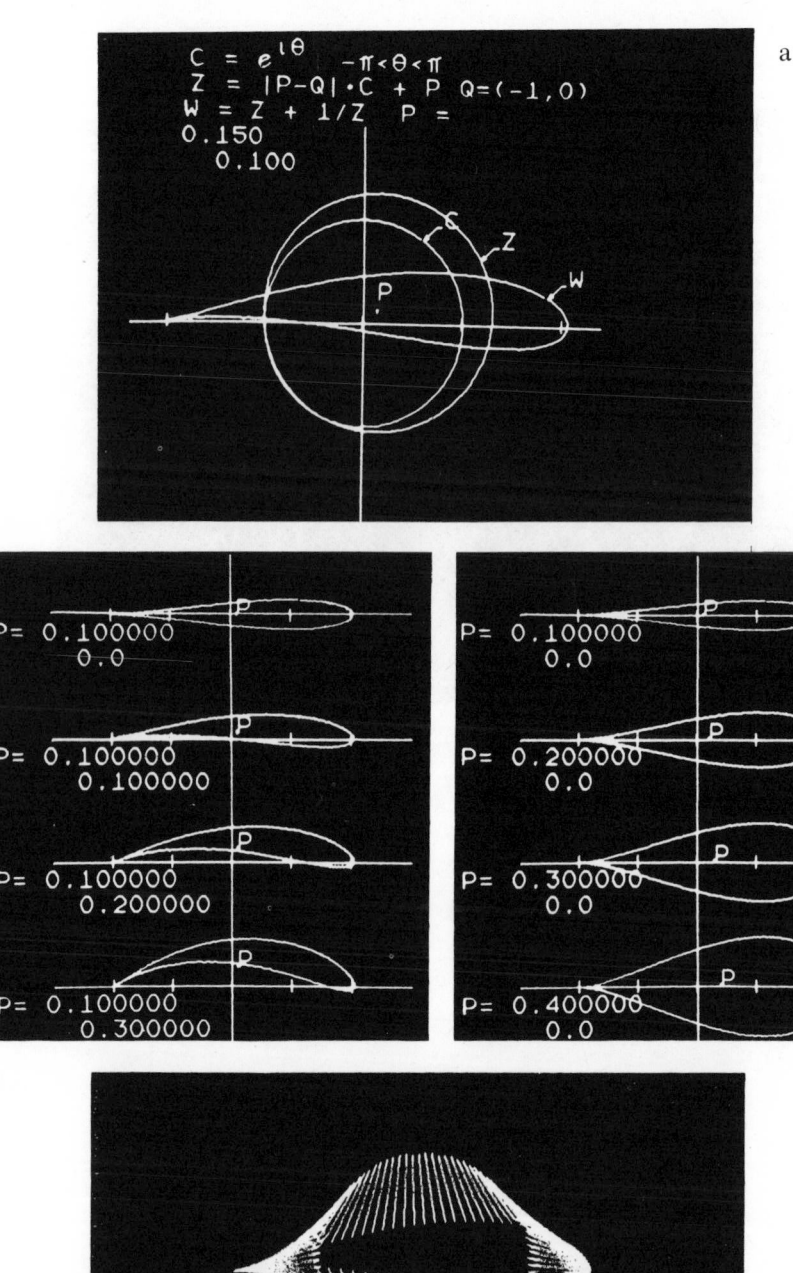

FIGURE 20. From Circle to Wings

a

Lateral motion of vesicle between cell walls 2000 angstroms apart over 2 milliseconds.

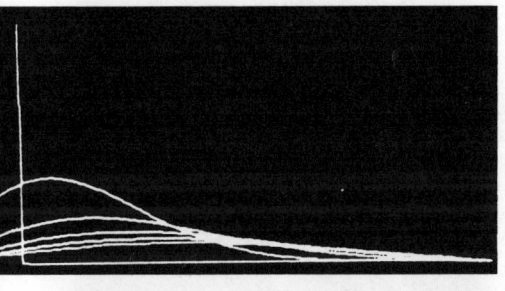

b

Concentration versus position between cell walls at 0.01 second intervals following injection at 300 angstroms from the left.

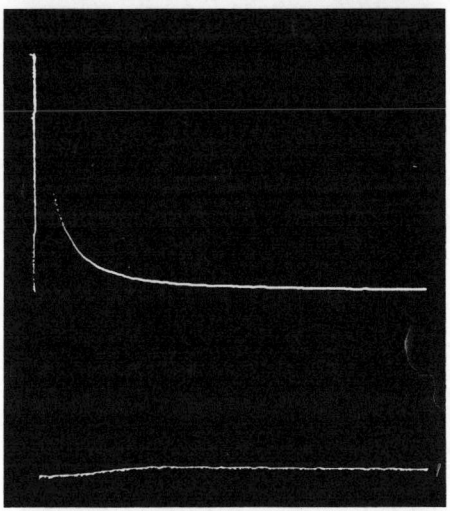

c

Flux out of left cell wall (top) and right cell wall (bottom) from time of injection to 0.07 seconds later.

FIGURE 21. THE BRAIN Acting out Fluid Transport in a Cell

FIGURE 22. Programmed Instruction on THE BRAIN

a

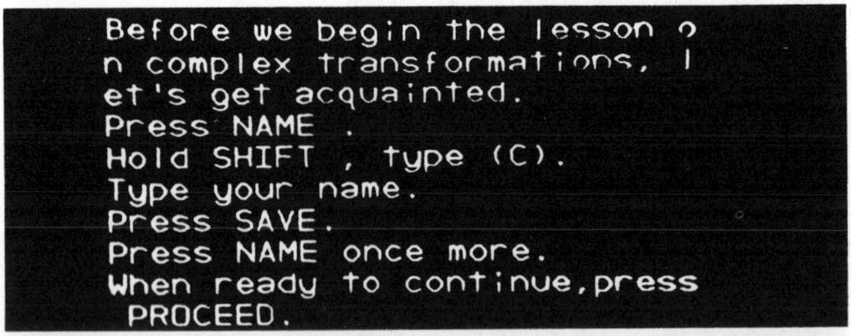

Before we begin the lesson o
n complex transformations, l
et's get acquainted.
Press NAME .
Hold SHIFT , type (C).
Type your name.
Press SAVE.
Press NAME once more.
When ready to continue,press
 PROCEED.

b

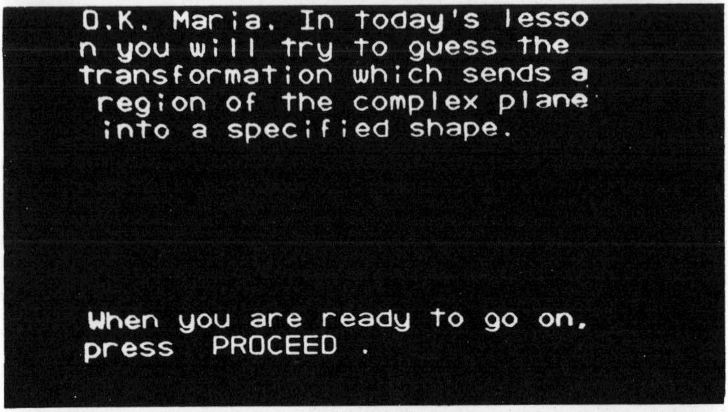

O.K. Maria. In today's lesso
n you will try to guess the
transformation which sends a
 region of the complex plane
 into a specified shape.

When you are ready to go on,
press PROCEED .

c

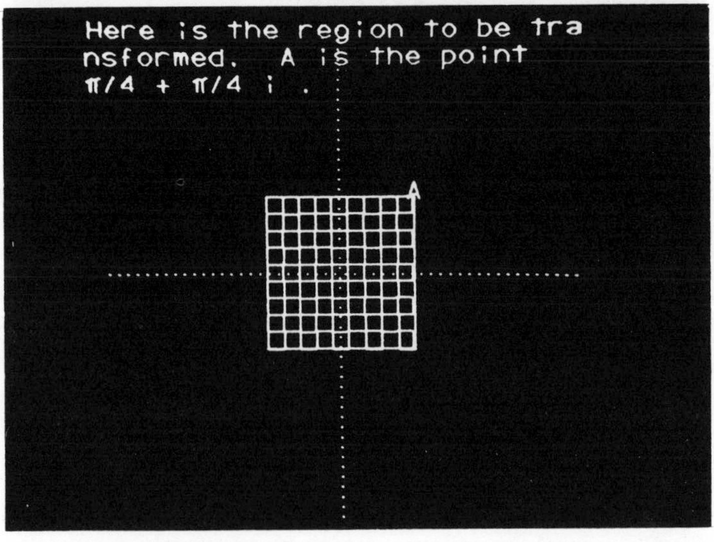

Here is the region to be tra
nsformed. A is the point
π/4 + π/4 i .

What transformation sends th
e square region into the fol
lowing?

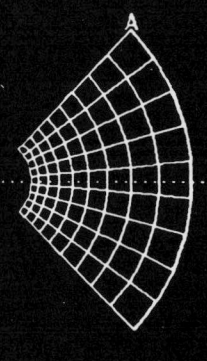

d

Choose one of the following
transformations by pressing
the appropriate button.

CHOICE A $w = z^2$

CHOICE B $w = e^z$

CHOICE C $w = \sin(z)$

CHOICE D $w = (\log(z))^{-1}$

e

ight on the first try,
aria.

Wrong guess, Maria. Your tr
ansformation yields the foll
owing region.

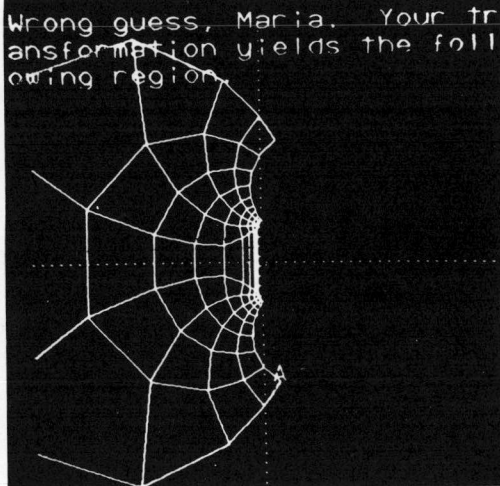

g

Our instrument's field of view is wide and variable. Through it we can see, as in Figure 19, a spiral in space and its projections as on walls meeting the floor at a corner. Or we can turn it toward the complex plane and explore, as a fledgling airplane designer might, the properties of the Joukowski transformations that change circles, like Z in Figure 20a, into wing shapes like those of Figures 20b and 20c. The role of P, as it enters the definition of Z in Figure 20a, is obscure to all but experts. But look how clearly anyone can see in Figures 20b and 20c how the wing shape changes as the point defined by P moves up or across.

What can it mean to anyone but an expert to say that circle Z in Figure 20a is changed into wing-shape W by $W = Z + 1/Z$? How immediate, how palpable, how intuitive this remote abstraction becomes when, in an instant, we turn our instrument and see, as in Figure 20d, the strings that tie points of Z to their images in W and feel how the plane has been pulled and stretched.

To explain a current research project to his students my colleague William Bossert has used THE BRAIN to act out the behavior of vesicles, microscopic spheres of intercellular fluid held within a membrane coat, in moving about the inside of a cell into which they have migrated.[28] The question is how much of the mechanism of fluid transport within the cell can be accounted for by Brownian motion, the random darting common to small particles.

Figure 21a shows one style of acting. The boundaries at left and right represent cell walls. The vesicle, played by a circle, starts somewhere between the walls, as shown at the top. At each successive time interval, played by successive positions downward, the vesicle takes a step at random to the left or the right. In the short time interval portrayed, not much has happened. That, in itself, is a lesson: this kind of imitative play-acting, called the Monte-Carlo method, is so tedious and expensive that it is used in practice only when all else fails, as in complex problems of nuclear reactor design.

In this case, man can endow the computer with the apparatus for solving differential equations, led by a diffusion equation. Figure 21b is a snapshot of a solution of such an equation at one point in time, showing the concentration, or distribution pattern, of many vesicles all assumed to have started at the same distance away from the walls. Most are still near the starting point, but some have drifted farther away. Whether or not diffusion is quick enough, and whether enough fluid may be carried to the walls this way to account for experimental results soon becomes apparent. Figure 21c shows how much flows out of the left side of the cell (top curve) and the right (bottom curve) in the time following the injection of vesicles initially concentrated as shown in Figure 21b.

Thus THE BRAIN has served us from a first baby-step to a frontier of research. It cares little who uses it: teacher, student, or expert practitioner. It can serve widely-shared goals — teaching of analytic geometry — or particular ones — exploring a unique research problem. The student may use it to solve prescribed exercises, or avail himself freely of as much of its mathematical and graphical power as he is able to use.

These are the possibilities I see. Programs for displays like the preceding may be prepared in advance, and copies mass-produced for use on any computer with THE BRAIN system. Or, they may be generated on the spot, as in answer to "what if" questions. Displays may be viewed by a lone learner or, when amplified by television camera and monitors, by a large group. They may be captured on movie or still film and, as in this book, stray far from their source in multiple inexpensive copies. This wide latitude should permit balancing needs and costs as appropriate in various circumstances.

Private tool for the learner, animated blackboard for the lecturer, or anything in between: THE BRAIN plays no favorites with processes. It may even be "customized" to create the illusion of individual tailoring, then greet you by filling the blank in "OK— — —" with a name it asked *you* to give it. The straitjacket of multiple choice may be strapped on the learner as in Figure 22 or he may be allowed an occasional escape into free play, or left entirely on his own. The choice remains, as it should, with the people, not the instrument.

Doing justice to the possibilities of THE BRAIN or accounting fully for its high cost or for its many technical limitations is beyond the scope of this essay. My aim here was not to claim an addition to current practice, but only to show explicitly one of the exciting promises that I see.

6 Where Do We Go from Here?

6.1 HERE

The roller coaster of aspiration and disillusionment is amusing to the extreme conservative, who thought the aspirations were silly in the first place. It gives satisfaction to the left-wing nihilist, who thinks the whole system should be brought down. It is a gold mine for mountebanks willing to promise anything and exploit any emotion. But it is a devastating whipsaw for serious and responsible leaders.—John W. Gardner, No Easy Victories*

We have seen that educational technology has not reformed—much less revolutionized—education as dispensed in our schools. Formal education is not ready for Alvin Weinberg's technological fix (p. 58). Numerous economic, institutional, intellectual, and technical barriers account for this failure. The formal educational system is bound to society in a way that is almost ideally designed to thwart change. Little *substantive* technological change is therefore to be expected in the next decade.

We have also seen, however, that various processes and devices do have great promise, although they are unlikely to

* New York: Harper & Row, 1968, p. 4.

contribute to widespread practice without further nurture in hospitable soil. My analysis of individualization has shown how limited progress can be made under carefully controlled conditions. The experience of Melbourne and Nova High Schools shows that steps can be taken toward individualization for creativity and independence when a powerful and wealthy segment of the community wills it. Given limited educational goals, rate tailoring can be done with people or with machines, as shown by the Pittsburgh and the Stanford experiments.

The Purdue experience demonstrates what can be done with human and material resources not generally available in the schools; THE BRAIN shows how computers can help to stretch human reason and intuition. Colleges and universities, which train future cadres, spend roughly ten times more per student than the schools, and are freer than the schools from disciplinary, scheduling, and other constraints; they therefore may well be the more effective proving grounds for educational technology and the more appropriate targets for early reform.

This essay has not dealt with still other patterns of successes and failures which suggest other alternatives; the restriction here to formal education in the schools means that I have not taken into account the strong but haphazard impact of various technologies, notably television, on the scope and the quality of *informal* education. The experience of military, industrial, and Job Corps programs is also relevant. Admittedly, the learners, the incentives, and the social contexts in these situations differ markedly from those in the schools. Nonetheless, a look at these situations may well suggest alternative patterns for formal schooling and life-long education.

Moving from limited success in the laboratory to useful

impact on practice hinges on understanding and removing barriers to this transition. Current attempts to integrate technology and education are dominated by faddish orthodoxy. When more and more federal money is applied to the dissemination of half-baked ideas, the return on investment is bound to be inconsequential. Rigid adherence to the dominant fad diverts both human and financial resources from both the basic research and the sustained development efforts necessary to evaluate and to apply diverse competing ideas. There is a serious danger that the frantic adoption of change in form will continue to block change in substance.

Pretending that the problem is solved surely does not help. ES '70's appeal for "massive and radical redesign" of the educational system reflects at best the kind of wishful thinking that draws cancer victims to men with miracle cures.

Aware that many questions remain unanswered, the Committee for Educational Development (CED) has called for a national commission on research, innovation, and evaluation in education, but charges it with familiar tasks. Aside from encouraging basic and applied research, the proposed commission "should stimulate developmental activities which will enable the effective employment of useful research findings and should disseminate the results in forms available for school use."[1] Such talk evokes a chilling sense of déjà vu in spite of the CED's expressed awareness of the problems of premature dissemination. As for its evaluation function, the proposed commission should apply systems analysis to "*large-scale* [emphasis added] evaluations of the product of the schools and the effectiveness of innovation in improving results." Granting the need to evaluate, we have yet to find and prove the means.

The U.S. Office of Education's new policy-research centers

217

are given little scope for imagination. One is charged mainly with preparing "an inventory of knowledge of human potentialities for growth and development." Another has been asked to "forecast probable roles of teachers, counselors, and administrators in education in 1988." The tasks of the others include studies of "economic consequences of changes in educational policy" and of "long term implications of rapid technological change for society, manpower needs and education."[2] In themselves, answers to such questions can only paper over the cracks in familiar old untenable positions.

Other partners in the educational enterprise are likewise hamstrung. University scholars have pleaded long but fruitlessly their need for stable long-term support. The non-profit regional educational laboratories, though newly created by the U.S. Office of Education, have quickly learned that "the problems confronting education cannot ... be resolved with a pauper's budget that turns on again/off again in periods of short term commitments. Laboratories, if they are to succeed at an optimum level, will need long-range commitment and support."[3]

Mirabile dictu, the same holds for private industry, though it seeks silent consolation in immediate profits. The late Lyle Spencer, president of Science Research Associates, has described SRA's hurdles for new ideas by a few critical questions.[4] First, were something available as a finished product, would it sell at all to school people *now*? This hurdle assures either the status quo or else that demand must be conjured up as for deodorants and mouthwash. Once over this hurdle, the product must further promise to sell over quite a long span of years to a sizable part of the school market. The economic rationale for this condition is obvious, and sound from the point of view of a firm. But the condition is sensible *for education* only if the efficacy of the product is proved. If not, this condition is diametrically opposed to the need for cycles of trial and error. The second critical question is how long it takes to develop a product and bring it to market. SRA demands *less than three years* from the time of a decision to go ahead. This limit puts a damper on major technological innovation, since the technical answers must all be known essentially from the start. The final critical question is how long it may take to recover investment with reasonable profit. The planning criterion is *five years.* This limits the level of investment. As described by Robert Locke, senior vice-president of the McGraw-Hill Book Company and David Engler, general manager of McGraw-Hill's Instructional Systems Division, industry therefore plays a passive role, concentrating "on what is likely to happen rather than on what life could be like if things went a certain way."[5]

Risks obviously rise in proportion to uncertainty in either technological factors or the state of the schools. The technology-there-is fails in the schools-as-they-are. No one can tell for sure how to marry the technology-that-could-be with the schools-that-might-be. Risks also increase with cost. The examples I have analyzed suggest that desired effects and costs will tend to collide no matter what specific form technology might take. It costs more to aim at particular goals than at universal ones. Tailoring costs more than mass production. Lone learners demand more facilities than groups. Without taking risks to find out how to use resources more effectively, the observed relapses into lockstep will remain inevitable.

Industry sees no alternative to minimizing its risks by taking as gospel "what is likely to happen" in a system prone to catatonic educational stability along with its social convulsions. On this rock, it builds mainly devices and processes that deviate as little as possible from either their predecessors within the educational system or their prototypes without, and which work only on lucky days. Risky experiments by other partners in the educational enterprise have been absent, short-lived, or prone to early, fatal exposure to planting outside the hothouse.

The schools haven't got any money. Universities, nonprofit creatures of the government, and private industry haven't got any ideas save the present innovation fad, which favors highly visible quickie approaches creating the illusion of progress. No one is able or willing to take time and risks. How might we progress?

6.2 GETTING FROM HERE TO THERE

The road to wisdom? — Well, it's plain and simple to express:
>   *Err*
>   *and err*
>   *and err again*
>   *but less*
>   *and less*
>   *and less — Piet Hein,* Grooks*

If the status quo is unacceptable, planning beyond the bounds of knowledge inane, anarchy irresponsible, and all three dangerous, how do we get from here to there? Tempered by our ignorance, hence with due regard for risk, we must

* Cambridge, Mass.: M.I.T. Press, 1966, p. 34.

develop and test several different visions of "what life could be like if things went a certain way."

Predictably, the basic needs are common to most enterprises: educational technology needs better ideas, better people, and more money. These needs may seem obvious, but many believe that science already has all the answers ready for immediate exploitation, that the right people are on hand but just not organized for action, or that education already costs much too much. These needs therefore deserve restating with specific justifications prior to broaching the really critical question, "How to get there from here?" The suggestions below are aimed at skirting in the future some of the pitfalls catalogued in the first five chapters:

First, every attempt to introduce technological change into education has revealed how profoundly *ignorant* we still are. We know precious little about the psychology of learning, and what we know is more relevant to the laboratory than to the classroom. Behavioral objectives with a strong taste of the explicit, the quantitative, and the measurable account for but a small fraction of the many effects we expect of schooling. We have dream devices which we cannot make work effectively. We think of reorganizing institutions, but contemporary social and political science, though abounding with static descriptions, tell us next to nothing about the dynamics of transition from one form of organization to another. There is a history of instruction in industrial, military, and, more recently, Job Corps settings, but its relevance and applicability to the *formal* education of children is unknown. The enormous educational influence of mass media, peers, and other informal agents is obvious, but no one knows how to control and to maximize this influence or how to balance the formal and the informal.

Second, systems analysts trained to think unthinkable, apocalyptic thoughts in the style of Herman Kahn, or to calculate the performance/weight tradeoffs for missiles, are ill-prepared to deal with more than the form of the educational system. Technologically illiterate educational leaders preside bemused over Hawaiian rain dances. Teachers ill-prepared and unrewarded even for good teaching in present classrooms are neither well-disposed toward, nor capable of contributing to, technological innovation. Teacher-proof educational schemes prepared by remote academic reformers sit unused on the shelf or are adopted in name only. Industrial designers are passive, and salesmen accustomed to other markets sell useless short-lived devices without profit to anyone save themselves. Professors of education practice little of what they preach.

Finally, the notion that any form of technology can make a significant contribution "at no additional cost or even at lessened costs per pupil" (p. 194) is an illusion. More books and better libraries cost more money. Greater individualization costs more money, no matter what the specific process may be. Better understanding and better-trained people cost more money.

Ideas, people, and money create little of value if used inefficiently. The importance of economic efficiency is evident from my observation that, by 1975, every additional dollar spent per child in a year adds $46.5 million to the national bill for education. How are the necessary resources to be allocated for economically efficient progress? Careful timing, a willingness to take and to share risks, and flexible decision-making mechanisms that encourage diversity seem essential. I therefore suggest the following policies as more conducive to economically efficient progress than current policies:

1. *If we want efficiency, we must support promising ideas longer than either private or government programs now permit.*

   The odds against success with quickie cures are great, unless one thinks of them merely as goads to prod people and institutions out of their accustomed molds. Overcoming our ignorance will require imagination and risk-taking as well as patience and continuity, not just pressures for immediate returns paid in the counterfeit currency of unviable, glamorous additions to current practice. It takes more imagination to get new ideas than new labels, and it takes time to try the ideas out. It takes time to train people. Developing new processes and devices from prototype to production model to payoff is both time-consuming and risky.

2. *If we want efficiency, we must support risk-taking and cushion failure.*

   Schools, universities and nonprofit organizations need stable support. Industry needs financial incentives beyond profits on safe short-term investments. Teachers need opportunities for real professional development. The young guinea pigs need assurance of a place to go after the experiment.

3. *If we want efficiency, then risks, resources, and responsibilities, the 3 R's of educational technology, must be shared by all the partners in the educational enterprise.*

We have seen how hopeless advance by one partner is without advance by the others. We know how dangerous exclusive control by any one partner can be. In our great ignorance, who can prescribe *the* right path?

4. *If we want efficiency, we must chart our course by human judgment, not exclusively by formula.*

We have seen that the realm of explicit quantitative analysis, the realm of the measurable, is yet but a small part of education. Forcing scientific technique beyond its limits is scientism, not science; obscurantism, not rationality. However solemnly couched in the terms of modern science, auguries from animal entrails are no substitute for the judgment of men.

5. *If we want efficiency, we must follow through in depth with a small number of diverse alternatives.*

Ignorance forces us to try anything. Lacking infinite resources, we cannot try everything. The present shotgun approach has been exhausted; it has few achievements to its credit. It would be better to apply resources in greater depth to follow fewer promising experiments through to probable failure or imminent success. A single ill-aimed authoritarian blast, one prevailing faddish orthodoxy, makes no allowance for ignorance or error. We need more than one chance.

What sort of mechanism might serve these policies? Both nature and the ideology of free enterprise suggest turning to pluralism and competition. The resulting processes should leave ample freedom to make choices consistent with broad local and national objectives.

Such processes are alien to the educational-enterprise-that-is. The Bundy Report to Mayor Lindsay makes plain how the components of a single school system vie with each other in the exercise of veto.[6] On the national scale, the educational enterprise has all the bureaucratic rigidity of a military service, without the countervailing central authority that can ultimately dictate some moves. At the same time, this enterprise has most of the fragmentation and the frustrations of small-scale organizations, without their redeeming flexibility and their freedom of initiative and response.

Education is not a buyer's market. Professional educators have neither the financial nor the intellectual resources to shape the processes or devices they must use. At most they may select from set offerings. Since the Supreme Court decision of 1954, the demands of parents and pupils have been in the national spotlight, but parents and pupils still have essentially no choices within the public school system and little choice between public and private systems.

My argument for competition in education is not based on atavistic faith in a pure market mechanism. Such faith has obviously declined in the many areas where deliberate public intervention and control has proved necessary. The argument stems from my belief that a system which is assured basic existence no matter how badly or how unresponsively it performs can benefit from *some* elements of market competition, with careful checks and controls built in.

The need for competition in education has been recognized before. Several proposals to that effect have been made in the past few years. None has yet come to fruition. A bill for state tuition grants which was defeated in Rhode Island proclaimed "the inalienable right and responsibility of parents to determine the kind of school their child attends."[7] Theodore Sizer and Phillip Whitten have proposed a Poor Children's Bill of Rights patterned on the G.I. Bill of Rights. Aiming frankly to "discriminate in education in favor of the poor," they would "quite simply, give money in the form of a coupon to a poor child who would carry the coupon to the school of his choice, where he would be enrolled." Significantly, they add that "the supplementary grant which the child would give to his school must be large enough to motivate the school to *compete* for it."[8] They quickly concede that their plan must be part of a package including other social reforms, the production of a new breed of professionals, new school buildings, better public information, and so forth. Other proposals, more relevant to the middle class, call for tax deductions for parents with children in school.

Aiming, like Sizer and Whitten, at a better and more constructive balance of positive power, the Bundy Report proposed decentralization of the New York City school system into smaller subunits more directly responsive to the needs of the people. It stressed, however, that decentralization per se will not improve health and welfare, eliminate teacher shortages, or tell us about the basic mechanisms of learning and teaching.

Mechanisms for catering to such a buyer's market can also be imagined. Let us visualize, side by side with evolving existing public and private schools, new enterprises that operate local schools as branch offices or as franchises under contract with the local school board. These new enterprises might be created as public, private, or mixed institutions. Competitive initiative would then be encouraged if pupils could at least have the option of going to a town-operated school, a school operated by a neighboring town, or a school operated at the will of the local board by one or another of the new competing institutions. Teachers also would benefit from a choice of employers.

Vertical organizations become conceivable. For example, a school operated by Raytheon might use the products of its subsidiaries: textbooks published by D. C. Heath, language laboratory equipment by Dage-Bell, science materials from Macalaster Scientific, and Edex devices for measuring responses. The need to sell products through multiple layers of professional associations, school boards, principals, and so on, is replaced by the need to compete with other schools and other suppliers for the presence of the satisfied pupils of satisfied parents and their money.

Horizontal associations are equally plausible. The oft-proposed educational park, combining all levels of education, perhaps with community services and some industry as well, would afford other patterns of cooperation in action, research, development, training, and evaluation.

Whatever the modes of organization, if effectiveness were assessed only by the direct market mechanism, then the classical democratic problem of faith in unsophisticated buyers would obviously arise. Sizer and Whitten hypothesize "that parents will send their children to the 'better' schools," conceding "that this is an hypothesis of high faith," but emphasizing that while they trust parents but little, they trust them more than they do "the present monopoly of lay boards and professional schoolmen."[9]

But national, state, or local public educational and social goals need *not* lose *their* market influence in order to leave a just share to pupils and parents. Contractual specifications, subsidies, tax reductions, and other controls or incentives can be applied to the various schools according to judgments made by someone other than pupils and parents. Thus, services for counseling parents on school selection, local school boards, professional or industrial organizations, philanthropies, state or federal agencies, or national commissions can continue to bring wider social concerns to bear on the management of the schools.

No one has yet explored in sufficient depth the implications for education, or for the polity, of proposals like the few preceding examples. Each such proposal addresses only a piece of the competition problem; each raises questions of class distinctions, racial discrimination, or church-state relations. How to give free enough rein to such new ideas without unbearable risks? How to reconcile them with conflicting ideals? How to combine them effectively into comprehensive systems without coordination or other euphemistic forms of coercion? How to tell achievement from worthless churning without imposing one's tastes or prejudices?

Existing government bodies like the National Science Foundation and the U.S. Office of Education have no directives or charters fitting them to tackle these questions. Private bodies, even the Ford Foundation, do not have enough money. The recent legislation which created the Model Cities program, the Job Corps, or the Communication Satellites Corporation abandoned the restrictive rule of absolute uniformity of treatment, and has also pioneered the channeling of public funds through private or mixed institutions for public purposes. This new flexibility raises the hope that effective new institutions can indeed be created.

The following are suggestions for one mechanism having qualities consistent with the previously stated policy objectives. Very likely there are other ways to achieve a kind of large-scale evolutionary effect through enough distinct trials to create a fair probability that different paths will be taken, that illuminating controversy will rage, that enough public control is exercised, and that real progress will result.

Imagine a government, mixed, or private body representing the major segments of our society. Call it the Educational Foundation, or by whatever other name, Council, Consortium, or Commission, that has the least pejorative connotation. Empower it to collect and to disburse public and private resources. Charge this body with giving birth to competition and keeping it alive long enough to assure a fair chance of survival. Ask this foundation to set priorities and to judge merit, but to dictate no specific courses of action. Assure from the start that the foundation must disappear with public fanfare when its job is done in the eyes of society, whether through success or through failure. Require it to report its actions fully, frequently, and publicly.

This foundation might then request proposals about, sponsor studies of, and eventually nurture the operation of competing educational systems by self-constituted groups. The latter might be horizontal, vertical, or completely unexpected combinations of consuming and producing, public and private, local, state, and national organizations and individuals, including existing schools or new ones. Each group would choose its own composition.

Work would proceed in stages. Each proposal to the foundation would specify the group's perceptions of the state of educational affairs at the start of a stage, explaining why it finds a need for further work; it would state the goals to be reached at the conclusion of the stage, and how these goals relate to whatever ultimate goals the group perceives. The means for comparing the results of a stage with the goals set for that stage—and the time of completion—would also be specified. Further, the source and the distribution of risks, resources, and responsibilities for the given stage would be stipulated, along with estimates for the next stage. The foundation would be permitted no narrower specifications in its requests for proposals.

The aggregate of the groups supported at every stage would reflect the maximum diversity consistent with achievement. Achievement at any stage would be judged against the goals of the proposal, by the means specified in it. Each supported effort would therefore be judged relative to its own goals, according to its own measures. The foundation would wield authority only in choosing the mix it supports; it would be responsible for keeping the mix diverse.

So long as goals are met and diversity remains, the continuity of efforts within the means of the foundation would be guaranteed. Any group grown capable of raising its own resources, and of assuming its own risks and responsibilities, would quickly be weaned from the foundation. Since lack of foundation resources may force casting out poverty-stricken but otherwise promising groups, there would be incentives toward weaning.

The *minimum* number of supported groups would be set when the foundation was created, as evidence of commitment to the nurturing of competition, and as a tripwire for the terminal fanfare. Should the foundation's resources drop to a level too low to support the minimum number of groups, this would be interpreted as society's judgment either that enough weaned competing groups were on hand for the foundation's work to be declared successful or else that the whole plan had failed. Either way, the foundation would automatically dissolve. The fanfare is to assure that all this would happen by daylight.

Alternative scenarios may prove superior. Whatever they may be, they will need better ideas, better people, and more money. But then, I am assuming that we really mean to reform education, not paper it over once more.

Appendix A
Visit to Small City

In January 1967 I visited a school system in Small City, the core of a substantial metropolitan area. A quick tour cannot claim even the same anecdotal authority as a thorough and exhaustive analysis by a substantial team. The observations recorded in this appendix should be prized for their immediacy. Such authority as they may command arises in part from their consistency with the few meager observations available in the literature. I took pains also to have the impressions reviewed by a responsible and friendly administrator of the Small City school system to whom the original draft of my trip report was submitted for comments. His commentary (in italics) is interspersed as appropriate among the record of observations. I was accompanied on the trip by Mr. Jan ter Weele, then a doctoral candidate in the Administrative Career Program of the Harvard Graduate School of Education, who collaborated in the early stages of this study and who is now assistant superintendent of the Hanover Supervisory Union, Number 22, in Hanover, New Hampshire.

Small City must remain unidentified and all names disguised in order to respect the wishes for anonymity of our sources of frank comments. This fact in itself is a significant commentary on why there is a difference between the picture of schools as drawn in the literature or in public pronouncements and the several layers of reality.

HISTORY OF THE COMMUNITY

The administrator provided us with the following description of Small City to set the scene.

For more than thirty years the school system sustained the quiet punishment of neglect except in one respect: the schools provided a broad field for local patronage. The neglect of the schools was quite thorough. The buildings were permitted to deteriorate and no new buildings were put up for a long period of time. Equipment, books, and materials were consistently inadequate. Teachers were drawn almost exclusively from a small teacher-training center in Small City. It was almost unheard of for a resident of Small City to go through the teacher-training center, apply to the school system for a job and not be appointed. The shortest roads to appointment to principalships and other administrative positions were reasonably long service and favor with appropriate political people. Everyone knew these rules of the game and the town was well adjusted to these rules. Little direction came from the central office and the principals ran their schools.

In the early 1950's a new political climate emerged. New and extraordinary energy and imagination infused all areas of city government, including eventually the schools. The original attention, growing out of a bias for redevelopment, was directed to the physical rehabilitation of the school plant. A long-range building program was launched and, within a relatively short period of time, new schools were erected and some old schools were renovated. Three new high schools were built; five elementary schools were built. With the exception of the first two high schools and two large elementary schools, all the new schools were built with a sharp eye for tasteful architecture. No school duplicated another. Two of the schools can be considered national showcases for school-building.

In the late fifties attention was shifted to the development of human resources. The mayor appointed a new breed of Board of Education members. A comprehensive city program was drawn up to deal with the human problems of urban centers. A considerable grant from the Ford Foundation made possible the establishment of a private community corporation to work in cooperation with city departments, the mayor's office, and especially the Board of Education. The head of this corporation had been president of the Board of Education for some years. Besides the Ford Foundation grant, the corporation attracted considerable federal grants to develop its programs.

A model community school program was established. A dynamic superintendent of schools was engaged and, suddenly, the rules of the game were changed almost completely.

During the post-war decades Small City experienced the familiar pattern of the massive immigration of poor, southern Negroes and the exodus of many middle-class white families. The school population shifted from a predominantly white socio-economic mix to one which is increasingly poor and Negro. At present the elementary school population is close to 50 percent Negro. The intermediate school and high school populations are close to 35 percent Negro, a percentage increasing at the rate of approximately 3-5 percent per year. As in other cities, no preparations for this significant change were made. Neither the school leadership nor the teachers were prepared to deal with this problem.

Only during the last five years have concerted efforts been made to cope with this problem. These efforts have been met with the usual resistance, confusions, fears, and lack of resources. But the superintendent of the Small City school system attracted new people to fill leadership positions in the system, and he elevated many within the system to positions of leadership without paying attention to the usual game of musical chairs. And considerable state and federal funds have become available to replace the Ford Foundation funds being phased out. But facing up to the system's problems is hardly equivalent to solving them. Most of the school principals are old-time appointees, and many of the teachers look back to the good old days.

THE PACK SCHOOL

We visited two schools, the Pack Junior High School, in a building left over from the old days, and the Grant High School, built by the new regime. The day began with a visit to the Pack School, whose principal is Mr. John Cudder. The school serves approximately 800 pupils from grades 7 and 8. Students are drawn not only from the immediate neighborhood, but also from a variety of more remote districts from which they are bussed. Although one of the aims of setting up the school was to effect racial integration, the current enrollment of the school is approximately 80 percent Negro.

GUARDIANS OF KNOWLEDGE

The teachers, the principal, and the city school headquarters unanimously concur in describing the school as a problem school. The principal's half-jesting characterization was: lots of activity and full of spirit. To illustrate the latter concretely, two boys whom we met in the hall were later the subject of a peremptory directive over the school's loudspeaker system: "Will James Thomas and Charles Wilkes report immediately to the office. This is an order!" The announcement came over the loudspeaker system while we happened to be having coffee in the teachers' room. The teachers responded to the squawk-box with intense jeering and other expressions of irritation, and greeted the specific nature of the announcement with mockery, while looking at us as if to say: "We told you so." In any case they treated the matter as entirely routine.

On one of our later trips through the halls, we ran across a teacher actively tugging a boy by the wrists. At the entrances from stairway landings to halls, boys with badges stood as traffic cops in white painted circles. All three doors to the auditorium were chained and padlocked.

In regard to the loudspeaker announcement ending, "This is an order," and the other factors indicative of close supervision and attempts for strict control: This is indicative of a mood in the school where the staff and administration know that the controls have to be largely extrinsic. The attitude of the students matches the attitude of much of the staff, namely that they're engaged in a holding operation. The students don't look upon the school yet as a place that will help them make it, as a place that is relevant to their needs. And the staff has a low level of expectation of these kids. This corresponds to their experience with teaching these youngsters. They're

237

applying the old standard program to youngsters for whom the program still doesn't make sense. The school is hardly geared to meet the wide range of problems it now faces.
I'm not referring particularly to peace-keeping practices. The entire curriculum must be revised and a new range of resources are necessary. Their absence leads to the displacement of educational goals by disciplinary actions and efforts at control of behavior. In effect it all adds up to a holding action. A large proportion of administrative and teacher energy is consumed simply in maintaining control.

ADMINISTRATIVE PROBLEMS

During the same time the principal indicated that one of the charms of his job was the unpredictability of his day: epileptic fits; boys suspended from class; boys skipping classes and wandering over to other schools, being held there and being brought back by the police. (Ter Weele thinks it significant that the pupils were brought back to the school rather than to their homes—the cops seem to look upon the school as an instrument for keeping the kids off the street in circumstances where the parents can't or won't.) That very morning, the normal start of the principal's day was livened by his need to deal with two boys who had had a serious fight in the school bus on the way to school.

As you note, in the case of the child being brought back by police, there is general agreement that the schools should contain these children. There is less recognition that the system needs reorganization to reduce the level of coercion necessary by making the school experience more relevant to the lives of these children. This is more simply said than done.

Since it would require changes in program and personnel and reeducation of personnel, there are financial and psychological costs which create considerable staff and community resistance.

SCHEDULING

When we arrived, we met the principal, who introduced us to his Director of Guidance, who stood ready to guide us around the school. One wall of the principal's office was entirely taken up by a classroom schedule, covering all days of the week and all rooms. The schedule gave some idea of the complexity of allocating resources and personnel. While we were in the office, one of the principal's assistants rushed in looking for an alternate room to which to send a teacher who, for some reason we did not understand, could not remain in the room where he was. A room was found; the method used was to take a long pointer to guide the eye and run it up and down and across the chart until an empty room was found. This operation took about two minutes. It should be noted that the consequences of delay might be more serious than one would think at first glance, since a group of pupils inhabiting the halls seemed to be the last thing any of the school administration would want to have on their hands.

We then discussed what kind of classes we might want to look in on. After the vagaries of personal taste and the master classroom schedule were taken into account, we decided to spend the first period with an eighth-grade art class. The art teacher, who was described to us by the principal as a "real mod," turned out to be just that, in the shape of a pretty wife of a student at Small City University.

ABILITY GROUPING

This art class was almost entirely white, with only one or two Negro pupils in it. Stepping out of the art class, we were led to a slow math class, which, in contrast, was inhabited almost entirely by Negro students, with the exception of one white girl and a boy of apparently Latin origin. Racial imbalance turned out to be rather common, both within the Pack School and, as we discovered in the afternoon, also at the Grant School. The mechanism for segregation within desegregated schools is simple: grouping by "ability." For example, the seventh grade is divided into echelons, ranging from class 7-1, the brightest, to 7-22. We should mention that we saw a high percentage of Negro teachers in both the Pack and the Grant Schools and that camaraderie among the teachers was high. In fact, although we were extremely conscious of student segregation, we were quite unconscious of race distinctions in our dealings with the staff. There was obviously great rapport and a feeling that "we are all in this together."

You also note that while the school has a mixed population, the classes tend to be segregated. The reason for the separation is obvious. Major attention is paid to teaching the youngsters subject matter, and the assumption is made that they will learn best in homogeneous classes.

As you go down the line in the tracks, not only are the students less able to achieve, but there is an increased concentration of youngsters who present problems. Hence, the negative attitudes in these classes are magnified. The students have negative attitudes toward themselves, toward their teachers, toward the school. The lethargy and apathy on the part of students express their perception of the irrelevance of what is going on in their classes.

NEW MATH

The math classroom we visited, like the rest of the school, was dingy and shabby, although in a reasonable state of repair. One light was out, and the general atmosphere was one of neglect. The geometry teacher was a young man in his first year of teaching at this school.

Ter Weele, as an experienced school investigator, lifted the cover of the desk at which he was sitting; I followed suit. The materials in the desks included a miscellany of chewing gum and candy wrappers, odd scraps of paper, and torn-up notes. The desks had evidently not been emptied either since the beginning of the semester or longer; they were about as full as they could have been without stuffing.

There were seventeen students in the class. Boys and girls were separated, but two trouble-making boys had been neutralized by isolating them among girls. The teacher pointed out to us at the end of the class that one of these boys had just come back after having been suspended. When this boy misbehaved during the class, the teacher made a passing reference to this suspension, threatening further disciplinary action.

The six boys who sat in the middle of the class volunteered among them only one response, rather late in the period. When called upon by the teacher, they either sat silently or mumbled in a way completely inaudible to us and, on occasion, audible to the teacher only with effort and repetition. The language spoken in the class was hardly the King's English. The teacher did not bother to correct any of this: he had much more important things to do.

The topic for the day was a review of a set of questions written on the blackboard. What is a segment? What is a line?

What is a ray? What is a polygon? What are parallel lines? How do we tell the size of an angle?

Two or three of the brighter girls were always eagerly raising their hands, or occasionally even interrupting. Others raised their hands rarely but responded when called upon by the teacher. By and large, the impression was one of student lethargy and apathy.

The teacher worked extraordinarily hard, in part perhaps to impress us, but later conversation with him confirmed our impression that on the whole he always took his job quite seriously.

The course was conducted from a fifth-grade book, and the teacher explained to us that these students could not be brought up to the level of algebra or, in fact, of any serious quantitative manipulation, but that he was trying to get across some basic qualitative concepts.

While sitting there, both of us formed a deep impression of utter futility, since it was so clear that most of the students cared little and had little use for what was being presented. Yet, there was much evidence of a good deal of innate intelligence among some of them. The teacher was trying to get across the notion that a line or line segment has an infinite number of points, and that points have no dimension. He distinguished carefully between the dimensions of his physical chalk marks and the abstract concepts he was trying to get across. Once, when he described a line as going to infinity in each direction, he promptly corrected himself to return to the jargon peculiar to the class, describing the lines as "going on forever."

In the course of the discussion of the number of points on a line, one of the girls asked how it could be that a line has length when the points which make it up have no length at all. The teacher muttered that this was by definition, which is not a bad escape, even in a graduate course at Harvard. In fact, it was quite surprising how much attention some of the pupils were paying, considering the nature of the subject (one reason for this is given in the next paragraph). At the end of the class we questioned the value of these subjects to the pupils and the teacher told us that he saw this as a problem in all of education. Indeed.

Although the students seemed extraordinarily apathetic and stupid in answering questions posed to them by the teacher, they exhibited great acumen and intelligence in raising questions that would divert the teacher from the path of the syllabus. These questions were frivolous in intent, but by no means frivolous in content: they showed a keen appreciation not only of human relations and of techniques for screwing up a teacher, but also of the unpleasant loose-ends of geometry. The matter of the undimensional point making up a dimensional line was the best example of this kind.

The teacher also frequently said, "Now does everybody understand that?" There was general assent. He would then ask several particular boys in turn, and each gave no response whatsoever or otherwise indicated absence of understanding. One of his techniques, once an answer was elicited from a student, was to ask the rest of the class if they agreed or disagreed. In most instances there was a random distribution of agreement and disagreement. As a principled non-Aristotelian, the teacher dispensed with the law of the excluded middle by asking, at one point, how many there were who didn't care. No hands were raised either, meaning that the sum total of hands raised on any of the three possible questions was less than the total number of pupils in the class. This indicates either the need for a fourth logical category, or a deep measure of apathy in the class.

During one of these episodes, the teacher pointed out in an aside to us that at least one of the boys would always follow the lead of one of the girls whom he knew to be a B student. Whatever she said, he voted for. The teacher described him as a good politician. The teacher then made an effort to get some of the pupils to give the reasons for the answer and, although some progress was made in that direction, subtle lawyers soon diverted the discussion into another path. One obvious predicament of the teacher was the fact that lack of preparation by the pupils frequently made it necessary for him to enter into an infinite regress of explanations of prior concepts, which again regrettably petered out somewhere along the path.

Your last paragraph, referring to the students' ability to divert the teacher from the path of the syllabus, is a very interesting one. Their "great acumen and intelligence" in doing so really illustrates that just as the staff has displaced its goals in regard to many of these kids, from one of education to one of discipline, the students, perhaps inadvertently, substitute for the goal of learning the goal of circumventing what they consider dreary efforts to teach them things they feel are irrelevant.

Socializing with the Faculty

By this time we had managed to shake off the Director of Guidance and were wandering around the school on our own. We ran into the pretty art teacher in the hall and invited her to have a cup of coffee. This subtle ploy was designed to get us into the teachers' common room, which, according to ter Weele, is the best place to find out what's really going on in a school. We maneuvered our way to a table inhabited by a tall Negro teacher, who was responsible for one of the "special-education" classes (that is, one for kids whose IQ's are below 70). This man, Mike Simpson, who was described to us later as an ex-basketball star without training in special education, had been on the staff of the school for a month. The other teacher at the table — Fred Perkins, male, white — was a science teacher.

This group was unanimous on one desideratum of a good school: DISCIPLINE. Fred, who ardently advocated rigid authoritarianism, told us of a priest who had come to teach at the school imbued with great democratic ideals but who, after two days, discovered the gospel of authority. It is hard to understand why these teachers are in the school, except for the art teacher, who's holding the fort while her husband is getting his degree at Small City University. The basketball player is eking out his living teaching while playing pro basketball. The science teacher seemed generally embittered.

All three of these people were young, in their late twenties or early thirties. We commented that all the teachers we had met and all those in the coffee room were young. The art teacher told us that the old types never seemed to come down and that in particular a Miss Widmerpool never seemed to eat. She was described as "being wedded to the school," having been with it for years and years, and she was obviously regarded by this group as a little bit queer.

You referred to a teacher of a special education class. You further note what is all too pervasive, namely that he too was not adequately prepared for that kind of class. You also note that he has a second job. Teachers with second jobs are quite common. It is obvious that this extra job further saps the teacher's energies for carrying out an educational program.

In regard to the question of the teachers' organizations and the teachers' feelings about their job, and particularly in answer to the question why do they stay. This will have to be answered in different ways for different teachers and administrators. Some, particularly those with long service, stay because they see no happier alternative. They are waiting out their time. In a sense, they face the same "rub" that Hamlet faced. This is even more true for the long-service administrators. Others stay on a short-term basis because they need the money. Some of these are Small City University wives who know that they will be moving on in a year or so. Some of them will try to get jobs in the suburbs next year. If they do, they move on; if they don't they will stay. Others remain because teaching is the kind of job that will permit them to carry on a second job, bringing in a reasonably handsome total income. For many, teaching is the first step up the middle-class ladder. Despite the frustrations of the job, they enjoy the prestige, the safety, under the circumstances perhaps I should say security, and the working hours.

A proportion, and I would be hard-put to judge it quantitatively at this point, but a good proportion, are there to do a job. Within the constraints, many of them do remarkably well. We should not overlook the fact that despite the dreariness of the building, despite the inappropriateness of the program, despite the inadequacy of supplies, despite the pervasive mood which was observed, and so forth, most of the children do learn. The failure of the system is not to be judged by what is accomplished, but rather by the nagging knowledge that the potentialities of so many of these youngsters are not going to come close to being realized.

BETWEEN CLASSES

The inter-period bell rang and Mike went off, telling us he was about to take on a class. We buzzed off ourselves to observe the halls during interchange. There was a fair amount of commotion, running, and yelling in the halls, although I could not describe it as superficially any more strident or violent than what I recollect from the halls of the Bronx High School of Science twenty years ago.

THE LIBRARY

During our wanderings we walked near or through the school library several times. On each occasion the library was empty save for the librarian. On one of the later visits, close to lunch period, we accosted the librarian and gave her our usual computernik cover story, which elicited a reply that anything computers could do to relieve overburdened librarians was all right with her. Each class in the school, according to the librarian, is scheduled for a library period at least once every two or three weeks. A film-strip projector was set up ready for a lesson on using the card catalogue. The librarian thought it essential to supplement this presentation with the presentation and handling of honest-to-God catalogue cards, since she felt that the students got more out of seeing a card in the flesh than out of an abstract image on a screen.

While we were talking to her, two boys came in asking to get some books and were peremptorily sent out on the ground that they were supposed to be in their room getting ready for lunch and that if they wanted books they should come back after lunch. Two girls momentarily appeared and busied themselves with something at a nearby table; they were described to us as library helpers who seemed to love to putter around the library now and then. Ter Weele says this is a good way of bugging out of class.

The librarian told us that students were free to borrow books, but hardly ever did; that the library was open after school for as long as the students needed it, but very few showed up.

The example you give of the library at work is an indication again of a resource which is available but is not properly used. In none of these instances would it be fair or wise to pass judgment on the individuals involved. This would deflect our attention from getting at the root causes as a guide to finding comprehensive solutions.

A COMMUNITY CENTER?

In response to our direct question as to whether the library was open to the community, the librarian replied emphatically, "No!" She said the collection was small and specialized to the needs of pupils and not of adults.

This attitude contrasts markedly with the labeling of the school as a "community school" and the impression, shared by the assistant principal at the Grant School, that the community schools were intended to serve the neighborhood adults, that the school facilities, including libraries, were open late at night and that such facilities as homemaking rooms, typewriter rooms, and so forth, were available to adult classes. In fact, the Grant School administrator complained that the community-school concept was fine in principle, in that it led to higher usage rate of school space, but that this affected the budget not at all, and that the school was given no more money for additional typewriter repairs, book purchases, or floor wax, in spite of hypothetical doubling of usage rate. We are puzzled by the discrepancy between his impression of the use of community schools and the testimony of the librarian.

You referred to the discrepancy between the librarian's view of her library and the general concept of the community school. Quite clearly, the concept of the community school is not yet generally accepted by the total staff. The operation of the community school varies from one school to the other. In some schools the programs are quite extraordinary. In these schools the principal and the assistant principals who are responsible for integrating the community school activities and the school activities work energetically and as a team. That this happy situation does not exist throughout the system is a fact and should not be surprising considering the length of time the program has been in operation and the length of time it takes to disseminate thoroughly any new program. This should explain your puzzlement. In fact, the integration of community-school programs with regular school programs is one of the remaining problems being worked on.

THE LOST CLASS

We then returned to the Pack School office to find out where Mike Simpson's special-education class was meeting, so that we might watch it. The principal cheerfully gave us the number of the room, but when we went there we found it vacant, although Mike's copy of *Hot Rod* magazine, which we had seen him carrying in the teachers' room, was now on the teacher's desk. We subsequently found Mike right back where he had come from, in the teachers' lounge. Even ter Weele, with his deep expertise, could not unravel this mystery. We asked Mike when he would be going to class, keeping a straight face all the while, and he replied that in twenty minutes or so something would happen with the intermediate lunch period and he would then meet his class. This would happen at 12:00. Meanwhile, where his class was is something he did not volunteer and we could not find out in spite of interrogating the lunchroom help. We are therefore somewhat puzzled about the nature of the scheduling chart on the wall of the principal's office. It is doubtful that whatever mystery lies behind it could be unraveled by a computer.

BOOK COVERS

While we were interrogating the principal concerning the whereabouts of Mike's class, we happened to tell him that we had been in the library, and he immediately launched into a panegyric on the virtues of the library. With pride he pointed out that, as a means to induce the students to use the library, bright-colored jackets had been bought to wrap around the old books in an effort to make them more attractive. This innovative spark kindled no great fire. As the principal ruefully pointed out, the kids didn't bite and kept going for the new books. Fairy tales, he told us, were in great demand.

Your reference to the techniques used to get students to read books, in the bright-colored jackets, etc., is self-explanatory.

SCIENCE

Somewhere in the course of the morning, we wandered into a science class, now being held for the pupils we had earlier watched in art class. The teacher told us that the class was in the process of testing rocks. The response to our question of "Why rocks?" was essentially a shrug of the shoulders meaning "Why not rocks?" There was an overhead projector in the class and also an analytic balance in excellent condition, indicating relatively little use. Upon questioning one of the students, we found that the analytic balance had been used in a demonstration earlier in the year, but not since. Most of the class was sitting around a U-shaped table. The teacher was busy making his way around to grade student reports on tests previously made on various minerals.

The interest of these children in their work and their general ability was obviously far higher than that of the other classes we observed, and ter Weele guesses that they correspond to the median or better in, say, the Watertown seventh or eighth grade. Many of them, however, were sitting around doing absolutely nothing, while two or three groups were either wrapping up the tail-end of an old experiment or beginning a new one.

One of the girls and a boy explained to us with considerable verve and a measure of understanding the procedures they followed, which consisted of trying to make a guess as to the nature of the mineral—a sound and intelligent procedure—and then following this up with a series of prescribed tests, at each step attempting identification through the use of a mineral test chart tacked to a bulletin board. Where identification was not possible, they went on to make further tests. Ter

Weele says it is obvious to him that the kids knew in advance what answers were expected. On the other hand, the children pointed out that the teacher did not dock them for, say, coming out with a specific gravity diverging somewhat from that expected on the chart. For example, one paper was shown to us where the experiment showed a specific gravity of 3.2 for a mineral whose specific gravity was listed on the chart as 2.5. This paper had an A and the student explained, in conversation with us, that he surmised that the discrepancy was due to impurities in his sample, which is not an unreasonable hypothesis, whether he got it from his own head or the teacher's. The fact that the measurement might have been imprecise was not mentioned, but it seems likely that the students in this class would have been introduced even to that concept.

Meanwhile, in the front of the room, on the single demonstration bench, other students were horsing around with a Bunsen burner next to a bottle of hydrochloric acid which had been left on the desk by some pupils who a few minutes earlier had been pouring some into a test tube as part of a test procedure. There was evidence of quite a bit of freedom for the pupils to work, although there were not enough rocks to go around, not enough equipment, not enough guiding materials. Also, it seemed as if the kids who were doing the work were perennial class operators, while the rest of the crew was rather passive, but we have no real back-up for this observation. On the whole, however, this class seemed seriously limited by facilities rather than by ability.

Your comment that "the class seemed seriously limited by facilities rather than by ability" I believe could apply to the system in general. Instead of the word "facilities," however,

*we ought to substitute "organization" and "program design."
In fact, there is much more talent in the system than is being
utilized. One might say we have the unhappy situation in
which the whole is considerably less than the sum of its parts.
(What can one say about the dreary look of the building as a
whole?) The fact is that the maintenance of the schools is
better now than it's ever been.*

*This, in a sense, is illustrative of the system as a whole. It
makes more sense to judge it in terms of where it came from to
the point it is in now, than merely to look at a status report.
Further, this school is illustrative of the influence of all of the
kinds of problems urban schools tend to face nowadays and a
low level of attempts to resolve the problems. There are
situations which are considerably happier.*

WOODWORKING AND UNIONS

The bulletin board in the outer school office had on it a
poster advertising the American Federation of Teachers, a
union affiliated with the AFL-CIO. We learned more about
unionism in the school when we stopped in the woodworking
shop just before leaving the Pack School. Throughout this
period we were completely unaccompanied, unannounced,
and unforewarned, in a school outside of our friendly administrator's domain.

We introduced ourselves to the shop teacher, who was
shellacking a drawer. Three or four boys were puttering away
at benches in another part of the shop and another three were
sitting at a bench, writing. All the boys were Negro.

The three writers apparently had misbehaved and couldn't
be trusted with the shop equipment. With the other students,

the teacher had a rather jocular if stern and paternal relationship. He kidded them when necessary—for example, when he noticed out of the corner of his eye one boy sawing away with a coping saw at a piece of wood held in his hand, he pointed out to him that he had better get the wood in a vise since he'd hate to have to waste a Band-aid on his finger.

When two boys wanted to leave the room, he told them they might do so as soon as the pass returned, and when the two boys ducked out without waiting for the pass, he let out a whoop-and-holler which brought one of them back; when the other did not materialize, he darted out into the hall after him.

The shop seemed well-equipped with the standard woodworking hand tools and also with an impressive array of power tools, including three lathes, a planer, a joiner, a sander, and a drill press. Had we been walking through on a more superficial tour, we would have been deeply impressed, but when the shop teacher caught our glances toward the equipment he quickly volunteered the information that the tools had been standing there for a year and a half and were unconnected to any power source. He also pointed to a stack of electrical cabling conduits on top of one of the cabinets, which he said represented some $800 worth of electrical equipment necessary to connect his power tools, but which had lain in its resting place for an equally impressive number of months. With some bitterness, he attributed this sad state of affairs to the fact that the entire school system has only four electricians who, at Christmas time, damn well had to go and get the mayor's Christmas tree lit up. He also told us that the work benches, which were new, had been on order for ten years. The machine tools, he said, had also been ordered a long time ago and finally appeared at a time when he had given up hope, but this manna was unaccompanied by the juice necessary to activate it.

Upon inquiry, the teacher revealed that he was a member of the American Federation of Teachers. In his estimate, some 50 or 60 percent of the teachers in this particular school also belonged to this union, while in other schools he estimated the percentage to be much lower, something on the order of 2-5 percent. When queried about his reasons for joining the union, his rejoinder was very simple: "I'm covered by Lloyd's of London for $100,000 in case I clobber one of the kids." He was rather bitter about the fact that the recognized bargaining agent for Small City schoolteachers was the state section of the National Education Association and that the rules of the game were so rigged that if he were to have to argue an appeal from an administrative decision, the lawyer from the American Federation of Teachers would not be permitted to accompany him unless an NEA representative was also present.

His total budget for materials for the year was $265. When asked how he made do, he pointed out that he bought the #3 grade pine used for framing houses, and used this to attempt cabinet work. His explanation of the high percentage of teachers in his school belonging to the AFT was that only the AFT was sympathetic to teachers in "combat schools" of this kind. He also made some general remarks about how lousy and fouled up the whole system is, and why anyone in his right mind would stay there. We did not have the nerve to ask him why he stays. His attitude about the Pack School seems shared generally by teachers, principals, and administrators alike. Every one of them realizes that he is in a hard situation. Some of the top administrators feel they are responding to the great challenge.

To end on an optimistic note, last year a new teacher organization was formed in town. It now consists of about twenty teachers. Some of them are members of the NEA and others are members of the Union. This organization was set up specifically to deal with professional problems. All of these teachers are deeply committed to making education in urban centers work. They have met consistently over the past year. Last week they invited the superintendent to one of their meetings. The superintendent was quite impressed with their analysis and set of recommendations. There is no doubt that these recommendations will influence future educational policy. In a sense I think that the ferment that Small City has gone through over the last decade is beginning to pay off educationally and that with a little bit of luck we'll be getting down to root causes and gut issues.

THE GRANT HIGH SCHOOL

The Pack Junior High School is housed in a dingy but reasonably well maintained building, vintage late twenties–early thirties. The only athletic facility we noticed was a large field of brown mud in back of the school, utterly empty save for one parked car. By contrast, the Grant High School is housed in a modern building, completed during the summer and opened in September of 1966. The school building is so new that it presently houses only grades 9 through 11. The twelfth grade is coming in only next year. The physical plant includes a separate athletic building with a swimming pool, a huge and well-furnished gym, and a variety of other athletic accessories. Both the main building and the gym building are of ultra-modern poured concrete construction.

The enrollment at Grant High School is presently about 1200, or approximately 300 students in each of the four "houses" of this school. Next year 400 more students will be added. The architecture of the school reflects its design as a school based on a house plan. The first floor is given over entirely to common facilities, including cafeteria, typewriter room, a physics and chemistry laboratory, a language laboratory, a central auditorium, and so forth.

The organization of the high school brought many innovations for the city that have significance for the future. Not only is it a distinctively designed school — the work of a renowned architect — it is also the first instance in which a principal was appointed some six months before the school was to become operative. Although not a new pattern for many communities, this was a startling departure for Small City. Further, the school architecture followed very specific educational specifications. The school was designed to accommodate a house plan. Most of the staff members at the school chose to be at the school. Housemasters were selected and began to function during the summer before school opened. The funds made available for equipment, supplies, and books were relatively generous.

Despite all this, it should be noted that the school opened somewhat before it was fully equipped and before such facilities as the gymnasium and the auditorium were ready. Since the staff and the student body were new to the school, there was much for everyone to learn about routine matters and also much effort expended to learn who was who in the school. Taking this into account, I would say the school was operating considerably more smoothly than one might have anticipated.

CANDY-COLORED DOORS AND GUM-COVERED FLOORS

A comment on the custodial staff. In the Pack School we saw a custodian moseying about the halls with a putty knife scraping gum from the floor of the halls. The gym teacher at Grant High had a very prominent sign at the entrance of the gym, saying "Gum-Chewing Forbidden in the Gym." We also saw many kids in both schools chewing gum in class, twiddling chains, sticking combs in their hair, or otherwise preening. At the Pack School, the geometry teacher felt it necessary to ask a girl not to comb her hair, while at Grant High, in a special-education class we visited, three boys proceeded to pull out combs and preen their hair while the teacher's back was turned. It should be pointed out that M.I.T.'s Project MAC has also had difficulty with computer consoles that have been literally gummed up.

The second floor consists mainly of ordinary classrooms, although we observed one laboratory-classroom apparently used for general science. All the floor areas on the second floor are covered with rugs, which greatly contribute to the reduction of noise level, although they bring with them the usual problem of static electricity discharge. Thus, in at least one respect, Negro children are in Small City introduced to some of the problems of executives of some of our largest and wealthiest companies. We did observe a rather nasty trickle leading from the door of one of the general science laboratories down the hall; whether this was water or hydrochloric acid we were afraid to determine.

The classrooms were all on the interior of the building and windowless. The four "houses" each occupied one of the four corners of the quadrangular structure. In the center of the structure, on the second floor, is a large room which we understood would become the library for all four houses, but which was not yet in operation. This large room has windows and a generally cheery atmosphere. Lockers for students were all around the halls and painted bright, cheery blues and reds—almost IBM-like.

Each house has a large room used as a study hall. Offices with entrances directly to this room are occupied by the housemaster, his secretary, and the house guidance counselor. We were told that, at present, each house has only one guidance counselor, although there are to be two by next year. The master of one of the houses explained to us that the students had scheduled study hours in the house study hall, and that he and the counselor used these periods for consultation with the students when necessary, rather than pulling them out of their regular classrooms. Students in each house are of all grades, all ability levels, all colors. In this school, as in the Pack School, segregation operates by a multi-track system according to ability level. Thus, one finds only Negro children in the special-education classes and only white students in the higher-ability classes, just as in the Pack School.

While we were talking with the housemaster in the study hall, the hall was crowded with students sitting at the tables, some working on assignments, others reading textbooks, some reading magazines, others staring vacantly. Ter Weele notes that there are copies of *Ebony* magazine in the common room. The housemaster pointed out to us that he does not discourage talking or whispering in the study room as long as study is not disrupted, and makes no special effort to bother those who are not reading or studying since, as he pointed out, if he gave them a book they wouldn't read it anyway. This was said without any malice.

The principal of Grant High School is Robert Terzaghi and the assistant to the principal is Frank Di Costa. Terzaghi is a product of the Harvard Graduate School of Education's Administrative Career Program. The superintendent of the Small City schools, Jim Amato, is also a product of this program.

PRIORITIES AND TECHNOLOGY

One of the major technological contributions to the principal's office was an enormous Bogen console for a master PA system, with buttons for switching to all classrooms and channels for radio broadcasts and God knows what else. A smaller version of this monster is found in the office of each housemaster. The pecking order is thereby clearly established. The principal can bellow at more people than any housemaster. With a gadget like that, who needs a computer?

AN INNOVATION

One innovation described to us by Di Costa was the use of overhead projectors in the classrooms. Apparently because of delivery problems, there were initially no blackboards in any of the classrooms. At this point the school officials scrounged up enough overhead projectors to add to those already allocated to the school in order to put "one in every classroom."

We were told that, even after the blackboards came, the overhead projectors remained and that, while the younger teachers had been enthusiastic about the overhead projectors not only as a primary tool under duress, but also as an aid even when the blackboard was around, the older teachers also responded to the emergency situation by adapting themselves to the overhead projector and continued to use it after the blackboards arrived. Di Costa did tell us, however, that the older teachers felt they had to have a pilot's license to use the gadgets. The master of one of the houses said there were only enough overhead projectors for half the classrooms and pointed out that in his house mainly the history teachers used them for overlays of one kind or another. The older teachers, he said, had essentially abandoned their use.

In reference to the overhead projectors: just for the sake of accuracy, the number of overhead projectors was approximately one for every two classes.

MORE ANNOUNCEMENTS

Di Costa also pointed out, in connection with the Bogen console, that he thought the things were a confounded nuisance and that the school therefore restricted their use to a five-minute period each day except for emergencies. Since we were exposed to such a five-minute period of inanity, which interrupted regular classroom business when a girl got on with announcements about who should be where for what sports or extracurricular activities, we can attest to the wisdom of this decision.

PROPERTY AND PRIVACY

Another interesting architectural innovation we were shown at this point was a room full of teacher carrels adjacent to the master's office and the student study hall for the house. Each teacher has a fairly comfortable and reasonably spacious carrel where he may keep his books, do his work, and so forth. The idea is partly to be nice to teachers, partly to destroy the proprietary attitude toward homerooms that teachers are prone to have in schools. There was no evidence as yet as to how well either purpose has been served; in any case, at the time when we visited the room, the teacher carrels were all unoccupied. There were, however, books on most of the shelves and one overhead projector in a carrel.

In regard to the carrels and the effect they would have on proprietary attitudes toward homerooms, let me say that they have been greeted in a very mixed manner.

ARCHITECTURE

One of the striking architectural features of the school, about which a great deal will undoubtedly be written in the press, is the auditorium. In keeping with the four-house motif of the school design, the auditorium is designed as a square with tiers of seats around the edges and an empty central floor. The floor evidently is intended for use as a theater-in-the-round, or, when filled with movable chairs, as a space for additional seating capacity. Furthermore, partitions rolling along the ceiling can be moved into the central space to divide the auditorium into four "socio-instructional areas." The entrances to these four areas are labeled Lecture Room 1, 2, 3, and so on. Di Costa also pointed out to us that the floor could be used for dances or other social activities, thereby avoiding firing up the whole gym building for a night. He contrasted this effective use of space with the old-fashioned auditorium, which is unused most of the time, except on those formal occasions where people sit in the usual row-by-row chairs. It was on this occasion that the question of community schools came up, and, while pointing out that the facilities of the Grant School could serve the community, he mentioned that the other schools, including the Pack School, were similarly intended.

At this point, Di Costa, who had been promoted to assistant principal of Grant High after having been principal of one of the lower schools, pointed out that in his previous job he had had a great deal of trouble with his staff concerning after-hours use of the school. Teachers resented coming in to find their papers disarranged, their desks moved two inches to the left, or, in the home-economics room, the pots and pans unwashed. Turning to the provision of carrels for teachers in the Grant School, Di Costa pointed out that he found teachers' regard for their homerooms as "their property" to be untenable in a situation where, after all, the taxpayers own the school. We had the feeling at this point that he was playing some internal phonograph record.

To a significant extent, the Grant School seems like the Pack School poured into a new bottle. Everything was more subdued owing to the carpeting on the second floor and the restriction of the first floor to adults on most occasions save lunch. Yet during lunch, the doors leading from the first floor to the stairwell to the second floor were barred by student guards who, when we sought to gain passage, explained to us that it was five minutes before one and not time to go up yet; they relented only when they noticed our escorts and realized our official status.

Ter Weele points out that the house plan is an excellent way to maintain control over the students. Since all of them are supposed to be in their respective houses most of the time, it is easier to keep track of them. Moreover, those who are not in class are in the study hall adjacent to the offices of the housemaster, secretary, and the counselors. Therefore, the feeling of loss of control that one has in the Pack situation, where patroling the halls and keeping track of pupils is exceedingly difficult, is lost in the Grant School, although we nonetheless saw quite a few students racing around the halls, their footsteps muffled by the rugs. While we were observing one class, however, the noise outside the room became high enough for the teacher to have to raise his voice significantly, but this was close to the end of the period and perhaps understandable.

Administratively, the house structure provides for additional supervisory and administrative manpower in the form of the four housemasters, their clerks, and their advisors. This situation, which frees the principal from routine administrative and disciplinary jobs, would be harder to explain and justify with more conventional architecture.

Your comment that "to a significant extent, the Grant School seems like the Pack School poured into a new bottle" brings us to the heart of the matter. The differences between the two schools are striking and yet you see much that is essentially the same. First, as to the differences: the principal of the high school is young, energetic, optimistic, and convinced that a high school can be made relevant to the lives of all the children in his comprehensive school. The staff of the school is likewise younger, more energetic, more optimistic, more open to change. The housemasters of the school reflect this spirit admirably. Two of the housemasters are extraordinarily well-educated, well-motivated, imaginative young peo-

ple. By and large, the department heads are of the same quality. Interestingly enough, the proportion of administrators new to the school system at this high school is extremely high. Hope for the system, like hope for the school, rests in the potential of these people. One can be optimistic about it because the superintendent of schools and the Board are equally forward-looking and determined to remake an old system. In other words, we want to pour new wine into newer bottles, to pour new wine into some of the old kegs that we have around.

Your observations underline how formidable these problems are. After five years of compensatory efforts, it is quite clear that we have not yet got to the gut issues. With all the striking differences between the two schools, what goes on in the classrooms is too much alike. That's why I have consistently stressed the importance of seeking change through (1) deepening teacher preparation, (2) changing the organizational structure, which should lead to (3) the design of significant programs which are relevant to the broad spectrum of children in a comprehensive school.

By the way, the staff relationships at the high school are extraordinarily good. I don't know if there's a school in the whole city where the staff has such a high degree of camaraderie cutting across all age groups and, incidentally, extending beyond the teaching staff to the other service personnel in the school.

SPECIAL EDUCATION

In most of our wanderings through the Grant School we were on our own, as we had wished. We had asked to see one of the special-education classes, since, for reasons related earlier, we were unable to see one at the Pack School. Di Costa gave us the room number where a Mr. Pinza was to be teaching. We came there and, miracle of miracles, the room was empty. We felt that fate was conspiring to send us to nonexistent classes of this kind, and wandered around the building a bit more.

When we returned five or ten minutes later, there was a class of seven or eight tall Negro boys and one tall Negro teacher, to whom we introduced ourselves, but who turned out not to be Pinza at all. He was the master of one of the houses, who, by some deal arranged with Pinza and totally unrelated to our appearance, had taken over the first five or ten minutes of the class in order to experiment with a new seating arrangement.

The subject of the lesson was to have been science, but through some lapse in communication the housemaster started them off on arithmetic. Pinza, whom we met later, commented on this lapse but did not react too plaintively. The students were working on problems involving the multiplication of three- or four-digit numbers by numbers like 2. The textbook was a fifth-grade-level textbook. The housemaster drew a blank when asked why 2134 was in the thousands. (It should be pointed out that the pupils in this class were between fourteen and seventeen years of age.) After writing on the board 134 and 34, he elicited from one of the boys the response that 2134 was in the thousands because there were four digits in the number. He thereupon asked, "How do you tell thousands?" and got the answer, "Four digits." "Hundreds?" "Three digits." And the point seemed to stick, at least with one member of the class.

The housemaster was a bit of a dandy, with precise and rather pedantic mannerisms. While the boys were working at their exercises, he came back to talk to us and explained that things would get a bit livelier in a while, but that right now he was trying to get the boys to communicate with him and with each other. His new horseshoe-table arrangement was an experiment aimed at eliciting better communication than is possible with individual seating or circular groups. He said it is important to communicate; communication is of the essence. He stopped just short of saying, "We teach communication, not subjects or children." This was bad enough addressed to us, but we felt nauseous when he returned to the front of the room and said, "Boys, let's communicate." The class reacted with utter apathy; when communication grew active enough for him to ask one of the pupils whether he had done the first exercise, the answer was a terse "No." Meanwhile, one of the boys was giggling because another boy was asking him how much 4 times 4 was, thinking it was 8, while *he* knew fully well that it was 16.

Your description of the class taken over by the housemaster was superb, but I should point out that this man is highly effective with certain youngsters and their parents. He obviously is someone who has a strong sense of having made it. He also has a strong sense of helping others make it. He has a bit of the preacher in him, which is quite obvious. He is also extremely thorough in keeping records on kids and following them up with considerable encouragement. He is very tough on those who he feels aren't being responsible. He is also very conscious of being formal and paying attention to the proprieties. He is extremely courteous and thoughtful in his relations with the youngsters. What I'm trying to say is that he is considerably more effective in general than this description of him would indicate.

The amazing thing to us was that the structure of the class was in many ways indistinguishable from that of more advanced classes. It is only when one realizes that these big strapping boys are dealing with fifth-grade materials that the horror of the situation dawns.

Meanwhile, Pinza, the regular teacher, tiptoed in and took his seat at his table at the front without making a sound. Ter Weele noted that when one of the boys raised his hand or motioned to Pinza that he had a question, Pinza signaled back to him to address his question to the housemaster, who was in control. The question remained unasked.

Since we found "communication" rather oppressive, we slunk out into the hall, motioning Pinza to come out after us, which he cheerfully did. We discussed the textbook with him and he pointed out that the boys regarded the use of a fifth-grade textbook as a great stigma; he therefore supplied them with junior high books to carry around in the halls and in the cafeteria, so that they could avoid losing face with their age peers.

He then showed us the grammar book he was using, carefully pointed out that nothing in the binding or labeling revealed that it too was of fifth-grade level and said, "See, you can't tell it from a junior-high book." The book was an interesting introduction to how language grows in response to needs of communication. The subtlety of this point might, however, well be lost on students of fifth-grade reading level. The book also laid great emphasis on the structure of the sentence: subject, predicate, parts of speech, and so forth. Ter

Weele asked Pinza why he thought it important for these children to know what a noun is. The reply was a startled look. We believe it had never occurred to Pinza that he might be teaching useless things.

This whole issue raises some very profound questions related also to the use of the junior-high book as a face-saver. In a situation where what a noun is is taught to middle- and upper-class children, it would be a denial of democracy to deprive these youngsters of the same knowledge, however useless it is to them in their situation and however ill-equipped they are to acquire this knowledge. In our subsequent description of an upper-middle-class geometry class, we will point out why we think that the same accusation could be leveled at much of high school education, whoever it may be addressed to.

We then returned to the class with Pinza, who took over when the housemaster departed, feeling that his innovation had worked out pretty well. To our eyes there was no discernible change after we returned to the room and Pinza took over. The matter of multiplying 10 times 9 was flooring one of the students and Pinza urged him to go to the board to draw 10 groups of 9 sticks or perhaps 9 groups of 10 sticks. Meanwhile, the teacher was showing us some textbooks he had not shown us before; the hair-combing episode described earlier took place during this interval. The student sent to the board made a feeble try, gave up, went back unobtrusively to his seat while we were talking to the teacher, and the issue never came up again.

Your first paragraph is quite perceptive and again illuminates the larger problems. Why should the structure of a class, the very slow class, be indistinguishable from that of the more advanced classes? How do you deal with situations where big strapping boys are working on fifth-grade materials? How do these things happen? How is it possible that they continue to happen? In brief, why is the institution so unresponsive to the obvious needs of its clients? Here we are not only dealing with a school system, but we're dealing with the society at large.

The students in the higher-level classes have a sense that somehow all of it will pay off in the long run. For the other students, who have no such hope, the whole affair is dreary and in many respects damaging. The teacher you noted who was working extraordinarily hard is not an exception. Many teachers do. Unfortunately, the program they have to carry out and the total setting within which they work is one in which they don't have too much hope and for which they are not adequately prepared.

The indictment of teacher preparation is all too clear and painful. The resilience of many teachers and youngsters withal is a hopeful factor and certainly the starting point for building new, more adequate curricula.

"Dirty stuff"

Mr. Pinza, the teacher of the special education group, is a multi-purpose teacher. When he is not doing arithmetic, he does science with his children, as well as grammar, and other subjects. He was telling us about a science class he conducted in which a description of the flowers, stamens, pistils, and pollen led to problems of eggs, and questions as to whether or not there were eggs in girls. He said he carried his explanation quite far but did cut it off short of the "dirty stuff." He obviously felt quite proud of having demonstrated his restraint.

I'm glad you can report that we don't teach any "dirty stuff" in the schools. Actually, there has been a citizens' group and a group from the Health Department working along with the director of curriculum and a number of teachers who have designs for pilot family-education and sex-education courses. A couple of these were tried out during the summer and were reported to have gone off pretty successfully. Obviously there are some teachers who would be prepared to teach such courses and other teachers who would be much too modest to engage in them.

TECHNOLOGY

In our discussions with Mr. Pinza, we raised the question of whether or not he thought that computers might be useful to him. For the sake of argument, ter Weele stated that computers would not be useful in the context of the special-education group we were observing. Pinza took a very positive stand to the contrary, arguing that for the kind of drill work that he was doing with his class, a computer would be far more effective, enabling the students to progress at their own rates, etc., etc. In other words, he fed back to us the gospel of the drill-and-practice computer-aided-instruction people, with, however, in his case an apparently fervent feeling that the conditions were right for the application of these techniques to his pupils. He confessed to a total ignorance of the techniques themselves, but thought they would be highly welcome in his case although he could make no guarantee as far as any other teachers were concerned. He did see himself, in case these things were to come in, in the role of "an educational manager," walking around assigning students to the proper programs, answering their questions, providing guidance, and so forth. He even volunteered to be a guinea pig for us any time we cared to use him.

HISTORICAL PERSPECTIVE?

We then returned to the halls and were intrigued by the sound, wafting out of an open door, of a social studies class in the throes of a discussion of the sociology of slavery. There were no Negro children in this class. The text was an anthology of American history with contributions by Arthur M. Schlesinger, Jr., and other noted historians, and the teacher was trying to elicit from the class some view of what biases might be discernible in the explanation of slavery. In particular he tried to draw some parallels between Southern bond slavery and Northern wage slavery, or something to that effect. The discussion was animated on questions of how many lashes the master of a plantation could administer to a slave, or on the observation that since marriage among slaves was not considered legal in Southern states, the owner of slaves could feel free to separate couples or take a woman as a concubine. There was not, during the period in which we were in this classroom, any discussion of the race problem as it is so sharply in evidence in that very school. When we raised this question a bit later in the hall with two of the girls in the class, asking whether they might have thought it incongruous to discuss these questions when there were no Negroes in the class, the answer was, "Well, there are one or two, but they're not here today." "Besides," one said, "the state of the class was fully accounted for by ability-grouping."

How were the people of Small City, and the people of the school system in particular, to know that their entire lives would be directly affected by what was happening on the farms in Georgia, Alabama, South Carolina, and who knows where else? Was it possible for Small City on its own to predict what was going to happen and take effective action in regard to it? The larger issue is perhaps revealed in the remarks made by teachers at one of the junior high schools which had been largely white middle class when the Princeton Plan was put into operation. They stated simply and succintly, "Why did they have to send them to us?" In a sense, the people of Small City could ask, "Why did they have to let them come to our city?"

What I think is revealed here is that we are dealing with a national problem which affects localities, and we probably will have to find local ways of resolving them with considerable national support. When I speak of national support, I am not speaking simply in financial terms. I am thinking more particularly about the kinds of national efforts that went into the design of new courses of study, setting up training institutes and so forth.

The problem of how to deal with segregated classes in integrated schools is a very, very complicated one, fraught with enormous emotional overtones. The teachers like homogeneous classes. The parents like homogeneous classes. The students like homogeneous classes. In the same way the community at large likes living in homogeneous packages. It will not be easy to devise ways of dealing with this problem. It will require in the first instance considerable re-training of teachers to change deeply established habits of operation. It will also require a re-education of students and their parents. Most important, it will involve the design of a curriculum that can do the job.

273

Still More Math

We then followed this class to its next period, which was a geometry class. The teacher there gave an assignment of several review-question pages and told the class that on the following Wednesday these pages would be used as a quiz in class. He made it quite clear that he was warning them as to the exact nature of the test and asked how many of them thought they would get 100 on the test. A good number raised their hands, but he pointed out that from past experience with them he expected only a 5 percent difference in the number of 100's on a quiz without warning and one with full warning as to time and content. One girl raised her hand and asked, "Will we have to prove anything?" and he reassured her that the test would be entirely true-false questions, fill-in, or multiple-choice.

For the rest of the class period during which we remained, the teacher went through a proof of the proposition that, for any arbitrary quadrilateral, the lines joining the midpoints of adjacent sides constitute a parallelogram. The class made suggestions concerning the basic properties of parallelograms and someone suggested an approach to the proof, whereupon the teacher quickly pointed out that this approach was predicated on an assumption of properties absent from a general arbitrary quadrilateral, such as equality of certain sides. Someone then reminded the class of a theorem that was part of the assignment for this day, namely, that in any triangle the line joining the midpoints of two sides is parallel to the corresponding base and of half the length of the base. With some further broad hints by the teacher, the class then constructed a proof of the theorem.

It struck both of us that here, as in the case of the geometry class at the Pack School and of the special-education group we had seen at Grant, the motivation was less than evident and that one was dealing with sterile material of the old school. At Grant High, however, the privileged children clearly accepted this game as part of the price for middle-class security and seemed to go along with it, in some cases eagerly, in most cases with at least some measure of attention, and with far fewer complete mental absences than at the Pack School.

It was noticeable that this class was much larger than the Negro classes we had seen. In both the Pack School and the Grant School, we were told that there were more students in advanced-track classes than in retarded-track classes, because of the fact that discipline problems were fewer, students required less individual attention, and teaching could proceed with fewer interruptions and less individual obstreperousness. This speaks well for the docility of the middle class.

As Fred Perkins pointed out to us at the Pack School, one or two disruptive students in a class are enough to throw the whole thing out of kilter and if he had his way, he would throw them out of the class. We did not pursue in any depth the question of where they would go. He made it clear, however, that he had to spend a very significant portion of his time dealing with these disruptive children, whereas it was equally clear that the teacher of the upper-middle-class geometry group had all his time free for going over geometry, however absurd it might be. The teacher and this class seemed quite untouched by the new math, pure or applied. The teacher's technique would obviously have been rated excellent by any supervisor, but there was little connection between his class and the real world, intellectual or material.

When you refer to how easy it is for one or two students to disrupt a whole class, you again point to a general problem, namely, how to deal with disturbing students. At this point there are inadequate facilities and inadequate personnel to deal with them. This, besides the fact that, lacking personnel and lacking facilities, we have not devised or tested any plan to deal with them.

INTEGRATION

The fact that this teacher was a real pro in the old tradition brings to mind something about the nature and selection of the teachers in the Grant and the Pack Schools. In both places we were struck, as we have said before, by the congenial collaboration between Negroes and whites. We have also mentioned the segregation between younger and older teachers at the Pack School. At Grant, on the other hand, young and old congregated freely at the tables in the lunchroom. In part, the effect may be due to the fact that the school was new and that all teachers were therefore new, having been drawn either from the outside or from other Small City schools by a process which obviously picked some of the best available faculty. Mr. Pinza did, however, in the discussion of technology reported on above, point out that he would not venture to guess anything about the opinion of other teachers concerning the use of computers in schools since no one knew anyone else very well yet. On the whole, the teachers at the Pack School seemed of lower-middle-class extraction, reasonably clean but shabbily dressed, exuding an atmosphere of Dickens or Gogol, while their counterparts at the Grant School were on the whole neatly dressed, very well-groomed, and full of a magisterial dignity more reminiscent of Sinclair Lewis and *Main Street.*

LANGUAGE LABS

We later found Mr. Di Costa, who opened up the language laboratory room for us. This laboratory, on the first floor, was not completed. There were thirty carrels and a master console, which, curiously enough, had provisions for four channels but only one tape drive. Unless some obscure technological tricks are being played with multiple channel tapes, this suggests either that somebody goofed technically or that a budget got arbitrarily slashed somewhere along the line, reducing more grandiose plans to a fancy lockstep with one single tape and, at best, four synchronized channels. Even under the best of conditions, a four-channel system merely divides a group of students into four equivalent classes, each of which is in lockstep.

We then wandered around the building a bit more, finding the physics and chemistry lab on the first floor locked, with a girl waiting outside for the teacher. The language laboratory, naturally, was locked as well.

MOBILITY

Over our luncheon conversation with Mr. Di Costa, several interesting facts emerged. Di Costa estimates that out of the total Small City school population of 20,000 children, some 1,100 a month are leaving one school in the system for another, or for one outside the system. Most of this rotation, which in a year accounts for 50 percent of the school population, is concentrated in a few of the schools, which therefore have an annual rotation of more than 100 percent. Some schools thus have a completely changing student body with, however, some old faces reappearing after a period of absence in another part of the city. This problem is something that has come to its present critical state over the last five years.

The mobility figure that you have down there, as I indicated before, is quite accurate.

Compensatory education

Di Costa also discussed with us the work-study program in effect at the high school. This, in essence, is a system to reduce drop-outs by using bribes provided by the Office of Economic Opportunity. The students are farmed out to state and local government agencies for a variety of work. As Di Costa pointed out, the program is no panacea. It has done a great deal of good for some of the pupils, made little difference for others. The pupils are well paid for their work-study program. For boys at the age of sixteen or so, the current pay is $1.75 per hour, and the starting scale for younger boys is $.75. Di Costa commented only partly in jest that the hourly rate for the older boys came perilously close to his own pay, if his salary is divided by the actual number of hours worked.

The work-study program is arranged to interfere as little as possible with the normal school program. The housemaster and counselor take care of scheduling to see to it that these boys have their basic courses in the morning hours and are therefore free to leave earlier in the afternoon than other pupils. The program is restricted to students whose families satisfy certain criteria of poverty. We raised the question of availability and usefulness of such a program for upper-middle-class children, and Di Costa pointed out that attempts were being made to interest local industry in training programs that would be of value both to industry and to the community. Apparently little progress has been made in this direction to date.

I would mention at this point that there have been efforts made to bring in compensatory forms of assistance. There is a work-study program which has been moderately effective in keeping down the number of drop-outs. It also keeps up the level of low-achieving students in the school. In the past these children were permitted to drop out. In the past these students weren't even referred to as drop-outs.

Here is another example of increasing the burden on the school without providing the school with adequate means to carry out the added burden. Funds also were made available to hire enough teachers to reduce the class sizes. You noted that the class sizes in the school were quite good. Try to imagine the situation as it was with much larger classes. There are also after-school tutorial programs. The students who attend the tutorials are inevitably those with stronger drive and higher aspirations, and those least likely to be disciplinary problems. The most difficult youngsters are not caught up in this program. In fact, the most difficult students are untouched by any of the compensatory programs. There are also recreational programs after school; there are adult recreational and educational programs after school; there are community liaison workers who help maintain contact between the school and parents; these are all aspects of the community-school program.

Although the community-school program has certainly, as you observed, not resolved any of the very serious problems, we don't know the level at which we would be operating if it were not for the support of the community-school program.

THE BUDGET

The school budget is sent for approval to the finance committee, which also operates under the mayor. Di Costa tells us that the finance committee not only makes recommendations concerning overall budget cuts, but has on occasion pointed at specific items. These items have usually been salary matters, because that is, in Small City as elsewhere, an overwhelming portion of the school budget. One wonders, given the structure of the policy and political decision-making apparatus, whether any suggestions for technological improvement would get anywhere, barring of course the possibility that these would support local industry. (This supposition suggests, for example, that the situation in Watertown might be altered radically if its major obsolete and now shutdown government installation were taken over by the electronics industry now characteristic of the Boston region. One can imagine a rather strong influence on the Watertown schools from an electronic computer-aided-instruction industry based in the town.)

Other facets of Small City school life emerging from the conversation with Di Costa include the fact that the school board is appointed by the mayor. Thus, City Hall has a good deal of control over school matters. This then leads to problems of nepotism in teacher appointments, suppliers, and so forth. (For example, the rugs in the school are 100 percent wool, a curious situation in the light of rather better-wearing qualities of some of the synthetics and, in any case, the absence also of allergenic tendencies in the synthetics. One surmises the work of a wool lobby, since the wool industry is a depressed industry in Small City's geographic region. The stuff costs $22 a square yard. This puts it in the medium-high quality range.)

No comment about the rugs. All I can say is that the Board member who rode herd on that and the school staff person in charge of it are both very straight and I believe knowledge-able people.

GRAFFITI

As we walked out, we passed by an empty classroom with chairs in neat array, a blackboard, and to the right of the blackboard a huge but empty bulletin board. On the bulletin board, lettered in bold print with blows from a blackboard eraser, we found "Fuck you." On the blackboard, in a smaller, rounder hand, the threat was made more explicit: "Fuck you, teacher." In a fit of middle-class morality, ter Weele erased both and we left the school.

As far as graffiti are concerned, I would say that our graffiti can match anybody's graffiti.

CONCLUDING COMMENT

You described the Grant High School very well. Your note about the seventh grade at Pack being divided according to echelons, providing a spectrum of students grouped carefully and homogeneously from the very brightest to the very dullest, is very interesting. I raised this question with a group of teachers and administrators at another junior high school. I asked how they could possibly manage to be so precise in their grouping and whether it really made sense. Their reactions ranged from surprise that the question should even come up to irritation at a challenge of so time-honored a system.

Change does occur here and there and in that junior high school the seventh grade is now divided into four houses. Each house is composed of a cross-section of the entire grade. Within each house the classes are organized homogeneously. As a result of this overall division, however, the separation of youngsters is considerably less severe. More important, this new form of organization has involved the administration and the teachers in a more thoughtful consideration of the grouping of youngsters and of the programs organized for their students. Likewise, it has resulted in much closer contact with both students and their parents.

I would end this by saying that it's instructive to get the impressions of somebody going through the schools. Those who see them every day and are involved in moving things along easily lose perspective. We have become increasingly conscious of how much effort it takes to move a little bit along the way. At the risk of being boringly repetitious, I would say that the rate of change will not increase appreciably until there is more radical reform of the school system's structure, until there is a more vigorous effort to upgrade the preparation of teachers already in the system, until the school situation attracts the best teachers to urban centers while at the same time implementing the new courses of study, etc., being developed and involving these teachers in overall curriculum development.

Appendix B

A Case Study in Reliability

The failure of appliances or automobiles is a common household experience. So are delays in repairs and failures of repairs. The light-hearted tone of industrial advertisements suggests that such experiences are isolated and extraordinary. The loss of the *Thresher*, the experience with the M-16 rifle in Vietnam, and the fire on the Apollo test suggest that the common experience is pervasive. The layman might be prepared to accept a share of the blame. Indeed, experience in the schools shows how markedly the pattern of education can be distorted by accommodation to the dictates of poorly designed or unreliable equipment when it is not simply ignored and left to gather dust. The experience recounted in this appendix is typical of the economic waste that the malfunctions, delays, and petty chicaneries associated with poor equipment design spread from the schoolroom to the launching pad.

I have a research project which, in keeping with the times, has a resounding title, Technological Aids to Creative Thought, and an acronym, TACT. The project deals mainly with computers, as described briefly in Section 5.5. Introducing our experimental subjects to the computer became a repetitive, tedious task, which we partially automated with tape-recorded instructions and synchronized slides showing what buttons to push, the effects to be expected, and so forth. Devices that play a tape and activate a slide-advance mechanism in response to tones recorded on the tape at the right point are commonly available. Having met my primary experimental need, I agreed to make the equipment available to my colleague, Professor William Bossert, for occasional use in an undergraduate course. The following is an account of his experience:

During the past summer Pat Harriss and I developed a program for the slide-sound units to explain the operation of the IBM 026 keypunch. The narration is a little less than 15 minutes in length and is accompanied by 30 slides. The program was given its first trial in Engineering Sciences 110, the introductory digital computer course, early in October. Since this was also the first general use of our Little Giant units by other than the project staff, I will describe my experience in some detail.

The most reliable of our Model XYZ units was selected for use. It refused to change slides regularly until the playback head was adjusted in height to provide adequate audio signal. The unit, along with a copy of the excellent operating instructions prepared by Adrian Ruyle, the tape cartridge, and the slide tray, was placed in the Engineering Sciences 110 keypunch room on the first floor of the Computation Center. The class, about 120 students, was shown the unit in a closed circuit TV tour of the Center and I advised each student to view the program while carrying out the first assignment requiring the keypunch.

Either I or one of the course teaching fellows stopped by the room every hour or two in the day, and once late in the evening. In two days of use we found the slide-sound unit in operating condition on only three of our checks. On these occasions the communication between the program and the students was impressive. The students followed the operations being described by trying them out on a nearby keypunch, even to the point of punching and using program control cards. About 20 students viewed the program in six known complete run-throughs. Most of them felt the time spent viewing the program was well rewarded, including several who had stayed on through unsuccessful attempts at a showing. There were at least ten such attempts, all involving a failure of the slide-sound unit. With one exception, in which the tape would not rewind, the unit stopped changing slides in these cases. This error was brought on in two different ways with about equal frequency. In the first, the tape head was shifted in position causing the slide-change audio signal to be inadequate even though the sensitivity control was at maximum. This shifting is to be expected from the flimsy and somewhat springy bracket that the head is mounted on, which also makes readjustment pretty much a chance operation. In the second, the hook on the slide change plunger became disengaged from the slide being projected so that it was not extracted when the plunger pulled out. This seemed to be due to the loose construction of the plunger arm and its lifting mechanism.

On the first day of use the students seemed to be willing to give up and go away when these failures occurred, or otherwise to sit rereading the operating instructions and staring at the constant slide until I came to repair the unit. On the second day, however, with the pressure of the assignment growing and frustrations building in those who had made previous attempts to view the program, the students began to try to remove jammed slides themselves. This caused some of the slide mounts to become slightly bent, which in turn made jamming more certain. On my first check the next day I found that the slide tray had been forcibly removed from the unit with a slide still stuck inside. The right angle brackets holding the tray carrier and plunger in place were bent, the slide tray and most of the mounts badly deformed, and several slides destroyed. I took the unit out of the room and substituted a mimeographed introduction to the operation of the keypunch. I have formed two strong opinions on the basis of this experience. First, the narrated slide program is definitely of value as a teaching aid. Second, the slide-sound unit we used is of unsatisfactory quality both of design and construction for regular student use.

Repair work was commissioned and proceeded rather slowly. Meanwhile, the following correspondence was exchanged with the manufacturer (who, like the slide-sound unit, is suitably disguised):

November 2, 1966

Dear Mr. Smith:

A few days ago I happened to see your glowing ad for slide-sound units. At about the same time a colleague completed the preparation of the enclosed memorandum* on an application of your equipment.

While your ad is correct in stating that the equipment is "used in leading colleges," I think that you should know that your equipment, in particular the Model XYZ is one of the most miserably performing kludges† I have had the misfortune to work with.

Moreover, after an initial period of sales enthusiasm, your regional representative proved hard to find in times of trouble, and local service arrangements most spotty and unsatisfactory

---

*The memorandum just preceding.

†"Kludge" is a term coined by Jackson Granholm of *Datamation* and now widely used by computer folk. It's meaning is obvious. The "u" is sounded as "oo".

in view of the unsettled state of the contract between your company and the local agent.

While the enclosed memorandum concentrates on the total unsuitability of the XYZ for student use, I must point out that the performance of all units is much less than satisfactory even under the most sheltered conditions. While the XYZ is so shabbily constructed as to give the most trouble, our ZYX has scarcely performed better. The instability of the relation between the reading head and the cartridge-holding mechanism is such that reproducibility of effect from one session to another from recording to the reproduction is most unsatisfactory. While this manifests itself most seriously in random slide actuation because of random sound level, and therefore random response to the control tones, the audio quality is generally poor and controls require resetting not only between sessions but frequently within one session.

The propensity of the slide-changing mechanism to jam is unspeakably bad. Even worse, retrieval of a jam is next to impossible, since there is no easy way to gain access to the inside of the mechanism. I was most embarrassed when I, myself, operated the equipment two or three months ago before a meeting of the local section of the Institute for Electrical and Electronic Engineers and found myself unable to use a planned sequence of sound/slide demonstration because of a poor slide-change control followed by a jam.

The principle of the device is sound. I should be most grateful if you could help us reduce the effects of its shabby execution to enable us to get on with our work, as by replacing the defective units with better-engineered models. Otherwise we shall be forced to regard our investment in one Model ZYX and two XYZ's as a total loss. Needless to say, if that were the case, we would feel no compunction about saying so loudly and publicly. Meanwhile, I think that professional honesty should compel you to withdraw this product from market or at least subdue the glowing style of your advertisements.

Sincerely yours,

Anthony G. Oettinger

November 8, 1966

Dear Dr. Oettinger:

This is in response to your letter of November 2, 1966, regarding the unsatisfactory performance you have experienced with our slide-sound equipment.

While your comments are discouraging, to say the least, I nevertheless thank you for calling the matter to my attention and appreciate the forthright nature of your remarks. My only regret is that you did not contact me sooner.

Our Eastern Regional Manager will be out here this week on a trip to our office and I intend to get into this thing with him.

I am sure you realize that the Little Giant Corporation is not a fly-by-night organization and as a division of Jones we have responsibilities to stand behind our products and make good.

Consequently, I will be writing to you again in about a week to work out a satisfactory solution to the problems you are experiencing.

Sincerely,

Melvin E. Smith

November 15, 1966

Dear Mr. Smith:

Thank you very much for your kind letter of November 8th. I am most grateful for your willingness to look into our problem, and I very much look forward to hearing from you soon.

Sincerely yours,

Anthony G. Oettinger

November 22, 1966

Dear Prof. Oettinger:

I understand that Mr. John H. Heeler, our Eastern Regional Manager, has contacted you since his visit out here last week.

Mr. Heeler informs me he is making arrangements to satisfy your requirements and we will cooperate with Mr. Heeler to the fullest in seeing that matters are worked out to solve problems that you have had plaguing you.

Sincerely,

Melvin E. Smith

December 28, 1966

Dear Mr. Ruyle:

Some time ago we prepared a rather clever little audio-visual program on how to record on the ZYX. It is out on loan most of the time but, as soon as I get my hands on it, I will send it to you to use for a couple of weeks. It might prove helpful in indoctrinating your people.

Your Model XYZ machines are ready for return to you except for new play-back heads which we want to install on them. These new heads are much superior to the originals and greatly improve the performance of the machines. The new heads have been on order for two weeks now and are due in our shop the first week in January. We should be able to ship the machines back to you no later than January 10. We will better this date if at all possible.

I regret the difficulties you and the people at Harvard have experienced with our equipment but, at the same time, I appreciate your patience and understanding and giving us the opportunity to correct matters.

Please feel free to call on Mr. Heeler or myself at any time.

Sincerely,

Melvin E. Smith

December 30, 1966

Dear Mr. Ruyle:

This is to let you know that I now have my hands on the program covering operation of our Model ZYX machine which was mentioned in my last letter.

In order to avoid any possible confusion, I would like to call a few things to your attention. First, this program has had a lot of usage and I noticed that about one-fourth of the way through the program there is one weak slide change signal on the tape. Therefore, if you notice the slides start running one frame behind the audio at that point, just push the manual slide change button once and the program will be back in sync. Second, this program was made several years ago and some minor changes have been recently incorporated in the machines which do not coincide with the pictures. The pictures show a machine equipped with a three position rotary switch in the lower left corner of the front panel. The four positions on this switch are "off", "audio", "visual", and "A/V." We recently replaced this rotary switch with a three postion toggle switch. Your machine may have the toggle switch and, if so, the instructions in the program will still apply relative to placing the machine in the A/V mode.

The pictures show a two position "INT"–"EXT" switch on the back panel of the machine above a two pronged slave projection plug socket. We recently replaced this socket with a four pronged plug which eliminated the need for the switch. If your machine is equipped with the four pronged socket and has no "INT"–"EXT" switch, you can disregard this portion of the instructions in the program.

> Sincerely,
>
> Melvin E. Smith

The situation described in the foregoing correspondence did not significantly improve. We have continued to use the units under sheltered conditions, both in the laboratory and in the course. For the latter, that means having on hand at all times a teaching assistant experienced in the care and feeding of the beast. I tried to find another supplier:

May 16, 1967

Dear Professor Smith:

For the last year or so I have been using a Little Giant XYZ Slide/Tape unit whose construction and reliability I have found to be generally poor.

A few days ago, after I gave a talk at the MIT Science Teaching Center, someone told me you have been using a similar unit by another manufacturer for several years and apparently without grief.

If this information is correct, I should be most grateful if you could give me the name of the manufacturer and a model number or similar description of the apparatus you are using. Many thanks.

Sincerely yours,

Anthony G. Oettinger

August 17, 1967

Dear Professor Oettinger:

Thank you for your letter of May sixteenth. In regard to your question, we have been using the Model ABC by Small Wonder. This unit has been satisfactory except for a special complex switch which has failed on numerous occasions.

I am sorry but I cannot highly recommend this unit for reliability and construction.

Sincerely yours,

George Smith

Notes

Introduction

1. New Orleans Conference on an Educational System for the Seventies (ES '70), March 6-8, 1968, "Conference Objectives," p. 1.
2. ES '70, "An Empirically Designed High School Program," p. 1.
3. ES '70, "Secondary Education in the U.S.: *A Status Report*," p. 2.

1. The School Setting

1. Charles J. Hitch, "Program Budgeting," *Datamation,* 13 (September 1967), 37-40.
2. Alvin M. Weinberg, "Social Problems and National Socio-Technical Institutes," *Applied Science and Technological Progress,* a report to the Committee on Science and Astronautics, U.S. House of Representatives, by the National Academy of Sciences (Washington, D.C.: Government Printing Office, 1967), pp. 416, 418.
3. John S. Gilmore, John J. Ryan, and William S. Gould, *Defense Systems Resources in the Civil Sector: An Evolving Approach, An Uncertain Market,* prepared for the U.S. Arms Control and Disarmament Agency (Washington, D.C.: Government Printing Office, July 1967), pp. 53-54.
4. Peter Schrag, *Village School Downtown: Politics and Education—A Boston Report* (Boston: Beacon Press, 1967), p. 117.
5. James W. Becker, "Run, Computer, Run: A Critique" (unpub. critique presented at the conference on the draft version of *Run, Computer, Run* held in Cambridge, Mass., May 1-2, 1968), p. 5.

6. P. Alper, R. H. Armitage, and C. S. Smith, "Educational Models, Manpower, Planning and Control," *Operational Research Quarterly,* 18, (June 1967), 102.
7. Robert R. Mackie and Paul R. Christensen, *Translation and Application of Psychological Research* (Goleta, Calif.: Human Factors Research, Inc., January 1967), p. 1.
8. Ibid., pp. 5-6.
9. Robert J. Schaefer, *The School as a Center of Inquiry* (New York: Harper and Row, 1967), p. 30.
10. James S. Coleman, *Equality of Educational Opportunity,* U.S. Department of Health, Education and Welfare, Office of Education (Washington, D.C.: Government Printing Office, 1966), p. 8.
11. "44.6 Million Pupils in Schools at Record $27.8-Billion Cost," *New York Times,* Jan. 2, 1967, p. 16.
12. U.S. Department of Commerce, Bureau of the Census, *Statistical Abstract of the United States, 1965* (Washington, D.C.: Government Printing Office, 1966), p. 107. U.S. Congress, Joint Economic Committee, Subcommittee on Economic Progress (hearings of June 6, 10 and 13, 1966), *Technology in Education* (Washington, D.C.: Government Printing Office, 1966), p. 213.
13. U.S. Department of Health, Education, and Welfare, Office of Education, *Projections of Educational Statistics to 1975-76* (Washington, D.C.: Government Printing Office, 1966), p. 44.
14. U.S. Department of Commerce, *Statistical Abstract of 1965,* p. 119.
15. U.S. Department of Health, Education, and Welfare, *Projections to 1975-76,* p. 17.
16. Leonard A. Lecht, *Goals, Priorities, and Dollars: The Next Decade* (New York: The Free Press, 1966), pp. 32-33.
17. Ibid., p. 157n.
18. U.S. Department of Health, Education, and Welfare, *Projections to 1975-76,* p. 70.
19. For the method used to convert 1965-66 dollars into 1962 dollars see U.S. Department of Health, Education, and Welfare, *Projections to 1975-76,* p. 109.
20. Lecht, *Goals, Priorities,* p. 157.
21. Ibid., p. 161.
22. U.S. Department of Health, Education, and Welfare, *Projections to 1975-76,* p. 70.
23. Ibid., p. 6.
24. City School District of the City of New York, Board of Education, *Annual Financial and Statistical Report, 1965-1966* (New York, 1966), p. 60.

25. Marilyn Gittell and Edward T. Hollander, "Fiscal Status and School Policy-Making in Six Large City School Districts," Part II of "Investigation of Fiscally Independent and Dependent School Districts" (unpub. ms., 1967), p. 208.
26. *Watertown: The Education of Its Children* (Cambridge, Mass.: Center for Field Studies, Harvard Graduate School of Education, 1967).
27. Ibid., p. 88.
28. Ibid., p. 124.
29. Ibid., p. 92.
30. Ibid., p. 91.
31. Ibid., p. 87.
32. U.S. Department of Commerce, *Statistical Abstract of 1965*, p. 336.
33. Thomas C. O'Sullivan, "Terminal Networks for Time Sharing," *Datamation*, 13, (July 1967), 39.

2. Educational Technology: The People and the Institutions

1. Bel Kaufman, *Up The Down Staircase* (Englewood Cliffs, N.J.: Prentice-Hall, 1964), p. 50.
2. Ibid., p. 121.
3. *Watertown: The Education of Its Children* (Cambridge, Mass.: Center for Field Studies, Harvard Graduate School of Education, 1967), p. 22.
4. Uri Haber-Schaim, "The PSSC Course," *Physics Today*, 20 (March 1967), 26.
5. *Harvard Project Physics Progress Report* (Cambridge, Mass.: Harvard Project Physics, January 1967), p. 26.
6. Educational Services, Inc., *A New Physics Program for Secondary Schools* (Newton, Mass.: Educational Services, Inc., 1966), p. 4.
7. James B. Conant, *The Comprehensive High School: A Second Report to Interested Citizens* (New York: McGraw-Hill, 1967), p. 55.
8. *Watertown: The Education*, p. 35.
9. Paul Brandwein, "Science and Related Areas," Chap. 13, Sec. B, in U.S. Congress, Senate Committee on Labor and Public Welfare, Subcommittee on Education, *Notes and Working Papers Concerning the Administration of Programs Authorized Under Title III of Public Law 89-10, The Elementary and Secondary Education Act of 1965 as Amended by Public Law 89-750*

(Washington, D.C.: Government Printing Office, April 1967), p. 282.

10. Daniel S. Greenberg, "The Air Force: Study Relates Troubled Relationship with Research," *Science,* 156 (June 16, 1967), 1463.
11. Nick A. Komons, *Science and the Air Force: A History of the Air Force Office of Scientific Research* (Arlington, Va.: Office of Aerospace Research, 1966), p. 68.
12. Ibid., pp. 69-70.
13. Ibid., p. 70.
14. Ibid., p. 91.
15. Arthur G. Wirth, Foreword to Robert J. Schaefer, *The School as a Center of Inquiry* (New York: Harper and Row, 1967), p. ix.
16. David Riesman, "Thoughts on Teachers and Schools," *The Anchor Review,* 1 (1955), 45.
17. "Innovators Need Support," *Educational Technology,* 7 (June 30, 1967), 25.
18. Lawrence M. Gariglio, letter to the Editor, *Educational Technology,* 8 (Aug. 30, 1967), 15.
19. William A. Rodgers and Lawrence M. Gariglio, *Toward a Computer Based Instructional System,* a Visiting PACE Fellows Publication (Saginaw, Michigan: Saginaw Township Community Schools, n.d.), p. 2.
20. Ibid., pp. 15-17.
21. Ibid., p. 17.
22. "Information Dissemination of Educational Innovations," is the title of a seminar announced by the Center for Communication Studies of the National School Public Relations Association, Santa Barbara, California, for February 2-5, 1969.
23. Myron Lieberman, *Education as a Profession* (Englewood Cliffs, N.J.: Prentice-Hall, 1956), p. 473.
24. City of New York, *Corridors of Challenge: Teaching in New York City* (New York: n.d.), p. 2.
25. McGeorge Bundy et al., *Reconnection for Learning: A Community School System for New York City* (New York: Mayor's Advisory Panel on Decentralization of the New York City Schools, 1967), p. 31.
26. Kaufman, *Up The Down Staircase,* p. 60.
27. Ibid., p. 169.
28. David Bazelon, *Strategy for Change. A Report on The Model School Division and Its Advisory Committee* (Washington, D.C.: District of Columbia Model School Division, April 1966), pp. 11-12.
29. Appendix A, p. 238.
30. Appendix A, p. 255.

31. Don Davies, "Teacher Education," Chap. 15, Sec. B, in U.S. Congress, Senate Committee on Labor and Public Welfare, Subcommittee on Education, *Notes and Working Papers*, p. 295.
32. Philip W. Jackson, "The Teacher and The Machine: Observations on the Impact of Educational Technology," prepared for the Committee for Economic Development, September 1966, p. 7.
33. "The Importance of Anonymity: The Work of The Components Designer," *Bell Laboratories Record*, 44 (January 1966), 33.

3. Educational Technology: The Processes

1. "Individual Teaching Plan Excites Experts," *Boston Daily Globe*, Oct. 5, 1967, p. 42.
2. John I. Goodlad, *School, Curriculum and the Individual* (Waltham, Mass.: Blaisdell, 1966), p. 33.
3. Glen Heathers, "Individualized Instruction," Chap. 7, Sec. B, in U.S. Congress, Senate Committee on Labor and Public Welfare, Subcommittee on Education, *Notes and Working Papers Concerning the Administration of Programs Authorized Under Title III of Public Law 89-10, The Elementary and Secondary Education Act of 1965 as Amended by Public Law 89-750* (Washington, D.C.: Government Printing Office, April 1967), p. 178.
4. Harold Benjamin, *The Cultivation of Idiosyncrasy* (Cambridge, Mass.: Harvard University Press, 1962), p. 9.
5. B. Frank Brown, *The Non-Graded High School* (Englewood Cliffs, N.J.: Prentice-Hall, 1963), p. 166.
6. Patrick Suppes, "The Uses of Computers in Education," *Scientific American*, 215 (September 1966), 218.
7. Patrick Suppes, *Computer-Assisted Instruction in the Schools: Potentialities, Problems, Prospects* (Stanford, Calif.: Institute for Mathematical Studies in the Social Sciences, Technical Report No. 81, Oct. 29, 1965), p. 11.
8. Launor Carter, *Personalizing Instruction in Mass Education by Innovations in the Teaching-Learning Process* (Santa Monica, Calif.: System Development Corporation, Report No. SP-2722, Jan. 27, 1967), p. 6.
9. John F. Cogswell, *Analysis of Instructional Systems*, final report of the project New Solutions to Implementing Instructional Media Through Analysis and Simulation of School Organization (Santa Monica, Calif.: System Development Corporation, TM-1493/201/00, 1966), p. 183.
10. Ibid., p. 42.

11. Jan C. ter Weele, personal communication, Nov. 30, 1967.
12. Heathers, "Individualized Instruction," p. 181.
13. Suppes, "The Uses of Computers," p. 217.
14. R. L. Bright, "Educational Technology and The Disadvantaged Child," *Educational Technology*, 7 (June 30, 1967), 7.
15. Appendix A, p. 268.
16. Bel Kaufman, *Up The Down Staircase* (Englewood Cliffs, N.J.: Prentice-Hall, 1964), p. 56.
17. Education U.S.A., "Promising Innovations Hit Snags," *Washington Monitor*, Sept. 23, 1968), p. 19.
18. J. Lloyd Trump and Dorsey Baynham, *Guide to Better Schools: Focus on Change* (Chicago: Rand McNally, 1961), p. 27.
19. Brown, *Non-Graded High School*, p. 70.
20. Ibid., pp. 72-73.
21. Ibid., pp. 98-99.
22. Ibid., pp. 57-58
23. Ibid., pp. 59, 61.
24. Educational Services Inc., *Teacher's Guide for Behavior of Mealworms* (New York: McGraw-Hill, 1966).
25. Ibid., p. 1.
26. Ibid., p. 13.
27. Ibid., p. 14.
28. John I. Goodlad, "The Curriculum," *Innovation in Planning School Curricula—Appendices*, prepared by the National Education Association (Washington, D.C.: U.S. Department of Health, Education, and Welfare, Office of Education, August 1966), pp. 29-30.
29. Ibid., p. 30.
30. "Nova High School: America's Galaxy of Educational Innovation," I|D|E|A brochure (n.d.), p. 5.
31. Helen Mattison, "Resource Center," I|D|E|A brochure (n.d.), p. 4.
32. Goodlad, *School, Curriculum*, p. 37.
33. Theodore Sizer, personal communication, Jan. 24, 1967.
34. S. S. Stevens, "Measurement, Statistics, and the Schemapiric View," *Science*, 161 (Aug. 30, 1968), 853.
35. Robert Glaser, "'New Myths and Old Realities'—Six Responses and a Reply," *Harvard Educational Review*, 38, (Fall 1968), 741.
36. Robert Glaser, *Adapting the Elementary School Curriculum to Individual Performance*, report of the Learning Research and Development Center, University of Pittsburgh, Preprint No. 26 (Pittsburgh: University of Pittsburgh Press, 1967), p. 5.
37. Benjamin, *Cultivation*, p. 28.

38. C. M. Lindvall and J. O. Bolvin, "The Project for Individually Prescribed Instruction (The Oakleaf Project)," Learning Research and Development Center, University of Pittsburgh (Pittsburgh: University of Pittsburgh, February 1966), p. 4.
39. Glaser, *Adapting the Elementary School*, p. 8.
40. Ibid., p. 7.
41. Ibid., p. 8.
42. Ibid.
43. Ibid.
44. Ibid., p. 9.
45. James W. Becker, "Run Computer Run: A Critique" (unpub. critique presented at the conference on the draft version of *Run, Computer, Run* held in Cambridge, Mass., May 1-2, 1968), p. 2.
46. Education U.S.A., *Individually Prescribed Instruction,* an Education U.S.A. Special Report (Washington, D.C.: National School Public Relations Association, 1968), p. 2.
47. Ibid., p. 3.
48. Bright, "Educational Technology," p. 1.
49. Glaser, *Adapting the Elementary School*, p. 19.
50. Education U.S.A., *Individually Prescribed Instruction,* p. 1.
51. Samuel Postlethwait, J. Novak, and H. Murray, *An Integrated Experience Approach to Learning* (Minneapolis: Burgess Publishing Co., 1964), p. 5.

4. Educational Technology: The Devices

1. John I. Goodlad, "The Curriculum," *Innovation in Planning School Curricula—Appendices,* prepared by the National Education Association (Washington, D.C.: U.S. Department of Health, Education, and Welfare, Office of Education, August 1966), p. 36.
2. Bel Kaufman, *Up The Down Staircase* (Englewood Cliffs, N.J.: Prentice-Hall, 1964), p. 35.
3. Philip W. Jackson, "The Teacher and The Machine: Observations on The Impact of Educational Technology," prepared for the Committee for Economic Development (September, 1966), pp. 3-4.
4. Patrick Suppes, *Computer-Assisted Instruction in the Schools: Potentialities, Problems, Prospects* (Stanford, Calif.: Institute for Mathematical Studies in the Social Sciences, Technical Report No. 81, Oct. 29, 1965), p. 1.
5. *Random Access Teaching Equipment,* Dage-Bell Corp. brochure (Michigan City, Indiana, n.d.), p. 2.

6. Stafford North, "Learning Center Gives Each Student a Study Carrel," *College and University Business*, 40 (May 1966), 48.
7. Walter Daugherity, personal communication, Fall 1966.
8. American Association of School Librarians, *Standards for School Library Programs* (Chicago: American Library Association, 1960), pp. 25-26.
9. Educational Electronics, Inc., a collection of brochures (circa 1967).
10. Karl Deutsch, "Government and Technology," a paper prepared for the Columbia University Seminar on Technology and Social Change, Oct. 13, 1966, p. 5.

5. The Computer in Education

1. Patrick Suppes, "The Uses of Computers in Education," *Scientific American*, 215 (September 1966), 207.
2. Ibid.
3. Ibid., pp. 212-213.
4. Donald F. Hornig, testimony delivered before a subcommittee of the Committee on Government Operations, House of Representatives, *Data Processing Management in the Federal Government* (Washington, D.C.: Government Printing Office, 1967), p. 146.
5. Technomics, Inc., *Computer System Support for Comprehensive Educational Advancement*, a study authorized by the School Board of the City of Philadelphia, in conjunction with the Brooks Foundation (Santa Monica, Calif.: Technomics, Inc., 1966, p. 3.
6. Ibid., p. 5.
7. Ibid., p. 3.
8. Samuel Feingold, "PLANIT—A Language for CAI," *Datamation*, 14 (September 1968), 45.
9. Patrick Suppes, "Another Look at the Problems of Computer-Assisted Instruction" (unpub. critique presented at the conference on the draft version of *Run, Computer, Run* held in Cambridge, Mass., May 1-2, 1968), p. 13.
10. Suppes, "Another Look," p. 19.
11. Stanford University, Institute for Mathematical Studies in the Social Sciences, "The Stanford-Brentwood CAI Laboratory Project" (n.d., circa 1966).
12. This is partly a consequence of state licensing laws that impose the equivalent of the presence of a fireman in every Diesel locomotive.

13. Technomics, *Computer System,* p. 3.
14. Ibid.
15. Ascher Opler, "The Receding Future," *Datamation,* 13 (September 1967), 32.
16. Lawrence M. Stolurow, "Computer Assisted Instruction (CAI)" (unpub. ms., Harvard University, 1967), p. 56.
17. Ibid., pp. 56-61.
18. Daniel Alpert and Donald L. Bitzer, "Design of Large Scale Computer-Based Education Systems," lecture given at M.I.T.'s colloquium series "Education and Computers," Feb. 14, 1968.
19. Gerald T. Gleason, "Computer Assisted Instruction — Prospects and Problems," *Educational Technology,* 7 (Nov. 15, 1967), 7.
20. Felix Kopstein and Robert Seidel, *Computer-Administered Instruction Versus Traditionally Administered Instruction: Economics* (Alexandria, Va.: George Washington University, Human Resources Research Office, April 1967), pp. 11-12.
21. Ibid., p. 24.
22. Ibid., p. 29.
23. Technomics, *Computer System,* p. 10.
24. Ibid.
25. Ibid.
26. Nina Gould, "Teaching Analytic Geometry Using THE BRAIN," in Project TACT, Report No. 4, *Applied Mathematics 271: Technological Aids to Creative Thought: Student Papers* (Cambridge, Mass.: Project TACT, Aiken Computation Laboratory, Harvard University, Spring 1968), p. 17.
27. Gould, "Teaching Analytic Geometry," pp. 20-21.
28. William Bossert, personal communication, Oct. 18, 1968.

6. Where Do We Go from Here?

1. Committee for Economic Development, *Innovation in Education: New Directions for the American School* (New York: Committee for Economic Development, July 1968), p. 20.
2. Education U.S.A., *Washington Monitor,* June 19, 1967, p. 245.
3. James Becker, "Regional Laboratory Presentation on Technology," speech given at the meeting of Directors of Regional Laboratories in Washington, Washington D.C., Oct. 5-6, 1967, p. 13.
4. Lyle Spencer, statement at the conference on the draft version of *Run, Computer, Run* held in Cambridge, Mass., May 1-2, 1968, pp. 172-173.

5. Robert W. Locke and David Engler, "Run, Strawman, Run" (unpub. critique of draft version of *Run, Computer, Run;* McGraw-Hill Book Co., April 1, 1968), p. 21 (presented at the May 1968 conference).

6. McGeorge Bundy *et al., Reconnection for Learning: A Community School System for New York City* (New York: Mayor's Advisory Panel on Decentralization of the New York City Schools, 1967), p. 3.

7. Rhode Island House of Representatives, Bill No. H 1462, "An Act in Amendment of and in Addition to Title 16 of the General Laws Entitled 'Education' as Amended" (January 1968), p. 16.

8. Theodore Sizer and Phillip Whitten, "A Proposal for a Poor Children's Bill of Rights," *Psychology Today* (September 1968), 60-61.

9. Ibid., p. 63.

FIGURE SOURCES

3: *Watertown: The Education of Its Children* (Cambridge, Mass.: Center for Field Studies, Harvard Graduate School of Education, 1967). 4-6: Superintendent, Watertown Schools, Watertown, Mass. 7-8: Program for "Three National Seminars on Innovation," Honolulu, Hawaii, July 1967. 10-11: Learning Research and Development Center, *Individually Prescribed Curriculum* (Philadelphia: Research for Better Schools, Inc.). 12: Learning Research and Development Center, *1967-1968 Reading Curriculum: Experimental Edition with Explanations* (1967). 13: Learning Research and Development Center, *Individually Prescribed Instruction: A Manual for the IPI Institute* (1967). 14: "Trails Blazing at Golden West College," *Audio Tutorial Systems Newsletter*, March 1967. 16-17: Nina Gould, "Teaching Analytic Geometry Using THE BRAIN," Project TACT (Cambridge, Mass.: Aiken Computation Laboratory, Harvard University, 1968). 18: Jean Harrison, "AM 271 Project: Definite Integral Approximations," Project TACT, 1968. 19: Robert Des Maisons, Project TACT, 1968. 20: Arra Avakian, Project TACT, 1968. 21: William Bossert, Harvard University. 22: Adrian Ruyle, *THE BRAIN Primer*, Project TACT, 1968.